SHAME ON YOU:

Unyielding Devotion to a Sister with Mental Illness

By

DE ANNA L. YEE,

M.A. (Clinical Mental Health),

M.A. (Politics & Public Policy),

B.S. B.M., LPC

SHAME ON YOU

Unyielding Devotion to a Sister with Mental Illness

DL Enterprises, LLC

1905 Serman Street Ste. 200 #1795, Denver, Colorado

Author Credentials: DeAnna L. Yee, MA (Clinical Mental Health), MA (Politics & Public Policy), BSBM, LPC

ISBN: 979-8-9991802-0-9

Printed in the United States of America

Credits: Cover and Logo Designs: DeAnna L. Yee (Conceptualized with Creative Direction) **Ahwho's Corner Logo; DL Enterprises, LLC Logo**

Formatting: Completed June 19, 2026

Medical and Legal Disclaimer: This book is a **memoir**. It reflects the author's personal experiences, memories, and professional insights as a **Licensed Professional Counselor**. The names and identifying characteristics of some individuals have been changed to protect their privacy, though the author **has received permission** to use certain real names and images. It contains some strong language; and sexual content as it relates to symptomatic features of mental health diagnosis.

The information contained in this book—including discussions on **Bipolar Disorder, Cluster B Personality Disorders, and trauma recovery**—is intended for educational and storytelling purposes only. It is **not a substitute for professional medical advice, diagnosis, or treatment**. Always seek the advice of your physician or other qualified mental health provider with any questions you may have regarding a medical condition or family system crisis. Reliance on any information provided in this book is solely at your own risk.

For my sister, Denice, and all your wonderful parts,

And, In Loving Memory of Mom, we all miss you deeply.

INTRODUCTION

We all carry stories. Some sit silently within us, tucked between memory and survival, while others scream for release, desperate to be heard—not for attention, but for liberation.

This book is a tapestry woven from moments too complex for simple conversation, and too powerful to be forgotten. It's a journey through mental illness, trauma, family systems, faith, healing, and the messy truths we often avoid. It does not shy away from the raw—the uncomfortable, the painful, the unjust—but instead embraces it, believing that in vulnerability there is strength, and in truth, there is light.

I did not write this book to cast judgment. I wrote it to create space: for empathy, for understanding, and for grace. For the silent heroes living in chaos. For the misunderstood souls navigating invisible battles. For the ones who love deeply but imperfectly. And for anyone who has asked, "Why would you tell everyone?"—this is why.

Because silence breeds shame. And shame breeds cycles. Cycles of isolation, of hurt, of hiding. By sharing what was once silenced, I hope to unravel the cords of generational pain and bind them with threads of compassion, honesty, and spiritual insight.

You will meet characters—some real, some symbolic—who reflect the inner and outer conflicts we all face. You'll see how mental illness rearranges relationships, how love can simultaneously wound and heal, and how the sacred and the psychological must work hand in hand to build wholeness.

This is not just my story. It's yours, too. In these pages, may you find the courage to look inward, the strength to speak outward, and the wisdom to forgive in all directions—backward to those who came before, and forward to those yet to arrive.

Welcome.

ACKNOWLEDGEMENT

This book is born from pain, truth, healing, and grace—and it would not exist without the many hearts that carried me when I couldn't stand on my own.

To Denice: your life, your battles, and your spirit live in every page. You are more than your diagnosis—you are a mirror, a lesson, and a force of compassion. I hope these words honor both your suffering and your resilience. Your strength and resilience shaped every page of this book.

To my mother, whose vulnerability and voice guided the rhythm of this story: thank you for your willingness to revisit the past and help shape the path toward understanding. Your strength, even in fear, gave me courage. Well done, as God's faithful servant.

To my family, my kids and their families, my husband, Jim, Denice's sons and families, our sisters-thank you for giving what you were able to give to help Denice.

To the helpers—those who stepped in and those who stepped away: each of you played a role in teaching me about empathy, boundaries, and grace. Whether your presence brought clarity or confusion, I am grateful for the lessons it taught me.

To my faith: the scripture, the silence, the sacred presence—thank you for being my compass in moments of emotional fog. This story leans heavily into spiritual truth, and I am anchored by the belief that we are all divinely guided, even through darkness.

To the readers: thank you for opening these pages with open hearts. May you feel understood, challenged, and uplifted. This book is not simply a telling—it is an offering. You are not alone, and you are deeply loved.

Finally, to every broken piece of my story: thank you for existing. From shattered moments came wisdom, and from wisdom, this book.

With deep reverence and love,
DeAnna L. Yee

DEDICATION

This book is dedicated to~
Denice and all of your beautiful parts~
Thank God they are with you to help you through;
My children and grandchildren~
you have all given so much for me to help my sister.
I hope I have given you, in return, the value of family ties;
Dad and Mom~
you taught me strength and compassion to never give up,
especially during the hardest of times;
My husband~
you have supported me more than I ever could have asked for.
Your generosity and kindness expressed throughout my journey could never be repaid.
And, thank you for all you do to help with photo memories,
this is priceless. Your help never went unnoticed;
My sister Debbie, her wife April and our sister-in-law~
you stayed beside me, kept me focused
and supported me throughout the journey;
Dan and Jim~
you are my brothers, my best spiritual friends, my protectors.
You guided me through a world that I was learning how to live in;
My nephew, Denice's youngest son~
you love your mother in the darkest of times.
Your wife stood by her side when I could not.
I love you all, you have filled my life with value, enriching my character in so many ways.

FOREWORD

In this journey, we arrive at a place where truth meets courage, and vulnerability becomes a bridge to healing. The exposure of *Shame On You* is not just a story—it's a challenge, a fear, and ultimately, a declaration of purpose. It echoes the voices of those who have suffered in silence, those who have watched helplessly, and those who have dared to speak when silence felt safer.

This writing is a testament to the power of storytelling—not for spectacle, but for salvation. It invites readers to confront the uncomfortable, to sit with the pain, and to recognize the humanity in every flawed, fractured, and faithful moment. It is a call to forgive, to understand, and to extend grace not only to others but to ourselves.

Here, the author bravely unpacks the complexities of mental illness, familial roles, and the emotional cycles that shape our lives. Through raw honesty and spiritual reflection, we are reminded that judgment is not ours to wield, and that empathy is not weakness—it is wisdom. The narrative challenges us to look beyond black-and-white thinking, to embrace nuance, and to see the divine in the broken.

This book does not offer easy answers. Instead, it offers something far more valuable: perspective. It asks us to consider the cost of silence, the weight of shame, and the transformative power of truth. It reminds us that healing is not linear, and that love—real, protective, unconditional love—is the most radical act of all.

As you read, may you find pieces of yourself in these pages. May you feel seen, heard, and held. And may you walk away with a deeper understanding of what it means to be human, to be connected, and to be whole.

TABLE OF CONTENTS

Chapter 1

Cultural Considerations

"A balanced inner calmness radiates from a peaceful center. It neither craves others' approval nor rejects others' presence. It neither pulls towards nor pushes away. It has a reverent attitude towards life and all its inhabitants."

— Donna Goddard, The Love of Devotion

As I contemplate how to begin the story of growing up with a loved one who has suffered her entire life from comorbid mental health diagnoses, I feel it's important to start with some cultural context about our family—because all of it shaped who we became.

Dad had a hard, but good life. He was born the eldest of four to a stern, hardworking father and a mother from a large, agrarian and labor-reliant family who did her best to care for her husband and children. Dad often tells stories of having to live with Aunt Minnie—his father's sister—when Granddad had to move the family frequently in search of work. Granddad was a blue-collar man, taking construction jobs to support the household.

Despite the challenges, Granddad seemed to understand the importance of stability for the two oldest children—Dad and our dear sweet auntie, as she liked to call herself when we were born. So, while he took Grandma and the two youngest on the road, he left Dad and dear sweet Auntie behind so they could attend school uninterrupted.

Eventually, the family reunited, and Dad went on to finish high school. He participated in ROTC, earned his pilot's license well before graduating, and began his journey into adulthood as a journeyman in the construction field—doing what he loved.

Dad was drafted to serve in the war because of his aviation skills, but he was rejected. He always laughs when he tells the story: "They asked me to read the chart without my glasses, and I told them, 'What chart? I can't see no chart!'" He says he was "blind as a bat." Mom was also pregnant with my oldest sister at the time, so the military didn't make him leave his growing family. Still, he always considered it a blessing—he got to do what he loved, and what he loved helped him support his family.

Mom was born the oldest of two girls, eventually, legally, three when my uncle was born. *(Side note: there will be several detours in this story. Some will have details that may or may not be essential to this particular journey. When that happens, I'll label them "a detour for another journey," as is the story of my uncle and the influence he had on my life.)*

Anyway, Grandpa, Mom's father, immigrated to America as a young boy. Tragically, he lost his mother to tuberculosis either during or shortly after their voyage to Ellis Island. Like many in our family, he was a hardworking man. He built a career at the State Highway Department and also ran a side business as a mechanic out of his garage. Grandpa often shared stories of being called out in brutal winters to clear snowy mountain passes and rescue stranded travelers.

Grandma, meanwhile, anchored the home. She worked as the church treasurer and did all she could to take care of Grandpa, the girls, and later, my uncle.

Mom grew up as a "valley girl" (not the L.A. kind, but a small-town version). She and her sister, cousins, and childhood friends still laugh when they get together, reminiscing about the pranks they played and the joy they shared. She played the flute in the marching band, worked as a lifeguard at the town pool, Splash Land, and waitressed at a local café.

She had a boyfriend away in the military, someone she planned to marry. That is, until one morning when Dad came in with her father, who he had recently started working for. He sat down at the counter and immediately began flirting—obstinately and confidently—with the new counter girl. He ordered basted eggs, fully aware that she had no idea what that meant. She served him eggs sunny side up instead.

Flirting with her, he gave her a hard time about the incorrect egg order. Later, she turned to the chef and said, "I feel sorry for the woman that marries that guy". What she didn't know was that Grandpa had already told Dad the waitress was his daughter. After that encounter, Dad was hooked. He began cruising the neighborhood where he knew Grandpa lived, hoping to spot Mom. She admits that she used to hide under the porch whenever she saw him coming, because at the time, she was still engaged to someone else.

Eventually, Mom found out that her boyfriend had been unfaithful. She broke up with him, started dating Dad, and about six months later, they got married. To this day, they both like to say that Dad graduated high school twice—once for himself and once for Mom as she admits she didn't work very hard or care about finishing school. She frequently had Dad write her papers as she had better things to do than homework.

Mom stayed home with us kids until I started kindergarten. After that, she went to work as the manager of the school cafeteria, making sure she stayed connected to me during my school years. I was never a latchkey kid, never went to daycare, and I've never experienced the reality of having divorced parents. The same is true for all my siblings.

From this brief explanation of our family's cultural background, I want to highlight just a few of the values we were lucky to inherit from our lineage: stability, loyalty, commitment, forgiveness, discipline, courage, humility, kindness, and perseverance. I'm sure there are even more.

So, if these values are so deeply embedded in our family, you may wonder why I feel compelled to write this story and expose such vulnerability. My answer is simple—mental health is important. It affects everyone. No matter the disability, disorder, or symptoms, we are all affected by the emotional and mental pain that mental illness brings. This has been true ever since the great fall of man, as told in the *Holy Bible* (*Genesis 3:1-24).*

When we hide our stories, our shame, and our struggles from one another, I believe we only help feed the darker forces that thrive in silence. Things like anxiety, perfectionism, judgment, greed, jealousy, laziness, and above all, the justification of misused anger.

My mother had genuine concern when she asked why I titled this book *Shame on You.* And rightly so. The very topic of shame is daunting in itself. Add religion to the mix, and it becomes downright painful.

We were raised in a fundamental Baptist church, learning every Sunday, Monday, Wednesday, and Saturday how to live as born-again Christians. We were taught to live in a way that would avoid shame—whether it was shame toward ourselves, our family, our community, or our church.

Shame is a deeply held human emotional state. Like all emotions, it serves a specific purpose. But before we dive deeper, let me tell you where shame lives.

Shame lives in my mother's right index finger.

Yes, you read that right. That is where it resides. And when I became a mother, it took up residence in my right index finger as well. I remember Mom pulling out the "shame finger" a few times, and when she did, it felt like the earth quaked beneath my feet. I'm sure many of you know exactly what I mean. Maybe you had one too. And maybe, like me, you inherited it.

Before we go any further, let's clarify two emotions that shape this entire story: *guilt and* shame. They are often confused, but they serve very different psychological and relational functions.

Guilt as defined by Merriam-Webster (Lipsher, 2025) is:

- The fact of having committed a breach of conduct especially one involving moral or legal consequences.
- A state of conscious wrongdoing, often accompanied by remorse.
- A feeling of deserving blame, whether for real offenses or imagined ones.

Guilt can also be used as a verb:

- to cause someone to feel guilty. Don't listen to mommy, she is trying to guilt you.
- to persuade through guilt: "Eat your green beans — there are starving children in Africa."

Now, let's talk about shame. In contrast, shame runs deeper. It is not just about what we have done—it is about who we believe we are.

In sharing our story, I'm exposing myself in the hope that it will help our family heal and that it will show others they're not alone in their struggles. I hope this exposure leads all of us on a journey of forgiveness—not just forgiving ourselves but learning how to forgive one another as we grow individually, as a family, and as a society. Bottom line, I hope for the end result to help us, step down from the pedestal of grandiosity, where we all hide our shame; and, to learn how to step up from the pit of shame to find our voice and express ourselves, living in a more balanced and healthy state, individually and relationally.

Yes, I recognize that sharing our experiences may bring about feelings of shame and judgment from others. People may scrutinize how we handled ourselves during those difficult times. But I believe that in the end, this vulnerability can lead to deeper understanding and connection.

Miriam Webster defines shame as:

- A painful emotion caused by consciousness of guilt, shortcoming, or impropriety
- A condition of humiliating disgrace or disrepute.
- A cause of regret or reproach

As a verb, shame means:

- to bring shame to someone or something
- to cause someone to feel shame
- to force action through emotional pressure.

There are both religious and scientific theories about where shame comes from and how it evolved in the human race.

According to the Bible, shame began with the acquisition of knowledge about good and evil, which came through the Fall of Man, when Adam and Eve ate the fruit from the tree of knowledge. Their punishment for disobeying God's one command was to be "banished from the garden and condemned to a life of toil and sorrow" (Velleman, 2001).

To me, this interprets into the idea that shame is the feeling of being devalued by God for not adhering to His command. It also opens the possibility that the serpent believed or knew that Eve would be more easily tempted to disobey. For whatever reason, I'll leave that to you to ponder. Through the lure of her ear, the serpent enticed Eve to question God's command and simply "just say no" (Velleman, 2001), choosing to disobey. As it's written in *Genesis 3,* Adam and Eve became ashamed. And with that, the birth of shame *(Holy Bible, NIV, 1974).*

From a scientific standpoint, Daniel Sznycer states, "The function of shame is to prevent us from damaging our social relationships, or to motivate us to repair them" (Sznycer, et al., 2016).

Either way, shame is painful and embarrassing. Yet, it is a part of our nature, helping us control our internal emotions and behaviors and guiding how we interact with others.

This book is built on the foundation of shame, an engineered emotion designed to help us avoid being devalued by others (Sznycer et al., 2016). It explores how shame affects us as individuals, as family members, and as productive members of society. Yet, we are all sinners trying to live according to the Word of God, striving to regulate our internal systems while constantly balancing between cultural norms that have shaped our sense of value and the unique sense of worth that has emerged from our own traumatic experiences.

I am not concerned with being devalued by anyone who reads this account of mental illness and its effects on our lives. Rather, my intention is to offer my family—and anyone who relates to living with or loving someone who has mental illness—a new way to understand and approach the issue. Mental illness does not pick and choose who it affects; it simply affects all of us, species-wide.

It is my hope that instead of ostracizing those who struggle more than others in balancing their internal systems, we stop using the conditions of the mentally ill as a means to feel better about ourselves by devaluing them. We must recognize that they are just as human as we are (Real, 2023). Ignoring them, hoping their problems will disappear on their own, only perpetuates the issue.

I pray that by exposing our story, we can help someone—many someones, or even everyone—stop, take a breath, observe, and proceed (Linehan, p. 425-427). We need to begin reevaluating how we are either contributing to or helping to reduce the mental health challenges that continue to develop in our human nature, generation after generation.

Please approach this work with an honest presence, a forgiving heart, a reasonable mind, and a peaceful spirit. Let these words be a reminder of divine comfort and guidance.

SHAME ON YOU

"I sought the Lord, and he answered me; he delivered me from all my fears. Those who look to him are radiant; their faces are never covered with shame." *Holy Bible, NIV, Psalms 34:4-5.*

"In you, Lord my God, I put my trust. I trust in you; do not let me be put to shame, nor let my enemies triumph over me. No one who hopes in you will ever be put to shame, but shame will come on those who are treacherous without cause. Show me your ways, Lord, teach me your paths. Guide me in your truth and teach me, for you are God my Savior, and my hope is in you all day long. Remember, Lord, your great mercy and love, for they are from of old. Do not remember the sins of my youth and my rebellious ways; according to your love remember me, for you, Lord, are good." Holy Bible, NIV, Psalms 25:1-7.

Chapter 2

Beliefs

In *The Prophet*, it is said that God is the Archer, children are the arrows, and parents are the bow (Gibran, p. 18). In our family, our parents did us a great service by providing a strong spiritual foundation, solidified by joining a church where we spent much of our time growing up.

Now, I sense some readers may have a skeptical reaction, as I do even as I write this. However, I've come to appreciate the religious influence we had, understanding that the leaders themselves are human, subject to the same shortcomings as anyone else. In our family, both parents were faithful followers of God, yet each had a unique exposure to Him. This led them to develop seemingly opposite approaches that, when blended together, brought balance to my own development of faith.

Mom was born into a religious, church-going family in a college town, surrounded by farmland that we referred to as God's country. After she graduated and got married, Grandpa and Grandma moved east over the mountains to a larger metro city, where they raised my uncle. Grandpa was a Godly man and served as a Deacon in their church. I remember watching him study in the evenings, with his Bible resting on his lap and the warm light surrounding him. He would sit in his chair, an aura of peace seeming to envelop him. We used to sing his favorite hymns to him while Mom played the piano, and I would see him cry tears of comfort as songs like *Precious*

Memories by J.B.F. Wright and *Amazing Grace* by John Newton moved his heart.

When I shared this memory with Mom, the mischievous side of her came through. She shared how she learned the art of manipulation to avoid doing the dishes after big meals. She realized that "playing the piano for Daddy" would be a fun way out, so Mom and Sis would end up doing the dishes instead. Grandpa would vouch for her, saying she was busy practicing, and it always worked in her favor.

Grandpa's faith influenced many of us. I remember years later watching him and my uncle study at our kitchen table as my uncle worked toward becoming a State Highway Patrol officer. He spoke with Grandpa about his internal conflict as he really wanted to become a pastor. My uncle eventually became both a State Highway Patrol officer and a pastor, showing me that I, too, could have more than one career.

This side of the family, for me, provided God as a natural part of my existence and shaped the part of me that can't imagine a life without God.

Dad, on the other hand, was a self-proclaimed Atheist-Agnostic. Please forgive any logical inconsistency in the order of these words—perhaps it should be the other way around—but the intent here is more about understanding his stubbornness than the logic behind it. Dad grew up not just without God but vehemently opposed to the idea of such a being or presence.

As their love story goes, Mom, who refused to marry an unbeliever, sprinkled her charm and beauty over Dad until he was head over heels in love and decided to pursue her. He began counseling with her father and, shortly thereafter, accepted the Lord as his Savior. They married after a six-month courtship and engagement, and today, sixty-four years later, he professes more love for her than ever.

Going to church on Sundays had its ups and downs. Yet, like clockwork, Dad was in the car every Sunday morning, honking the horn to get us all inside as not to be late for Sunday School. I remember feeling like our real life on Sundays was chaotic—fighting, yelling, and disorganization—until we pulled into the church parking lot. That's when we magically transformed. The pretty, friendly, "everything is perfect" version of us appeared. We'd all exit the car, walk into the church, and suddenly become the good Christian family, each of us heading off to our respective Sunday school classes.

After Sunday school, we reconvened as a family for the main church service. I always wanted to sit next to Mom so I could sleep on her lap, until Dad said I was old enough to stay awake and listen. Near the end of the service, Mom would always get up to play the organ for the benediction. Sometimes, Dad would scoot me closer to him, still about arm's length away, and gently scratch my shoulder in affection.

Once the pastor said "Amen" at the end of the final prayer, it became a race to the car with Dad, who would watch everyone leave the church, growing more and more upset because Mom was "always the last one out." I could tell how the afternoon would unfold based on a few signs. If we turned right out of the parking lot, YAY! We were going out to lunch—except for the occasional times when Dad just changed the route for some reason. If we turned left, my mood immediately dropped to sadness, fear, and agitation because it meant we were just going home.

If we got home and the football game was immediately turned on after lunch, the afternoon would be a little better. At least Dad would be yelling at the television instead of us—unless, of course, we were too noisy in another room.

Dad was a Godly man, but there was definitely a difference between him and Grandpa. This side of "being a good Christian" helped me understand how someone like Dad could seek, learn, understand, and choose to believe in something as profound as God, despite the fact that He hadn't existed in his life before meeting Mom.

Looking at the historical union in my family, I see it as a living example of the three elements: mind, body, and spirit. Dad represents the mind—his logic and analytical thinking; Mom represents the body—simply put, she's an empath, intensely connected to the senses; and together, they provided us with the spirit of God, offering us free will to choose.

God has been my Archer, providing me with a very strong yet flexible bow that bent at just the right times but remained firm enough to never break, despite all of our experiences—mental illness being one of the many challenges, as described herein.

Chapter 3

Family of Six

We were always a family of six, at least that's how I remember it—Dad, Mom, and four kids. I was the baby, with two older sisters and one older brother, who was the only middle child until I came along. Each of us had our nicknames from our brother. Mine was "pudgy cheeks," and then "scream baby." Eventually, he and I clicked, and we became very close. He taught me things like how to pickpocket, how to shoot an arrow, how to play darts, and how to throw the bread and butter over the fence so Mom wouldn't know we didn't eat it when he and I sat outside for dinner.

He was diagnosed with Amyotrophic Lateral Sclerosis, better known as ALS, at thirty-five. He struggled with the terminal nature of the disease and fought hard against the inevitable. I remember one day he called me while I was in a meeting at work in the labor and employment division—something unusual for him to do during the day. I stepped out of the meeting to answer the call, and I'm so glad I did. He wanted to talk to me about his desire to go to college and get a degree, hoping it would help him earn more money for his family. At that point, he had come to terms with having to quit his job as a mechanic because his hands, weakened by the disease, could no longer hold a wrench.

We had a long, difficult, and honest conversation about the pros and cons of his desire to use the few years he had left to pursue a degree, with little time left to secure a higher-paying job. In the end, instead of going to school, he transitioned to a job that didn't exist at the time. He would have someone place a small dot on his forehead when he arrived at work. This dot connected to the mouse on his computer, allowing him the technology to continue working without his hands. He would take phone calls from customers with automotive questions, offering advice with his expertise and research skills. He worked until the day he was hospitalized due to a complication. After almost twenty years of marriage and raising two daughters, he lost his final "something" to the disease he called "Always Losing Something."

This marks a very difficult loss in our family's history, the loss of a significant other—one that will forever remain etched in our hearts.

My second-oldest sister, Debbie, had a difficult childhood, struggling to fit in. After high school, she joined the Navy. Looking back, she tells me she did it partly to prove our brother wrong—he once told her she would never accomplish anything. Unfortunately, during her time in service, Debbie experienced a significant sexual assault while stationed in Iceland. She reported the assault to her superiors, but instead of receiving support, she was met with disbelief and trauma. Not only was her assault denied, but she was also re-victimized by the implication that she must have done something to deserve it.

Debbie fought to maintain her sanity in the face of this injustice, but her battle was far from over. She was dishonorably discharged from the military due to the mishandling of her case. After her discharge, she married a man she met during her deployment, had a child, and helped raise his children from another marriage. But her trauma resurfaced, and for many years, she struggled with her inner demons. Eventually, she divorced her husband, came to terms with her true identity as a gay woman, and found happiness with a wife she's been with for sixteen years.

Debbie's experience was the first in our family to be identified as a mental health struggle, with diagnoses including Malingering and suspected Borderline Personality Disorder. It was also the first time a family member came out, and the family fully embraced her same-sex marriage. Before the end of her marriage, she also suffered the devastating loss of her home in the hurricane that destroyed Homestead Air Force Base in the 90s, marking another layer of trauma from a natural disaster.

Today, I'm happy to share that Debbie found the strength to challenge the way her situation was mishandled by the Navy. After a long fight, the Navy overturned her dishonorable discharge and restored it to honorable status, allowing her to receive full Veteran's benefits for her service. She is now able to receive the recognition and support she always deserved.

My oldest sister, Denice, represents the second and most significant mental health disorder in our family. Diagnosed in her early thirties with Bipolar Disorder, and later with Cluster B Personality Disorder (specifically Histrionic Personality Disorder), Denice's struggles didn't truly present until adulthood, leading to official diagnoses. However, I firmly believe her mental health issues began much earlier, when I was seven and she was around fourteen.

I am convinced that Denice's initial struggles were triggered by religious trauma we all experienced, but particularly her, when a well-known "end times" evangelist visited our church one summer. During that week-long revival, his message, full of fear, shame, and guilt, deeply affected us as vulnerable children already struggling with imperfections in our daily lives.

At the end of one service, Denice asked me to "go forward" with her for counseling—a practice often done in Baptist churches at the end of services. We found ourselves speaking directly with our pastor in the Junior High Sunday School room. Denice was terrified, believing she had never truly been saved. The evangelist's message about Salvation led her to conclude that, because she had never experienced the "peace that passes all understanding" after accepting Jesus into her heart, she must not have been saved. This fear, instilled by the evangelist's preaching, was the catalyst for what I believe was the beginning of a lifetime of internal turmoil for Denice.

This family trauma, marked by multiple attempts to prevent, manage, and recover from her episodes over the years, is at the heart of this book. It reflects the immense cost that shame and guilt have exacted on our entire family due to the experiences of mental illness.

Denice's oldest child was found guilty of vehicular homicide at seventeen, leading to a prison sentence followed by a lengthy probation period. This became the first indexed family trauma involving legal consequences. Soon after, her youngest child suffered life-threatening injuries in a motorcycle accident just as he was approaching legal adulthood. This marked the first severe experience within the family of someone clinging to life, undergoing extensive rehabilitation, and learning to walk and talk again.

Two years later, we faced our first—and, we pray, our last—death by suicide. My beloved brother-in-law, unable to bear the weight of his own pain, took his life. Denice, already burdened by so many tragedies, found him. This loss added to the heavy toll on our family, testing our strength in ways we could never have imagined.

Now, it is my turn to share my story. I bring the first and second indexed divorces to the family, along with a period of rebellious behavior that challenged my parents' marriage. For many years, I fought against their bond, wishing for them to divorce, and at times, I even wished for my dad to die so we could be freed from his strict hold. Today, I thank God that those immature, emotionally broken wishes were never granted.

In my search for healing during those tumultuous years, I clung to unhealthy relationships starting at the age of fourteen. The first of these relationships subjected me to severe daily physical, verbal, and emotional abuse. After two years, I was forced to choose between abortion or adoption for the baby created in this relationship. Despite my disdain for my dad at the time, he played a significant role in guiding me through this decision at just fifteen years old. It became a defining moment in my lifelong journey toward healing.

The day I left that relationship, a pivotal moment occurred. I was picked up by my "knight in shining armor," who saw a damsel in distress. I moved in with him on my eighteenth birthday, married him that summer, and had two beautiful children together. However, in marrying my first husband, I unknowingly introduced elements of criminal history, incarceration, and drug use into our family dynamic—a detour in my life that may one day shed light on why I became the "hero child" in the family.

I begin with these tragic family experiences—though they're far from the entirety of what we've endured—to provide you, the reader, with a foundation of the trauma we've faced. It's my hope that by sharing these vulnerable moments, you'll better understand our struggles. Our story is one of survival, both individually and as a family, through many traumas, and my hope is that it will offer a sense of solidarity to those of you who have faced similar challenges. You are not alone in your journey.

Chapter 4

Tragedies, trauma and Trauma

Tragedy is defined as an event that brings great suffering, destruction, and distress—such as a serious accident, crime, or natural catastrophe (Wikipedia).

Trauma, on the other hand, is the emotional response to such terrible events. These may include accidents, crimes, natural disasters, physical or emotional abuse, neglect, witnessing or experiencing violence, the death of a loved one, war, and more. In the immediate aftermath, shock and denial are common. Over time, individuals may experience unpredictable emotions, flashbacks, strained relationships, and even physical symptoms like headaches or nausea (American Psychological Association, 2025).

In recent years, society has introduced the term "small t" trauma to describe less severe experiences that still cause significant emotional distress—things like a breakup, job loss, or bullying. These events may not seem traumatic to everyone, but they can still negatively affect mental health (Newport Institute, 2022).

What's crucial to remember is this: what causes a trauma response in one person may not affect another the same way. Every response to trauma is personal and valid. Judging someone for their reaction—or the intensity of it—is not only unhelpful, it's hurtful. It can re-victimize and shame someone who is already suffering.

Life will inevitably bring tragedy. Our family, like so many others, has experienced its share. In fact, tragedy is one of life's few certainties.

By our very human nature, we are vulnerable to devastating natural forces—earthquakes, tornadoes, tsunamis, floods, avalanches, volcanic eruptions. You get the picture.

And because of free will, we are also vulnerable to harm inflicted by others—both those who choose not to contain their harmful impulses and those who try, but fail.

Then there's the spiritual reality: because of the Fall of Man, we are subject to every human affliction—physical, emotional, and mental pain—all leading ultimately to death, what the Bible calls the "wages of sin" *(Romans 6:23).*

Death.

It is the one certainty that unites us all. We don't know when it will come, or how, or where—but we do know it *will*. And we know *who* it will touch.

Still, when death arrives, it often feels unreal. We grieve. We feel shock, disbelief. And then, we begin to process—sometimes together, sometimes alone.

We try to comfort others while also craving comfort ourselves. We offer understanding while searching for it. We confront our own mortality, sometimes feeling a quiet relief that it wasn't us—and then wrestle with the guilt of being the one who survived.

Enter emotions—a vast, often overwhelming wave of feelings that crash over us, leaving us unsure what to do with them all at once. Trying to sort through the tragedy, trauma, and Trauma is daunting. There are so many words to describe what we feel, but when all those emotions hit at the same time, it can feel impossible to make sense of any of them.

Add to this the complexity of our unique, individual experiences—the lens through which we interpret what's happening—and we each end up on a very different path, trying to navigate our own way through the pain. What might help one person cope may not help another. Yet, one thing remains the same for all of us: it's difficult. It's painful. And that shared difficulty may be the only common thread that allows us to normalize the tragedy in some way.

From there, things begin to diverge.

Each person's ability to cope—shaped by their skill level, their logic, their reasoning—varies greatly. And with that, we step into the intricate, often misunderstood realm of mental health.

Tragedy and trauma push us all to search for something that feels "normal." But in doing so, we often start measuring others against our own version of what normal should look like. We start judging. We question why someone else is reacting "that way," forgetting—or perhaps never realizing—that their lens is not our lens.

Because each of us brings our own history, personality, pain, and healing to the table, the definition of "normal" becomes highly personal—ranging from minor nuances to major differences in perspective.

As a result, we find ourselves in conflict with those we once thought were on the same page. We seek out people who seem to share our experience, people who "get it"—only to feel jarred when they say or do something, in their own grief or anger, that suddenly doesn't bring comfort anymore. That emotional connection we felt begins to fray.

When the person is someone we're not deeply tied to, the relationship often fades quickly. But when that person is a loved one—someone close, someone we see and interact with every day—it gets much more complicated.

Now, not only are we trying to heal from the tragedy or trauma itself, we also have to cope with the disconnect. We must find a way to navigate the disagreement, the emotional tension, and the breakdown of shared understanding. And that... that is not easy.

I'm not here to debate the chicken-or-the-egg theory of mental health. I'm simply offering a normalized starting point—a way to begin making sense of something that has long puzzled me: how, despite growing up in a family that has remained intact for over half a century, I've heard from both of my living sisters—and suspect I would have heard the same from my late brother—that we somehow had *different* parents.

We were all born to the same two people, whom we each lovingly call Mom and Dad. So how is it possible that our experiences feel so fundamentally different?

Maybe it's because I'm the youngest. Maybe it's genetics, or some unique blend of nature and nurture. Maybe I came wired with more emotional resilience. I don't really know. But for whatever reason, it seems I took on what the mental health world refers to as the "hero child" role in our family dynamic.

I didn't understand this until I was well into my own parenting journey. But at some point, I began to notice a quiet refrain spoken among the younger generation—my kids and their cousins: *"Don't tell Aunt DeAnna... you know she'll just fix it."*

At first, that statement caught me off guard. But in time, it became a revelation—and I don't use that word lightly. It made me pause and consider the roles we're assigned (or assumed) in our families: the hero, the scapegoat, the enabler, the mascot, the lost child, the golden child. These labels are more than theories—they're lived identities. And I want to speak to each one of you now, whoever you are and whatever role you may have carried. I want to speak with compassion and care, not from a place of superiority, but from a place of "joining through the truth" (Real, 2018).

I believe that through truth—not blame, not shame—we can begin to release the overwhelming guilt and confusion many of us have carried for far too long. My hope is that this story, as raw and painful as it may be at times, can become a part of your own healing. That it can help lead you toward a more emotionally profitable life.

What you are about to read is vulnerable. It is painful. Not just for me, but for my family. So before we begin, I ask you—the reader—to pause with me and pray:

Dear God,

Please grant me the strength to write what this reader needs to hear—without shame, without fear. Give me the discipline to share my story with clarity and organization, so I don't lose the reader in the mayhem of mental health. Help me to honor You as the Archer of this experience—and to honor my sister, another arrow, and my entire family.

Please allow this reader to journey with me—open-hearted and open-minded—so they can absorb what they need for their emotional healing and mental well-being. And let them gently release what they don't need, without judgment toward me, my experiences, or any member of my family.

Thank You, Lord. And thank you, dear reader.

Namaste.

Chapter 5

In the Beginning, Mine that is

A Place for Open Disclosure

As I begin to write about this journey—one that began nearly fifty years ago—I find that I'm still struggling with waves of emotion. Anger often blankets what's beneath: sadness, disgust, surprise, and fear. These emotions stem directly from my lived experiences, and I expect they will rise to the surface as I continue to tell this story.

Let me be clear: this is *my* emotional truth, shared from within *my* experience. And while I will do my best to remain emotionally regulated while writing, part of my hope is that you, the reader, will also benefit—by witnessing and perhaps learning emotional regulation through my example, as you journey beside me.

It is my Wise Mind Adult—the grounded part of me—who is telling this story. She holds the steering wheel, guiding us forward, even as she allows space for the voices of my adaptive teenager and wounded child to speak their truths. They are heard, but also protected by me in the process (Real, 2008, p. 87).

As I mentioned in Chapter 3, I believe this story begins when I was around seven years old. That summer, our church hosted a visiting "End Times" evangelist during one of our regularly scheduled week-long evangelical meetings.

His method of bringing people to Christ? Pure hellfire and brimstone. Fear.

I couldn't tell you what messages were preached that week—I was only seven, after all. But I *can* tell you this: I remember the terror. The emotional chaos. The spiritual mayhem his visit stirred in my family.

What was said from the pulpit that week sparked something destructive. And what began as a spark ignited flames—flames that have burned through the emotional and spiritual landscape of my family for the past five decades.

Even now, as I write, a deep anger rises within me. The thought echoes loud: "How dare someone weaponized God against me, my sister, my family... using fear as a way to convince us to be 'good little people' for God."

And under that anger? There's a storm of emotion—intense disgust, grief, shock. Along with all the secondary and tertiary emotions that branch from those core feelings.

This memory comes straight out of what feels like the gates of Hades. The overwhelm is real—the kind that comes when religious methods are used to control, to manipulate, all in the name of "saving souls." As if the Kingdom of Heaven keeps score... as if someone's worth is based on how many notches they've tallied in a spiritual win column to present at the Pearly Gates.

Okay.

Now that I've said that—let's take a deep breath.

Let *me* take a deep breath. Let *us*, the parts of me, breathe.

Let's sit with the angry ones for a moment. Let them feel heard.

I remember these little red books—tracts, they were called. Imagine a matchbook-sized pamphlet, maybe six inches square when opened, filled with enough fear to alter the course of a child's entire life.

The images were cartoon-like, appealing in a way meant to draw us in. On the pages, people went about their everyday lives—walking, talking, shopping. But then, suddenly, there it was: the mark of the beast.

Bold, black ink. 666. Stamped across the forehead of someone who looked just like us, standing right beside us in the crowd.

We were told to hand these little red books out, to *witness* to others about the end times. It was our job to "win souls for Christ" and keep people from eternal damnation. We were just children, yet we were given this heavy responsibility with promises of prizes in heaven if we succeeded.

One of the images showed a man shopping for groceries. Instead of paying with money, a bar code on his forehead was scanned by the cashier. We were told that soon, the government would require us all to have numbers tattooed on our foreheads. These numbers, they warned, would eventually expose the Antichrist—someone *born with* the mark of the beast.

And we believed it. How could we not?

For those of you reading this who are younger—wow, yes, I know this sounds strange. But let me give you some context.

Back then, grocery checkouts worked like this: a cashier stood at the register and manually typed in the price of every single item. You stood there, waiting ten, sometimes twenty minutes while they totaled everything up. Then you handed over *cash*, or if you were fancy, you wrote a *check*.

Credit cards weren't a thing—not like they are now. If anything, you might have had what was then called a Master Charge card. But using a credit card to buy food? That was absurd. People would laugh at the idea. Debit cards did not exist either.

So, you can imagine how *futuristic* it seemed when we were told that a time was coming where you'd scan your forehead to pay. It was unbelievable. Terrifying. The idea of lasers reading bar codes? Numbers embedded in your skin? It all felt like a dystopian prophecy.

I remember, around that same time, the government started requiring each person to have their own unique number. I still recall Mom taking us down to the government office to receive ours. We stood in line, innocent and unaware, getting our identity reduced to a string of digits.

Was it all a coincidence? Maybe. Maybe not.

Maybe that's when I first started to understand what a *coincidence* even was. When I started to question fate, destiny, purpose—those big, grown-up ideas that arrive early when fear is handed to you too young.

A few months later, the news announced that grocery stores were implementing a "faster" checkout system. It used laser scanning devices to read a series of lines—barcodes—that contained the item's name and price. A computer processed the information and printed your receipt on strangely smooth paper. And just like that, the prophecy from the little red book didn't feel so far-fetched anymore. It felt real.Even the bags changed. No more brown paper sacks. Now, they had plastic bags with handles. That was it. That was when the utter fear set in.

The End Times are here. And I'm only seven. Already out of time. Already behind in the competition for a good spot in heaven. I would lie in bed at night, unable to sleep, consumed by the fear of burning to death in a fire because I hadn't won enough souls to Christ. I didn't even really understand what that meant—but I knew it was urgent. I knew it was eternal.

Eventually, I'd drift off somehow, only to wake up the next morning with a fleeting moment of joy: The "thief in the night" hadn't come for me. But almost instantly, that joy would be replaced with a fresh wave of anxiety. *I only have today.* Just this one day to try to be good enough, to say the right things, to save someone. Because if He comes tonight and I haven't done enough—I might be left behind.

That was my daily internal rhythm. Waking with dread. Living with fear. Sleeping with worry. Being a "good kid" wasn't the hard part—not really. That stuff? That was easy. Don't lie. Honor your parents. Follow the rules.

Yes, I lied sometimes. I stole a piece of candy from the bin at the store once. I was human, a sinner. But I *knew* Jesus lived in my heart. At least... I was *pretty* sure.

Even if I never actually *felt* Him knocking on that little wooden door in there. Even if I didn't hear the squeaky hinges creak as the door opened and He came inside.

But God—the Father? Nope.

He was terrifying.

He was the one who sent the floods. He caused the fires. He was angry.

And as long as I kept my head down, stayed quiet, and didn't attract attention, maybe—just maybe—I could survive

His wrath. I could manage the anxiety of trying to be good enough if it meant staying beneath His radar. That became my daily survival strategy.

Looking back now, I realize... Our Dad—*my* dad, *our* dad—he *was* that angry God. The God of Wrath. The one you didn't cross. The one whose silence was as loud as thunder.

And Mom? Maybe she was the embodiment of Jesus—kind, loving, soft, protective... maybe.

Chapter 6

In the Beginning, DeNice's that is...

I feel it is important to introduce some of the traumatic experiences Denice had in her developmental years that professionally speaking, would attribute to the development of mental illness diagnosis. One account that mom has described occurred when Denice was very little. Denice had been playing on a swing set and seemed to have knocked the wind out of herself. When she went to get help from Mom, she had fallen and hit her head on the concrete patio. She sustained a serious head injury that Mom, to this day, still tearfully cringes when recalling the incident. "Her little head was so bad, it was soft and bruised where she hit it", Mom recounts. "I took her to the emergency room and they told me that she had a concussion and to watch her for while", she adds, "I was so scared and felt so bad for her, she really was a hurt little girl". Research has increased over the last decade to show that traumatic brain injuries for children can lead to adult-onset mental disorders showing "people with TBI are 28 times more likely to have bipolar disorder. This is especially true if the head injury happened between the ages of 11 and 15. It is believed that TBI causes brain inflammation, which can lead to mental health issues" (Altuwairqi, December 29, 2023).

Another developmental trauma Mom recollects was when she took Denice to a dentist, I believe before the age of five or so. It was a new dentist that was supposed to specialize in working with kids. Back then, there were not the same protective practices in place for children and this event left Mom with a great deal of trauma as well, feeling extreme guilt that she should have responded very differently than she did. Mom recalled hearing Denice screaming from the dentist chair when she was getting cavities filled. The office staff at the time, consoled Mom and her worry telling her that kids are usually scared when visiting the dentist and that Denice was fine. Little did Mom know until after the dentist finished that he did not provide numbing agent for Denice when he was drilling out the cavities. Mom said "after he was done, he told me that she needed to experience what getting cavities felt like so she won't eat sweets". Mom was shocked and devastated at what she had just learned happened to Denice. Needless to say, Mom found a different dentist after that and didn't realize the trauma of that experience would play out over time for Denice. We all know that if this would have occurred in today's society, the outcome of that dentists actions would have been dealt with much differently. This experience plays in to how generational experiences and how they are addressed differently over time can lead to misunderstandings between parents and children. It also leads to the need for ending the blame for those who came before us, as they likely were doing the best they could with the resources and knowledge that was available to them at the time.

That said, even things like how our grandparents felt it funny to scare us and then laugh at our reactions as children being traumatized. For Denice, Mom mentions things such as her having a clown cake for one of her toddler age birthday's and big gorilla feet slippers, both where she reacted toward with utter terror. Mom recalls "rather than them backing off and realizing that she was terrified by these things, your grandparents chose to continue laughing and teasing her to illicit an continued reaction from her". She continued "I finally looked at your dad and took her out of the room…I told him that his parents are not allowed to treat her that way…I was so mad". Children are vulnerable and should be protected, however it is not always possible. For Denice, these events along with others could very well have contributed to the onset of mental illnesses that she had carried with her throughout her life.

Now that I've shared some of Denice's early trauma and my experiential filter of religious trauma, let's rewind to the *evangelical meetings*—the week that preacher came to town, declaring the "End Times" were near. This, now added to the trauma Denice experienced before my recollection or existence for that matter, is where I begin in an awakened state of starting to understand Denice.

It was customary at the close of every service for the preacher to invite anyone in the congregation to come forward for special counseling, or simply to pray at the altar until the service ended. I remember one of those nights clearly. My oldest sister, Denice, tapped me on the shoulder and whispered, *"Go forward with me."*

So I followed her.

I vaguely recall the pastor requesting someone—maybe one of the elder women of the church—to come pray with us. That part is fuzzy. What I do remember clearly is that we somehow ended up in the junior high Sunday school room, alone with the church pastor. That could only have happened after the service had fully ended.

The conversation that followed was seared into my memory.

Denice was riddled with fear. She was questioning her salvation. She was overwhelmed with anxiety because she had never felt that sense of peace people described—never experienced the warm, quiet assurance of having Jesus in her heart. She was terrified she had unforgiven sin and, because of it, she'd be left behind when Jesus returned. She wept as she spoke, barely able to get the words out. The fear was so thick in the room, even I, at seven years old, could feel it pressing down.

I didn't understand the depth of her fear then—not yet. My own terror hadn't developed. Not at that point.

So all I could do was try to comfort her. I tried to connect. I tried to understand.

I thought, surely, now that she had talked to the pastor—the one with the answers, the one with the guidance—that everything would be okay. That's what pastors were for, right? To help us understand, to help us find peace.

But as time passed, I began to realize: that moment was only the beginning.

Looking back now, I can see signs. Signs that mental health symptoms were already starting to surface in my sister's life, and in her personality.

In the years that followed that intense evangelical week, certain behaviors began to show up—patterns I didn't fully understand at the time, but that I now recognize as part of a much bigger picture.

Of course, I couldn't have known then. I was just seven. But now, with decades of hindsight, I can begin to piece together how those early spiritual experiences—those moments drenched in fear—were part of the foundation that led us to the revelations we're sitting with today.

When Dad bought our family home in 1973, Denice, as the oldest child, got her own room. So did our brother. Debbie and I shared the bigger bedroom next to Mom and Dad's room.

Not long after that—right around the time fear began to settle into me—Denice started asking me to sleep with her in her room at night. Looking back, it was as if I had become her security doll, her living "dolly," there to keep her safe from the thief in the night. I wasn't just her little sister anymore; I had become her comfort object.

She started bringing me places with her—to meet her friends, to Wednesday night church services, Saturday night youth group events, and Sunday night after-service "singspirations." I don't think I fully understood it then, but I had become her emotional buffer. Maybe even her emotional anchor.

Our cul-de-sac was full of kids, and we all played outside together—kickball by day, hide-and-seek by night. Denice developed a crush on a neighborhood boy her age. Each evening, she'd send me over to his house to ask if he wanted to come outside and play. She worked hard to get me to express how much she liked him, hoping it might nudge his feelings. But his response was always the same: he liked her—but not like that.

Still, he'd come out sometimes. And when he did, it felt like a small win—for her, and weirdly, for me too. Eventually though, he stopped coming out. And not long after that, so did she.

I remember another moment from her high school years. She had a friend who agreed to come visit our church—but only if Denice would attend a service at her Pentecostal church in return. We were roller skating in our unfinished basement when she told me about it. She was nervous about asking Mom for permission. We were raised to believe that all other religions were wrong, and only the Baptist church held the true way to salvation in Christ.

But eventually, Denice did get permission, and she went with her friend.

After that visit, something about her seemed... different.

She tried to explain the experience to me—how the people at that church spoke in tongues. She said that part confused her, but otherwise, the service felt familiar. Still, something about her had shifted. I couldn't put my finger on it, but I could feel it.

At the time, I didn't understand what was happening. I was still too young. So I just observed. Quietly, carefully, I watched.

I attended youth group roller skating nights, where we'd ride the church bus out to a rural skating rink with a wooden floor that creaked under our wheels. After a couple of hours circling the rink, we'd head upstairs to the loft for food, fellowship, and a Bible service.

That version of spiritual expression—community-centered, active, casual—felt right to me. I fit in there. It made sense.

But I never really found God inside the actual church building, even though I was there all the time. Monday and Wednesday nights. Saturdays for youth group meetups—

unless it was an overnight event, which I wasn't allowed to attend. And then Sundays, which belonged entirely to the church, except for the short break between morning and evening services, usually filled with lunch and football games during the season.

I remember one Saturday in particular, when I was about ten. Denice got me ready for the youth skating night. She dressed me in my brand-new jeans, carefully cuffing the bottoms so both sides matched perfectly—because that was the style. She let me borrow her pink terrycloth tank top, the one with the light blue and white silky heart patch stitched onto the upper left side.

She curled my hair and pinned it back with barrettes on both sides. One up and one down, she said, was not allowed "because that was how sluts wore their hair". I wasn't allowed to wear makeup yet, but she let me use her Luscious Lips roll-on gloss. It gave my lips a shiny glow, without color. I felt... cute.

That night, after we finished skating and were upstairs for fellowship, Denice told me I could go back down to the skate counter to say hi to the cute boy who worked there. So I did. I wasn't gone long—maybe a few minutes—when the bus driver, who also gave the Bible messages, came to find me and bring me back upstairs.

I still don't know what happened while I was gone. I didn't feel like I'd done anything wrong. I was just doing what I'd been told I could do.

Later on, I got to go on snow skiing trips with the youth group, too. Those trips were all-day events and gave the junior high kids a rare chance to tag along with the older youth. I liked that. There were some really cute junior high boys from the neighborhoods around the church who only showed up for the "cool" events—skiing, mostly. That made it worth showing up.

Sometimes my dad would go skiing with us. I really liked it when he came along on the trips.

As I got older and continued attending the Senior High youth events, I started to learn the hidden side of it all. The unspoken rules. The secrets. I learned how the older kids snuck Peppermint Schnapps onto the ski trips to "stay warm." I saw the heavy petting and make-out sessions that happened in the dark back rows of the church bus.

I learned a lot.

Denice started sitting at the front of the church, but on the "other side"—the opposite side from where our family usually sat. That shift happened around the time she began developing a fondness for the lone, tall guy who always came to church by himself. We all came to know him as Big Jim.

He was the youth group bus driver and the guy who gave the Bible messages during activities. It felt like Denice grew more confident when I was with her, or maybe people interacted with her more when I was around. Looking back, it was probably a little of both.

Big Jim started coming over between Sunday services for our family spaghetti dinners—and he never really left. Denice had captured his attention. He eventually became part of the family when they married on October 16, 1982.

We were now a family of seven.

I can't recall if I had asked to go with Denice on all her school and church activities or if she had just always wanted me there. Either way, the activities were fun, and it just became "our thing." I was her tagalong, but I didn't mind.

As I neared junior high, though, things began to change.

One evening, I was dressed and ready to go on a youth group outing. I remember hearing Mom and Dad talking in the family room. Out of nowhere, Dad said, "Well then she can't go."

I froze. What did I do wrong?

Mom came to talk to me. She explained that some people at church were upset that I was attending the senior high youth group activities when I technically belonged in the junior high group. They said it wasn't fair.

That was the beginning of the end for me—at least when it came to church.

Eventually, my lack of interest became a concern to one of the male elders at church. He told my parents I was a "black sheep who had wandered."

And that's when I started to understand what jealousy and envy looked like—how they could be dressed up in concern, or control, or righteousness.

Chapter 7

Establishment of DEFCON 3 – Hyper Religiosity

You're probably wondering—what is DEFCON, and what happened to One and Two?

In our family, we reimagined the acronym as a way to navigate life with Denice's emotional spectrum. For us, DEFCON stood for *Denice's Emotional Framework CONtainment*. It became a lighthearted but incredibly helpful tool we used to communicate with each other, giving us a shared language to recognize and respond to the varying intensities of her emotional states.

It helped us stay connected to her without always walking on eggshells or anxiously scanning for signs of an episode.

The naming of it came a few years ago, almost accidentally, when her oldest son once casually said, *"If Mom has a boyfriend, she's at DEFCON 4."* And just like that—it stuck.

Now, for those readers who appreciate accuracy: yes, the U.S. military DEFCON scale counts *down* toward war, with DEFCON 1 being the most extreme level of threat. In our family's version, we flipped the script. Our DEFCON numbers count *up* as Denice's emotional escalation rises. (More on the definitions of DEFCONs 1 and 2 later.)

There were three absolutes for the family when it came to using the DEFCON system:

Stay in your Wise Adult self

Don't get blended

Check your facts;

followed by three rules of DEFCON. It took years to even get to this point, and to be clear—it's still not foolproof. It requires all of us to stay grounded, self-aware, and humble enough to admit when we've been "hoodwinked" into an emotional entanglement.

That part—realizing we'd fallen for something said mid-episode and acting on it—was especially hard for me. My protective instincts ran deep. I had decades of involvement, of showing up for her, of believing I *should* step in. Letting go of that role—even a little—wasn't easy.

Rule Number One: There must be transparency. No more secrets. No more protecting confidences based on who said what to whom. I know—this one sounds harsh, especially when you think about trust and privacy. But unfortunately, for us, that concept had to be completely removed—for the sake of our family's sanity.

In our system, secrecy became a breeding ground for confusion, manipulation, and emotional chaos. So, we agreed: everything would be out in the open. It was the only way we could maintain balance while still trying to support Denice.

Rule Number Two: We must all be on the same page. This is where the DEFCON system really helped. Before it existed, things were harder. It meant tracking conversations, connecting dots, managing information between episodes. It took real effort from everyone.

In the early days, the main players were me and Jim. I can't count how many times he'd call and say, *"Can I bring her over for you to observe?"* Or *"Will you come here and help me figure out if this is an episode starting?"* We became a team—watching, listening, comparing notes. We got good at identifying the early signs.

Eventually, Mom was brought in too. That was hard. She struggled, understandably, with accepting how skilled Denice was at manipulating the narrative when she was mid-episode. For Mom, it was painful—watching her daughter suffer, witnessing the unraveling of *De-"nice"* into someone else entirely.

Rule Number Three: We must present a united front. This one took time. Each new episode drew another family member in, and with each addition came a responsibility to bring them up to speed—gently, but clearly. Many conversations happened. So did many family meetings. Each one was rooted in love, not control.

We weren't trying to box Denice in—we were trying to hold her, safely, within a system of support. And that speaks volumes about how deeply loved she was, and how devoted we all were to her care.

Now, for the episode that first brought true illumination to her mental illness—we have to travel back in time again.

I remember a Vacation Bible School activity in the park. One of the crafts that day was making a little book (yes, another little book). This one was made from squares of colored felt, each representing a step in the process of salvation—how we are redeemed by the blood of the Lamb (Revelation 7:9–17).

So here goes as best I can remember:

Page 1 - Black: Our hearts are full of sin;

Page 2 - Red: till we were cleansed when Jesus' blood was shed and we let him in;

Page 3 - White: and He made our heart white as snow

Page 4 - Blue: We are baptized in the water's blue;

Page 5 - Green: and grow with Him in the pastures green;

Page 6 - Yellow: till we meet Him again on Heaven's paths of gold.

Fast forward to the summer of 1993—what we now refer to as the beginning of the first episode. By this time, Denice and Jim had been married for twelve years. They were deeply involved in an Evangelical church they'd attended for years, and they'd built a family of their own: two boys, around eight and seven years old at the time.

There had been a few concerning moments before, when the boys were toddlers. I remember Mom and I going over to Denice's house to check on her. Her behavior had raised red flags, but things seemed to improve after we helped her with some laundry and tidied up her kitchen. Looking back now, it's clear she was in a deep depression. Jim had grown concerned, too—he noticed she spent her days glued to her favorite soap operas, neglecting the house, skipping preparation of meals, and not fully caring for the boys while he was at work. That was the first time I stepped in to help in a significant way—watching the boys and trying to clean up the house as best I could.

Now, really back to that summer of 1993. Denice and Jim were on a church mission trip in Chicago with their youth group. Both had been active leaders for years, committed to mentoring the younger generation. Then came a call that changed everything. Jim phoned Mom with news—something had happened. Denice was being flown home early.

That summer marked Denice's first mental breakdown, although at the time, no one fully understood what had triggered it, or even an understanding of what was happening. Later, when I talked with her while chronicling her episodes, she told me she remembered being overwhelmed with worry. She said she was desperate to know if people attending the mission event were truly going to heaven. She even claimed to see deceased individuals—people who appeared to be "floating," their feet not touching the ground. It was one of the earliest signs of what would later be diagnosed as a condition involving visual and auditory hallucinations.

Jim managed to get her on the flight home, but it wasn't easy. He told Mom that Denice refused to listen to anything he said, and he had worked nonstop to keep her calm during the flight. He also shared that, during the event itself, Denice had repeatedly run up and down the aisles, speaking gibberish—as if she were trying to speak in tongues.

When they arrived back in Denver, they went straight to the emergency room.

I believe it was a Saturday afternoon when Mom called to tell me what was happening. I told her I'd get a ride to the hospital from my neighbor. Her husband had kindly agreed to watch my two kids, who were three and two years old at the time.

My friend and I arrived at the ER—I think just before Denice got there. After waiting a few minutes in the lobby,

Mom came out from seeing her. She looked upset, confused, and completely dumbfounded.

"She keeps screaming that she needs to pee and they won't untie her from the bed," Mom said, her voice strained. "So I told her to just pee the bed." Then, with her jaw clenched tight, she added, "And when you go back there with her, you get that damned bracelet off her wrist and away from her. It's like she's worshiping that stupid thing, like it's got some kind of spell over her."

I had never seen Mom this angry before—not with Denice. Her frustration was boiling over, but it wasn't clear who or what she was mad at. Maybe the hospital. Maybe the situation. Maybe the helplessness. Denice was acting in a way none of us had ever seen before—completely inconsolable, irrational, unreachable.

To this day, it's unclear what exactly triggered that initial episode. But when I went back to see Denice in her ER room, it was clear she was intensely fixated on a handmade beaded bracelet. That bracelet—a faith bracelet—was crafted at the youth retreat. The colored beads symbolized biblical concepts, the same ones from a book I'd made back in Bible school.

She was visibly agitated that Mom had tried to take it away. As I stood by her side, she kept repeating the meanings of each bead, her voice rhythmic, ritualistic:

"Black—for our hearts, black with sin. Red—for the blood that was shed. White—for the robe of righteousness that makes us white as snow. Blue—for the throne of heaven. Yellow—for the streets of gold."

It was like listening to whispered prayers in a church with the hollowness of vaulted ceilings causing whispers to swim freely, echoing all around. She repeated the phrases over and over. When I tried to talk to her, she turned toward me, still chanting—only louder, as if trying to drown me out with her recitation.

That's when I noticed her eyes.

Denice has Mom's green eyes. But that day, there was no green at all. Her entire eyes were black—not just the pupil or the iris, but the whites, too. The sclera.

The room was brightly lit, as ER rooms always are. She was lying on the gurney, strapped down for her safety and the safety of others, with nothing covering her lower body. There was no scientific explanation I could find for what I saw. But when I leaned in, nose to nose, close enough that my eyes were less than an inch from hers—it felt like I was staring straight into her soul.

I said quietly, "You need to trust me. Right here, right now. Give me the bracelet. I'll keep it safe for you."

She paused. The chanting stopped. And then she said, "Okay."

She let me take the bracelet without resistance. After that, she began cooperating with the medical staff and was admitted.

I think it was the Monday after Denice had been admitted when I went to visit her at the hospital after work. A staff member escorted me to the area where she was being held. Before we reached the room, he warned me about what I was about to see—to help soften the shock.

He led me to a window, where his desk offered a constant view into her room below. When I looked through the glass, I saw Denice. She was naked, in a room with padded white walls, pacing like a caged tiger. She would walk back and forth, stopping at the window in the door each time, glancing out, then continuing on her path.

Despite the staff's warning, my heart sank. I stood there watching her, and my eyes filled with tears. It was all I could do not to fall apart right there. But through the sadness, one thought crossed my mind: *She's safe in there.*

The staff explained that her clothing had been removed for her own protection. She had been making attempts to harm herself, and standard protocol was to remove all objects—including clothing—until a patient in her condition stabilized. In later conversations, as I worked to chronicle her experiences, Denice told me she remembered trying to slash her wrist with the jagged edge of a plastic yogurt container. After that, they only gave her Styrofoam cups.

That was the first time I truly learned what a "72-hour hold" meant—or so I thought. There was nothing we could do but wait. She was being legally held for observation and treatment for seventy-two hours, and the staff would let us know what came next once the hold was over.

Eventually, she stabilized enough to be transferred to the hospital's mental ward. She stayed there until she "reset," mentally. We all exhaled. *Whew.* We thought it was over. We tried to go back to our lives.

But this episode became the first we would later define as *DEFCON 3.* The patterns, which we came to recognize over time, included: a fear of losing her salvation, an overwhelming worry that others weren't going to heaven, claims of hearing God speak directly to her, reports of seeing ghosts or angels invisible to others, behaviors marked by extreme jubilation and abnormal expressions of joy, hyper-fixation on religious objects, bible verses, and the idea of salvation.

Chapter 8

Establishment of DEFCON 1 - It's All In How You Play the Game

In the last chapter, we started with DEFCON 3—not because it was the beginning, but because it followed the natural progression of the story. I encourage you to see it as a starting point, especially for those who prefer structure. It offers a simple way to begin understanding just how disorderly and overwhelmingly chaotic mental health conditions can be—for those directly affected, and for those walking beside them.

DEFCON 1 came when we began noticing the inconsistencies in Denice's stories. She would tell different versions to different people, offering selective truths depending on what she wanted them to know. This behavior led to manipulation and division, fragmenting support in order to achieve a specific outcome. Dad would call this behavior "lying," whether by commission or omission.

To help myself make sense of it—and to cope—I started thinking of her actions as a chess game.

Full disclosure: I joined the chess club in elementary school after watching Dad play. Something about it drew me in. I think it appealed to my analytical side—the part of me that enjoys strategy, future thinking, and reaching goals. Still, other parts of me often took over, and truth be told, I remain a novice at best. But even now, I have a strong appreciation for strategic thinking, and I believe I'm fairly good at it.

So is Denice.

That raises an important question: What separates strategic thinking from outright deception?

The problem begins when strategy is used to manipulate. When the intent behind planning involves using others—without their full awareness—to carry out actions that serve a hidden purpose, the line gets blurry. It's like setting up a chessboard not just with the right pieces, but with people who can be persuaded that the moves being made are in their best interest, when in reality, they're fulfilling someone else's secret agenda.

As I write this, I can hear parts of myself—and maybe some of you—thinking, "Oh my God, this makes Denice sound evil." Especially if you know her personally.

To those concerned parts, I offer this reassurance: I don't believe any of us are inherently evil or bad. We are all human. We make choices. If I may refer to the Fall of Man and Woman in the book of Genesis (3:6), it reminds us that we are constantly making decisions shaped by what we've experienced. Every one of us has a unique set of filters—formed by our past—that influences how we respond to the world.

Those filters start forming early in life, especially during childhood, when we are most vulnerable. During those years, we rely on people who are also imperfect and human. Their mistakes, intentional or not, can leave emotional and mental wounds that we try to process through a child's understanding and a child's heart. That's where the earliest signs of personality or behavioral disorders may begin.

Most of us want to believe our parents did everything right in raising us. We hold on to the idea that they must have loved us—after all, they brought us into the world. For those who were adopted or raised in foster care, perhaps someone loved you enough to choose you, to want you. At our core, every human being has a deep need to feel wanted and loved.

That said, experiences vary greatly. I want to pause here and honor that truth—especially for those who were adopted or fostered. Your journey is uniquely yours.

Regardless of how we were raised—by birth parents, adoptive parents, or guardians—we all carry our own experiences of pain and trauma from being raised by imperfect, human caregivers. Each of us developed our own patterns of attachment, or lack thereof, to our primary and secondary caregivers. The trauma and pain we experienced during those crucial developmental phases were never the fault of our inner child.

To survive, we created internal systems—coping mechanisms that helped us get through the pain. These survival strategies, whether they served us well or not, became embedded in us. And the truth is, we carry them into adulthood. Sometimes, they help us. Other times, they hold us back.

When our inner children are triggered and allowed to take over—through our thoughts, behaviors, and emotional responses—all hell can break loose. Relationships suffer. Our careers take a hit. Our sense of self feels shaken. If we haven't learned how to manage our triggers, how to regulate our emotional responses in a healthy way, we end up causing harm. We hurt others. We hurt ourselves. We disrupt our own lives.

This begins a painful, familiar cycle: harmony followed by disharmony. Protecting ourselves, then licking our wounds. Then harmony again, and once more—disharmony. Round and round it goes.

What's often missing from this cycle is repair.

True repair is hard. It takes courage, effort, and emotional maturity. It requires us to take responsibility for the role we played in the disharmony. And let's be honest—who really wants to do that? It's so much easier to point the finger, to see clearly what someone else did wrong. It feels simpler to say, "They made me feel this way," or "They're blaming me for what happened."

But the truth is, as adults, it's our privilege, our right, and our responsibility to manage ourselves. We are responsible for our own reactions. We must contain ourselves—not to suppress, but to prevent causing harm to ourselves or others. It is also our responsibility to model healthy behavior for our children and for the children around us.

Childhood is over. It has passed. And sometimes, we must accept that—radically accept it.

This doesn't mean we silence or abandon our inner child. It means we stop letting that child run the show. As adults, we are called to show up with maturity, not hide behind anger or disguise our wounded parts in the mask of adulthood. Yet, as humans, this is something we often struggle to grasp.

The *Diagnostic and Statistical Manual of Mental Disorders* (DSM-5-TR) defines a personality disorder as "an enduring pattern of inner experience and behavior that deviates markedly from the norms and expectations of the individual's culture, is pervasive and inflexible, has an onset in adolescence or early adulthood, is stable over time, and leads to distress or impairment" (p. 733). The manual further categorizes various personality disorders, noting that "personality disorders represent maladaptive variants of personality traits that merge imperceptibly into normality and into one another." These disorders can manifest in behaviors that are odd-eccentric, dramatic, or anxious-fearful (p. 734).

Now that we have a clearer framework for understanding the potential roots of these behaviors and the survival skills they develop from, we can turn our attention to the behaviors we began noticing in Denice. These behaviors became a signal to us—something that prompted us to pause, observe more closely, and pay greater attention. Over time, it became an almost instinctual skill, a finely tuned inner sense, or a gut feeling for those of us who have worked with her through these difficulties.

This skill of recognizing and understanding her behaviors also became a critical tipping point, a moment where we knew we had to gather enough evidence and address it thoroughly as a team. Why? Because once we enter DEFCON 1, we've already crossed into the threshold of a DEFCON 5 disaster.

I believe I speak for everyone involved—especially Denice—when I say that the desire to avoid a DEFCON 5 situation at all costs is indescribable. And yet, we also know that if we choose to ignore it, or if certain family members continue to bury their heads in the sand, we are doing Denice a tremendous disservice. By avoiding the issue, we risk letting another catastrophe unfold for her—and for everyone who is involved, even if indirectly.

Much like parenting, we can't shield others from the pain that comes with experience. What we can do is walk alongside them, offering comfort and support, so they don't have to face it alone. This requires a strong sense of Self-protection and balance, especially for those of us accompanying them on this journey. The need for protection becomes even more crucial as Denice's DEFCON levels rise—each level demanding more of us in order to stay grounded and resilient.

When strategy is mixed with desire, and then sprinkled with jealousy or envy, the result can be manipulative and controlling behavior. A character that comes to mind to illustrate this is Veruca Salt from *Willy Wonka & the Chocolate Factory*. At its most overt, this behavior shifts quickly from being sweet and charming to demanding and destructive—just like in the iconic scene when she shouts, "I want it now."

As we begin to hear similar things from Denice, they may start to sound unbelievable, a little far-fetched. Once our inner alarms go off, it's time to compare notes with others who may be in contact with her. This is where the institutional rule of transparency—being on the same page—becomes essential.

The strategy of divide and conquer is a tactic many military leaders have used throughout history. It's easier to win a war when you can win multiple smaller battles. How does this translate to Denice's behavior?

When Denice sees something she wants that others have, and the desire to obtain it overpowers her, she enters what feels like a battle—a battle to do whatever it takes to win. The situation crosses the line into DEFCON territory when her focus shifts solely to what she wants, and she begins seeing others as mere tools to help her get it.

This is where the behavior starts to take on characteristics of odd-eccentric traits. Denice may begin dressing in louder colors, adopting more flamboyant and eccentric styles, and behaving in more dramatic ways. These shifts can include increasingly overtly flirty behavior and actions designed to draw attention. Alongside these changes, there is often an increase in anxious affect—her words and tone become more urgent, as if to convince others that something must be done immediately. She implores people to listen and share in her fear of what might come next. In some way, it seems she may be in a version of first level consciousness, focusing on survival skills to overcome fear of not having something she wants, where the want has become a belief that she needs it, and includes someone to help her get the believed needs.

As much as it may feel negative to consider the possibility of entering DEFCON 1, I submit that whether or not Denice intentionally manipulates and controls others to get what she wants should not be the focus of judgment here. What I hope to highlight in this moment is this: Thank God for the behaviors that present in DEFCON 1. These behaviors are essentially no different from the warning lights—what I learned to call "idiot lights"—on a car's dashboard, signaling that the vehicle needs attention. If we choose to ignore those warnings, the car will eventually, and sometimes rapidly, break down and stop working.

For someone with a personality disorder, especially if undiagnosed, they may lack the tools and skills to repair their own "vehicle." Just like many of us—thank God for those of you who are mechanics by trade—we are often unequipped to notice, diagnose, or fix what's broken. Whether Denice knows it or not, and whether we like it or not, when she's in this phase, her internal system is blinking warning lights for herself and for others. These warnings signal that she is heading toward a breakdown if the issues aren't addressed, redirected, or corrected.

As an adult, Denice is ultimately responsible for herself, just as the rest of us are for our own lives. During DEFCON 1, it's crucial to hold her accountable for her decisions and to offer guidance when necessary. At the same time, it's important to maintain enough distance to allow her the space to make her own decisions, hoping that what she chooses will help keep her from slipping into DEFCON 2.

Unfortunately, due to the stressors triggering her, it's often very difficult to predict what will happen. As a result, we continue to live our own lives but with heightened attention to Denice's life. We ramp up communication within the team, comparing notes about what each of us is currently experiencing in relation to Denice.

The observed behaviors during this episode that became defining signs of DEFCON 1 were: manipulation to acquire things from others, covert expressions of jealousy and envy, incongruence in statements and conversations, eccentricity and dramatic presentation.

Chapter 9

Paranoid Delusions

Someone is following me, Denice tells a police officer who had responded to a 911 call. The caller reported that a female had entered her garage and was talking to nobody. This incident took place in September 1997, just two days after the death of Princess Diana of Wales. For reasons unknown, this worldwide tragedy seemed to capstone the stressors building up for Denice, triggering yet another mental breakdown. This marked at least the third episode since the first one in 1993.

The night before, Mom received a call from Denice's mother-in-law, asking her to come and stay with Denice and the boys. According to Mom's recounting, Denice's mother-in-law explained that she had witnessed Jim "whip" their oldest son "with a garden hose for the last time" and was planning to "disown Jim and leave." She also mentioned that the younger son and the neighbor girl had gotten the older son into trouble again.

At this moment, I want to pause and ask you, the reader, to please reserve any judgment you may feel or want to react toward what you've just read. I'm not asking you to excuse any abusive behavior toward a child, for any reason. I simply request that if you continue reading, you do so with an open heart and an open mind. Consider not only what mental health does to the person who has a diagnosis, but also how it affects those who love someone struggling with their trauma.

At the same time, I ask you to hold compassionate and loving space for Denice's sons, particularly the oldest son. It is evident that both of them have also suffered great emotional and physical wounds throughout their childhood development, not only at the hands of Denice's mental illness, but also at their father's hands, while he was dealing with his own mental health difficulties and trying to help manage Denice in her episodes.

Jim's mother further explained to Mom that Jim had asked for someone to stay with the boys because he didn't feel comfortable leaving them alone with Denice due to her abnormal behaviors. He had to go to work, but his shift at the U.S. Postal Service was the graveyard shift, and he couldn't take time off. Between his own health issues and Denice's, Jim was often out of sick time at work. Denice was presenting with active delusions. Her triggered, irrational, anxious, and fearful thought processes had her convinced that she was unsafe—that she was going to die, just like Princess Diana had days earlier. In a follow-up conversation with me, she said, "Because my life is exactly like Princess Diana's."

Let me share the similarities Denice was using to convince herself, leading her to experience such overwhelming fear and ultimately becoming paranoid and delusional.

Denice and Princess Diana share the same birthday, July 1. Jim and Prince Charles were both thirteen and fourteen years older than Denice and Princess Diana, respectively. Both couples became engaged and married in the same year, and both marriages produced two children—both boys. Interestingly, Denice's oldest son was born three days before Princess Diana's youngest, Prince Harry. At the same time, both Denice and Diana were pregnant.

Mom went to relieve Jim's mom and stayed with Denice so Jim could go to work. By the time Mom arrived, Jim's mom had already left the house. Mom journaled Denice's behaviors and activities throughout the night, noting that Denice kept wanting to leave the house, but Mom wouldn't let her. There was no logical reason for Denice to go anywhere, yet for some reason, she kept trying to leave. When Mom finally got her to go to bed, Denice kept getting up every hour to check her blood sugar levels, convinced she had diabetes. (This will be unpacked further in the chapter on somatic symptoms.)

Jim had recently been diagnosed with diabetes and had begun educating himself about how to control it through diet rather than relying on insulin. He started going to the gym regularly, and Denice joined him, making it a good activity they could do together. He made significant dietary changes and worked hard to improve his health. Jim purchased all the supplies needed to regularly check his blood sugar levels, and it seems Denice had started to learn this practice as well. While this wasn't a bad thing for people to do for their health, Denice's mixing of this knowledge with her paranoid delusions led to abnormal behaviors, as Mom observed that night.

Denice also kept wanting to sleep with her youngest son, who was eleven at the time. She would try to wake him up throughout the night. Mom recalls having to repeatedly get Denice out of her son's bed so he could rest before school the next day, the first day of the school year for the boys. Denice was not oriented to person, time, or situation. Jim was right—Denice was unable to take care of herself, let alone her boys, in her current condition.

After a long, restless night, the morning brought even more heightened levels of paranoid delusions. Denice was convinced that something terrible was going to happen to the family. Realistically, she wasn't entirely wrong—there was impending danger, but not in the way she believed. Denice became adamant that her oldest son was not going to get on the school bus and began grabbing him, trying to keep him inside the house. This was just days before his thirteenth birthday. Mom told her to let him go so he could get to school. She can't recall where my younger nephew was at the time, but he was likely either gathering his things for school in another room or already outside.

After the oldest boy finally managed to leave for the school bus, Mom worked diligently to keep Denice in the house while waiting for Jim to come home from work. Denice eventually decided to take a shower so she could go with Jim to his doctor appointment when he returned. Mom, exhausted yet determined, sat down to continue journaling what had transpired during the night and morning. She must have known that recording Denice's erratic and abnormal behaviors was critical, showing excellent foresight even in her weary state. I've always admired this about her—she's the one from whom I inherited my historian skills.

When Jim returned home, he went to take a shower in preparation for his appointment. Denice, now finished with her shower, came downstairs and saw Mom journaling. Suspicious of what Mom might be writing, Denice asked what was on the page. Mom, fearing Denice would escalate if she told the truth, wasn't safe revealing the reality of what had happened the night before. So, she told Denice she was writing a grocery list—Mom even started one, just in case Denice insisted on seeing it. But Denice, convinced that Mom had been documenting her behaviors, believed the truth. Later, in a conversation with

Denice, she recalled feeling that Mom was trying to get her into trouble with Jim, almost as if she were tattling.

At the time, Mom was also unsure of Denice's safety if she left the house, so she refused to give Denice the keys, even as Denice insisted she needed them. Denice went upstairs, only to return moments later, waving Jim's keys at Mom in a childish, taunting manner, like a young child teasing another with a "Na Na Na Na Boo Boo" chant. Denice then sprinted out the door to get into the Jeep Cherokee. Where was she going? No one knew.

Mom rushed to follow her, terrified that Denice might drive in her unstable condition. As she reached the door, she noticed neighborhood kids gathering at the bus stop around the corner, which only heightened her concern for their safety if Denice got behind the wheel. Mom positioned herself between Denice and the car, trying desperately to prevent her from driving. She reached for the horn, hoping Jim, still in the shower, could hear the sound and come to her aid. But Denice, growing more agitated, became physically violent. She punched Mom in the left side of her face, knocking the glasses from her face.

Stunned and shocked—Denice had never been physically violent during an episode before—Mom bent down to retrieve her glasses. In that moment, Denice ran off, sprinting down the street, away from the house. Before Mom lost sight of her, she recalled seeing Denice scale an eight-foot wooden fence. "I kid you not," Mom says to this day. "If I hadn't seen it with my own eyes, I would never have believed it."

Apparently, Jim must have heard or sensed something was wrong and came out of the house in his underwear, asking Mom where Denice was. Shaken, surprised, and teary, Mom replied, "She hit me and then ran off." When Jim saw the bruise on her face where Denice had punched her, he rushed inside to call the police. While Jim was on the phone with the 911 operator, he was informed that another call had come in from a woman in a nearby neighborhood. The caller reported that a strange woman had shown up at her house, asking to use the phone to call for help. The police were en route to that location to pick up the woman before coming to Jim and Denice's house to sort everything out.

It turned out that the woman the police picked up was, in fact, Denice. At some point during the encounter, Denice had told the woman who helped her, "I need help because I think I just killed my mother-in-law," clearly recalling the assault on Mom but mistakenly thinking it was Jim's mom she had attacked. After a brief investigation, the sheriff, who had arrived to take custody of Denice, decided to have her transported to the hospital ER at Jim's request. He revealed to the police and Mom that he had taken Denice to the ER just a few days earlier for a mental evaluation, but she had been discharged without being placed on a mental hold or given any medication for her mood swings.

This experience marked the beginning of a frustrating pattern for Jim and me. We began to recognize Denice's "tipping point" as the critical moment when she needed care and could be placed on a 72-hour mental hold for further evaluation. Unfortunately, if we took her to the hospital before reaching that tipping point, she would present well enough—acting calm, coherent, and saying the right things—to avoid being held. We soon learned that this tipping point was, essentially, her DEFCON 5.

Chapter 10

Establishment of DEFCON 2 – Somatic Symptoms and Behaviors

The DSM-5-TR classifies certain disorders related to somatic symptoms, including conditions where symptoms are either factitiously created or genuinely experienced, but the individual becomes highly distressed and experiences significant disruptions in daily life. This often results from excessive worry and fear about what they believe is happening to them (p. 349-370). For Denice, this became part of a recurring pattern. She would either fabricate symptoms of diseases she believed she was suffering from, worry that others had diseases they hadn't been diagnosed with but were showing symptoms of, or become overwhelmed with the belief that something was seriously wrong with her body. In some cases, she would exaggerate the symptoms to prove that doctors had misdiagnosed her.

Common illnesses like congestion, a runny nose, or a slight cough would spiral into her self-diagnosis of a terminal illness. There was no consideration that these symptoms could be due to allergies or environmental factors—only the belief that something far more serious was happening. Complicated, right?

Now, I'm not a doctor, nor have I ever wanted to be one. However, through my experiences of raising my own children and working with Denice for decades, I found myself having to stay on top of medical knowledge to help manage her anxieties and symptoms. I sometimes joke that I could probably CLEP out of all the classes and pass the exams to be an M.D., but the Wise Mind in me laughs at that thought.

We all face conditions as part of being human. We get sick—sometimes with a common illness, other times with a terminal one. It's a part of life. As Americans, we're fortunate to have access to quality healthcare, and I believe it's crucial for each of us to take control of our own medical needs. Doctors are human too, and I haven't yet heard of any "magic pill" that works for everything.

Denice has certainly had her share of illnesses. She's dealt with persistent bouts of Irritable Bowel Syndrome (IBS), sinusitis, bronchitis, and the ever-painful and irritating Urinary Tract Infections (UTIs). The usual advice from doctors for these common health issues includes medications, dietary and environmental changes we can control, and healthier living practices—such as reducing stress. Sounds simple enough, right? Not so much.

When we're sick, many of us begin negotiating with ourselves. We promise we'll do anything to get better because, in that moment, we feel terrible. We vow to change our habits, live cleaner, improve our diets—anything to avoid feeling this way again. It's easy to make these promises when we're vulnerable and physically weakened. But here's the big "but"—when we start to feel better and get back to our normal routines, what happens to all the bargaining we did with ourselves? It often gets thrown out the window. We realize how difficult it is to change long-held habits, give up creature comforts, and soon enough, we forget how miserable we felt.

As adults, we have the right to choose, and we exercise our free will. We all tend to take advantage of that right, slipping back into old patterns until the next time we fall ill. So, let's explore when this cycle becomes detrimental to mental health, and how it escalates for Denice.

To understand DEFCON 2, we need to look at the diagnostic criteria for Somatic Symptom Disorder (DSM-5-TR, p. 351) or Factitious Disorder (p. 367), whether imposed on oneself or another. I want to clarify that I'm not attempting to diagnose Denice with these disorders. Rather, I'm using these references to help illustrate the behaviors I've observed in Denice and others while trying to care for her during one of her episodes. The language in the DSM-5-TR is useful in describing what happens.

DEFCON 2 is essentially defined as when Denice begins to act out in ways that reflect her belief that she—or someone close to her—is seriously or critically ill, or even near death. Her thoughts about the symptoms she experiences become disproportionate and persistent, fueling a sense of extreme anxiety. She becomes belligerent toward others who try to offer logical perspectives or reality checks regarding her situation. In her mind, these symptoms demand attention, and she devotes excessive time and energy to them.

This often leads to what I term "fishing for agreement" from doctors—hoping they will eventually prescribe a medication she believes will serve as her "miracle cure." Unfortunately, this behavior not only strains her relationships but also impacts her credibility. When she genuinely faces physical symptoms, her past overreactions sew disbelief and judgment about her pain tolerance, making it difficult for others to differentiate between genuine illness and emotional distress. (More on this in the chapter for DEFCON 5.)

As this behavior blends with the mindset of DEFCON 1, we begin to see a road leading to chaos.

Once her fear extends to others being sick, Denice starts looking for signs in those around her to validate her growing concerns. At one point, she became convinced that Dad had full-blown Alzheimer's disease. She would point out every little thing he forgot, trying to convince Mom of this fabricated diagnosis. The more she pushed, the angrier she became with Mom for dismissing her concerns, feeling unheard and disregarded.

I worked with Denice to help her understand that, whether or not Dad had Alzheimer's, there was nothing we could do about it. If he later developed the disease, our role as his children would be to support him through it—not to accuse him of forgetting things to prove our point. I reminded her to focus on herself, trust that God would handle Dad's health, and accept that we weren't in control of the outcome.

In her second marriage, Denice took a similar approach, excusing what she perceived as her husband's lack of intelligence. She would say, "He's never been diagnosed, but I just know he has Down syndrome, so we accept him as he is." In public, she elevated herself by positioning him as someone who needed constant protection and care, mirroring the nurturing role our mom had with Dad. This, she thought, showcased her skills as a wife, just like Mom's.

However, what Denice failed to see was how everyone else viewed her behavior. She treated him like a servant—ordering him around with demands like "Get me this" or "Go get that," and he would comply without protest. This dynamic resembled the way Mom had catered to Dad. In this marriage, Denice had found a way to feel superior, elevating herself by positioning herself as both a nurturing wife and, in her eyes, a competent one, mirroring both parents in this relationship.

Another memory that stands out in this phase of Denice's behavior development occurred years ago when my daughter was about five. I was driving Denice to the credit union, and my daughter seemed a bit down for some reason. When she expressed her sadness, Denice immediately turned to her from the back seat with a tone that was both luring and persuasive. She said, "Well, when *we* get upset like that, *we* just go and make ourselves feel better by eating a HUGE meatball sandwich from Subway."

Not only was she suggesting that I make Subway our next stop (and, by the way, that I should pay for it), but this conversation opened up a whole new issue for me to later unpack with my daughter. I had to explain why *we* don't eat our emotions away. In that moment, Denice's influence over others, especially with her words and behaviors, began to wake me up to the disordered symptoms and signs that were becoming more apparent.

Since Denice's 1997 episode, where she was convinced she had diabetes, she had managed to obtain a prescription for Metformin, a medication designed to treat Type 2 and gestational diabetes. It's also used as a weight loss aid to help prevent diabetes. Don't get me wrong—the pursuit of this medication was not entirely misguided. However, when an illogical mind twists something logical to prove itself "right," or when an adaptive child part within a mentally unhealthy state hijacks the person's internal system (Schwartz, Sweezy,

2020, pp.40) the medication subtly becomes a "magic pill." The thinking becomes: take the pill, do nothing else. The adaptive child part running the show refuses to exercise, practice healthy eating habits, or manage portion control.

An individual in an Adult Wise mind state would process the potential side effects of such medication. A simple Google search for Metformin reveals common side effects, including:

"Nausea and gastric distress such as stomach pain, gas, bloating, and diarrhea are somewhat common among people starting up on Metformin." (Kadanoff, 2019).

This is where the hyper-fixation on irritable bowel syndrome (IBS) began.

Once again, the common affliction of IBS that many people suffer from is far from pleasant. There are many causes, such as consuming foods that aren't compatible with one's digestive system, overeating, side effects from medications, genetic conditions, and more. Stress levels are also strongly associated with IBS, which makes it particularly difficult for those of us who struggle with it. Most of us tend to address IBS with common remedies: Pepto-Bismol, Tums, avoiding irritating foods, and, ideally, lowering stress.

However, when IBS is compounded by the escalating fears of death or running out of time, we find ourselves needing to move Denice from DEFCON 1 to DEFCON 2. This change in status prompts the team to increase contact with her and intensify efforts to help her de-escalate and manage her fears. We would aim to do this through logic-based tools like Socratic questioning, guiding her toward reducing the overwhelming fear that she's going to die.

To truly understand Denice, it's crucial that we approach her with non-judgment, using the 8 C's of IFS (Schwartz & Sweezy, 2020, p. 49-54): curiosity, connection, compassion, clarity, creativity, courage, calm, and confidence. Normalizing her physical state, Denice is a Caucasian, cisgender female, approximately 5′1″ in height. She is physically healthy, with a normal heart rate and rhythm, low to normal blood pressure, and healthy oxygen levels in her blood. Her cholesterol levels are in the normal to high range, and her lung capacity and function are good. Overall, she is in good health—aside from being told her bone structure is "soft, like chalk," despite being morbidly obese since mid-adulthood.

Denice also suffered from a severe head injury as a toddler, lost a front top tooth in a youth group hayride accident, and tore her right leg's MCL and ACL during a skiing accident in her youth group years. Over time, this injury became increasingly problematic, especially as the natural aging process took its toll. Her obesity contributed to the deterioration of cartilage, leading to bone-on-bone pain in her knee for many years. Eventually, after much mental stabilization and some weight loss (as required by her orthopedic surgeon), she underwent knee replacement surgery in 2018.

Now that you have a better understanding of Denice's physical health, let's explore the experiences when she enters DEFCON 2 during a mental health episode.

In the summer of 1999, Jim called me one evening and asked if he could bring Denice over for me to observe and validate or invalidate what he was seeing in her behavior. My son was at their house, supposed to stay overnight. He and Denice's youngest were very close, often referring to each other as "brother from another mother." Since the birth of Denice's children, I had become a surrogate parent, often helping care for them when they were small and during times when Jim needed to focus on managing Denice's mental health. When their youngest son suffered a near-death motorcycle accident in 2006 and ended up in a coma, Jim made me medical power of attorney for their son. This allowed me to help Jim make decisions for their son while he was incapacitated, especially since the stress of the accident could trigger an episode in Denice.

Back to the evening for a cousin overnight. Denice's son would have been about fourteen, my son around eight, and my daughter about nine. I told Jim to bring Denice over, and he planned to make up a reason to convince her that it was necessary to come to my house. This might seem underhanded, I know, but at the time, a DEFCON system hadn't been established yet. Jim and I were still figuring it all out. From previous experiences, we both knew that if Denice felt accused of "going crazy," she would become extremely angry—especially if she had indeed entered an episode. Since Jim suspected she was already spiraling, we agreed that we needed to handle things carefully, without triggering an outburst if we could avoid it, especially while he was alone with her and our sons.

Looking at it from Denice's perspective, with a healthy and wise mind, of course, the idea of being accused of "losing it" would be hurtful, infuriating even. It's natural to want to defend oneself in such a case. But when viewed through the lens of her mental illness, this situation could quickly escalate into a DEFCON level event—requiring a much larger response. Jim wanted my help because he was fairly sure she had entered an episode. Thus, the need to keep the real reason for bringing her over between us was crucial.

Jim told Denice that my son was having breathing issues—that he had asthma and needed to be taken home for a nebulizer treatment. This wasn't a lie; my son frequently experienced asthma symptoms, and they became more noticeable whenever he visited their house, where animal dander and severe dust buildup were constant triggers.

At the time, my husband and I had just purchased our first brand-new home the summer before. I had prepped both my husband and daughter with the reason we were expecting Denice and Jim, and we all resumed our activities while waiting for their arrival. When they finally got to the house, my husband, daughter, and I were in the kitchen, and Denice and Jim joined us. Meanwhile, the boys had resumed their usual goofing around on the living room couch. The family room was dimly lit by dusk, but the kitchen was bright and illuminated. I had yet to decorate, so the light reflected off the white walls and linoleum flooring, creating a crisp, clean space. My home didn't have a basement; the foundation was simply a prestressed concrete slab, making the kitchen floor a concrete surface covered in linoleum.

Hold on to these details—they'll be important later.

My husband was sitting at the kitchen table, his back to the sliding glass door. My daughter, as I recall, was standing between him and the peninsula gas fireplace. As I prepared the nebulizer treatment for my son, I kept an eye on Denice's behavior. She seemed to be lost in her own world, not really engaging with anyone, but appearing to have an intense, silent conversation with herself. She also paced between the kitchen table and the living room couch, where the boys were, moving in a way that reminded me of a tiger pacing in its caged zoo environment.

I moved over to join Jim, who had positioned himself at the other end of the kitchen, leaning against the sink. To give you a clearer picture, these two rooms together made up about ninety-five percent of the livable space on the very open-design main floor, which measured roughly twenty-five feet by twelve feet.

As Jim and I started talking, I quietly told him that I could definitely see the behaviors he was concerned about. We began making plans for him to take her to the ER for further observation. And then—*SLAP!* The noise echoed loudly in the vaulted space. In what seemed like mere milliseconds, we saw Denice go from standing to lying flat on the hard kitchen floor.

Now, we've all either seen someone pass out before or perhaps pretending to pass out. Pretending to pass out means that a person is still aware of their surroundings and instinctively tries to protect themselves from injury while falling. But this time—this *SLAP*—was different. Denice went from vertical to horizontal so quickly, there was no doubt that it wasn't a typical fainting spell.

How do we know she wasn't truly unconscious? When someone passes out, they are typically unable to regain consciousness immediately. And yes, we considered the possibility that she might have collapsed from dizziness, but no. Jim was well-trained in first aid, and I had my own experiences with passing out and being around people who had passed out. This was not real—it was pretend.

Of course, in our experience, it seemed like she was pretending. But for Denice, who had clearly entered the early stages of an episode, this was her maladaptive and illogical way of expressing her overwhelming fear that she was dying from a heart attack. Unbeknownst to her—or to us at the time—she was having a full-blown panic attack, which mimics the symptoms of a heart attack. In her mind, no one was listening to her claims that she was dying. So, she dramatically collapsed, holding her eyes shut so tightly that her eyelids twitched, and clenching her mouth closed while holding her breath to convince us that she wasn't breathing and needed CPR. In her mind, she was sure this would prove to us that she was dying.

As I kneeled down next to Denice, fully aware that it was all dramatics, my husband was working, though not very hard, at suppressing his laughter. Even my nine-year-old daughter, watching the scene unfold, found it funny. If we had been in an acting class, I'm sure most of the audience would have found the dramatics entertaining—if the storyline were a comedy. Up until this point, my husband and kids had never witnessed the behaviors Denice displays before or during an episode.

In an effort to contain the situation, with everyone around me finding it comedic, I aligned with Jim and reminded myself that this was a tragedy, not something to laugh at. I had to be careful not to let Denice think she could manipulate the scene any longer. So, I sternly turned toward the laughing crowd and, with a serious tone and facial expression, said, "Stop laughing, this is not funny."

I believed my husband, as an adult, would understand the gravity of the situation and serve as a role model for my daughter and the boys. It wasn't until much later, when talking with my now adult daughter, that I realized how much that moment affected her. She felt terrible about her natural, childlike reaction of laughing, not fully understanding what was happening. And, of course, she hadn't been shown how to behave appropriately in such a situation by my husband.

Jim and I now faced a crisis that needed immediate attention. We had to remain calm, avoid overreacting with fear or anger, and keep our heads in the game. In the blink of an eye, I found myself using a skill I'd later learn was from Dialectical Behavioral Therapy (DBT), known as STOP (Linehan, 425-427), observing as noise echoed around me, through the reprimand of the laughter, to observing Denice on the floor—it couldn't have been more than twenty to thirty seconds. I measured the time based on how long someone can hold their breath, which Denice was doing. Kneeling beside her, my hand on her chest, feeling her heartbeat, she barely turned her head toward me, opened her left eye just enough to see me, and then, in a forced exhale, she said, "I'm dead, I just had a heart attack." Without missing a beat, she quickly resumed squinting her eyes shut and holding her breath again.

To be fair to the laughers, I too had to exercise a tremendous amount of control in that moment because a part—maybe many parts—of me wanted to laugh as well. However, staying in my wise mind, I addressed Denice matter-of-factly: "No, you are not dying. You are having an episode, and we will help you get medical assistance if you cooperate with me right now and let Jim take you to the hospital."

After a few moments, Denice finally complied. She got herself off the floor, deciding when she was ready to stand. Forcing or demanding her to act sooner would only delay things and escalate her again.

We loaded her into Jim's emerald green Cadillac and headed north on the interstate to the hospital downtown. As we headed north on the highway, daydreaming, looking at the newly added decorated concrete retaining walls, I realized I had just naturally joined him without even realizing it. Jim and I were already certain this would result in another 72-hour mental hold, giving us a chance to reset for a few days while Denice could rest and receive the help she needed to regulate.

But things didn't go as planned.

After resting in the waiting room, I ran through the events of the evening in my mind, trying to stay calm and patient while waiting for Jim to come out with the news we expected: that they'd admitted her for a mental hold. Instead, I saw him exit the ER doors, his face filled with disbelief—only for my confusion and anger to set in as I saw Denice following closely behind him.

My mouth probably dropped open in shock. Jim approached me, already processing Denice's release to go home, and said, "They said there's nothing wrong with her. They told me to take her home."

"WHAT? Did you tell them what just happened at my house? Did you explain her behavior?" I kept searching for something he might not have told the doctors—something that could make them see what we had just witnessed. "What do you mean, there's nothing wrong with her? That's BULLSHIT!" I said, struggling to keep myself composed.

I had to radically accept the reality: she was going to get in the car with us and go back home. Jim and I both knew that within three days, she'd escalate again, and we'd be back in the ER, likely transitioning into another 72-hour mental hold at whatever behavioral hospital had an open bed. "What a waste of time and energy, again, to be told she's fine," we both thought and said to each other.

Jim drove me home, then took Denice back to her house, leaving my nephew with me for the night. This created another opportunity for me to check in on Denice the following day. And, as we expected, Denice was hospitalized within days of being released from the ER.

It was during this episode that her medical records finally reflected an established diagnosis of Major Depression, although Bipolar Disorder had not yet been ruled in or out. I now understand the process of ruling out diagnoses as a Licensed Professional Counselor, but at the time, from the perspective of a family member, not having clear answers was incredibly difficult. Jim, myself, and the rest of the family struggled to comprehend what was happening to Denice and how to "fix her," as Dad would often say.

Chapter 11

DEFCON 2 On Steroids

Another, more recent episode, one that began with a collision of DEFCONs 1 and 2, unfolded in the early months of 2022. Before diving into it, let me set the stage by sharing where Denice was in her journey at that time. The decade leading up to this will be explored in other chapters. For now, I ask that you join me in navigating this story as it unfolds somewhat out of order. This non-linear approach mirrors the often chaotic nature of mental health struggles, so let's walk through it together with compassion and a willingness to understand.

By 2022, Denice was living independently in her own apartment and working as a daycare teacher, a role in which she was deeply loved by the children, their parents, and her coworkers. She had a natural gift for nurturing young minds, and her patience and warmth shone through in all she did. She drove an older Subaru station wagon and earned just enough to support herself, especially when supplemented by an annual withdrawal from an annuity she had acquired.

Remarkably, she had gone six years without a full-blown episode. There were close calls, of course, moments that made us hold our breath, but overall, she was doing well. Really well. She was managing on her own, or at least as much on her own as was possible.

Back in 2016, during a previous episode, I had been drawn back into the family circle. Our sister-in-law had reached out, practically pleading for me to return and help. That call marked a turning point, not just for Denice, but for all of us.

In 2009, I made the decision to reevaluate my life. My second marriage had fallen apart, and not long after, I met my current husband. Yes, he's number three. With him, I found the kind of life I had always wanted—one I had never been able to achieve on my own.

Unfortunately, the emotional discord I was dealing with created a space where I withdrew from my family, except for my children, for six years. When I finally reintegrated into the family—especially under the circumstances that led to my return—I knew I had to set clear boundaries and conditions to feel comfortable stepping back in.

Where Denice was concerned, these rules were non-negotiable. If I was going to help her navigate the challenges of her mental illness, which at that point had escalated to DEFCON 5, then I would be the one making the decisions for her. I would lay out the plan and the process, and everyone else would need to follow it. That included full participation from each family member in whatever activities were necessary. Whether it was family meetings, brainstorming solutions, or signing up for specific responsibilities, everyone was expected to show up, contribute, and commit.

I think you get the picture. I was now in charge. Mom and Dad would remain active participants, offering guidance and insight, but from that point on, anyone involved had two choices: volunteer willingly, or be voluntold what needed to be done.

There was only one thing that would not be tolerated: opting out after committing to assist. Anyone who chose not to participate in Denice's care by changing their mind after committing —and in doing so, risked becoming a detriment to the progress we needed to make—would be voluntold to get the hell out.

I was operating in a state of equal parts fury and laser focus, determined to reorganize, clean up, and clear out the chaos that had engulfed Denice's life. Her years of untreated mental illness and poor decision-making had left behind a mess. And while those choices may have started as her own, the damage had rippled outward. The reality I walked into was not just her disorder—it was the entire family spiraling in what I would soon come to call DeNaughtyland. (More on that later.)

Everyone was given the choice to participate in Denice's care to the extent they were able, or to opt out without judgment. Very quickly, a core management team formed. It included Denice herself, our sister Debbie and her wife April, our brother's widow—whom we had adopted as a sister after his death—and Denice's youngest son and his wife.

With the support of this team, I filed for legal guardianship and conservatorship of Denice. These legal roles allowed me to act on her behalf, making critical life decisions and managing her finances. Taking on these responsibilities was both a blessing and a curse, but I'll share more on that later.

Now, we're back in 2022. It was late February. My husband and I were in Phoenix for a business retreat, enjoying lunch on the patio of a nice Mexican restaurant. That Saturday afternoon, I received a call from Denice. We were scheduled to fly home Monday, having decided to spend the weekend relaxing in Phoenix.

The moment I heard her voice, I knew something was wrong. Her tone was off—clearly DEFCON 1, maybe DEFCON 2. I was shocked by her condition. I had no idea something had triggered her, and as usual, the call blindsided me. She began sharing what she had been up to during the week prior, and I could feel my heart drop.

Honestly, a part of me didn't want to believe it. I wanted to stay in denial just a little longer, knowing that if she was really at DEFCON 2, we were entering another episode. That meant we needed to start preparing for war.

Coincidentally, on the global stage that same weekend, Russia invaded Ukraine. For Denice, this was not just a geopolitical event—it was a spiritual sign. In our childhood, we were taught that Russia would be the one to start World War III, marking the beginning of the "end times." Her belief in this added fuel to the fire. We were rapidly approaching DEFCON 3.

During that phone call, Denice was ecstatic. She was proud of herself for taking initiative and going to see a doctor—a new provider in her insurance network. Convinced she had COVID due to a persistent cough, she had managed to get treatment for what she believed was a serious case.

The doctor prescribed her an Albuterol inhaler to help her breathe more easily, over-the-counter Flonase to clear her sinuses, and something she referred to as "coughing pearls" to suppress her cough reflex. She was thrilled, completely satisfied with the outcome.

But the reality was different. She didn't have COVID. She never did. She didn't even have substantial symptoms, just a bit of sinus drainage—normal for the season. Still, she had worked the system with convincing ease, and that phone call marked the start of something far more serious than a misdiagnosis.

Knowing that I was out of state, Denice admitted she had taken the opportunity to see a doctor without telling me. She often used the passive-aggressive line, "You're so busy, I didn't want to bother you," as her justification for making decisions that always seemed to end in disaster. I'd always respond with something like, "Just keep me posted," hoping she'd stay in touch, but knowing full well that "keeping me posted" often meant I was blindsided.

During this call, Denice was unusually proud of herself for consulting with her doctor and obtaining the medications she believed she needed for her "COVID symptoms." She eagerly listed the medications she'd been prescribed, along with all the instructions her new doctor had given her. Of course, this doctor had no history with Denice, no background on her mental health issues, other than what was in her medical records—which noted she was on what we referred to as her "mental meds."

Denice went on to mention the warning the doctor gave her: "Albuterol can mess with your mental meds, so you need to keep an eye on how you're feeling." The doctor also told her that Albuterol was an "emergency use" medication, to only be used when she was having trouble breathing.

What caught my attention was Denice's proud declaration: "I already discussed these concerns with my coworkers, and they're on board to let me know if I start acting strangely." Of course, what she didn't realize was that she already was acting strangely—completely unaware of how out of sorts she had become.

Just as quickly as the conversation had shifted to her medical plans, Denice changed the subject. Another indicator that she is not regulated-abruptly detouring the subject of conversation believing it went unnoticed. She excitedly told me about a lunch date she'd planned with an old high school friend. She'd been talking about him for a while, and most of our family knew him, so at the time, this news didn't raise any alarms. She ended the call just as abruptly with, "Okay, I'll keep you posted."

Knowing that Denice had clearly escalated, I reached out to the team to sound the alarm—DEFCON 2, possibly DEFCON 3, with the potential for DEFCON 4 within the next 24 to 72 hours. If we could just get her through the weekend and back to work on Monday, I would be home that evening to intervene. But, of course, it didn't happen. The cat-and-mouse game had begun, and all team members were now on high alert.

By this point, we were all well-versed in the steps necessary to get Denice into an ER where she could be placed on a 72-hour hold. With alarms being raised and DEFCON 5 looming, the situation boiled down to pure luck and a whole lot of praying—hoping that Denice wouldn't hurt herself or others during this breakdown.

That Saturday evening, I remember Mom telling me she had gone over to Denice's apartment to check on her. As usual, it was a mess. This time, it also appeared that Denice's hoarding behavior had flared up again. While I'm not diagnosing her, it's important to understand the severity of her mental disorders. Denice meets the diagnostic criteria for Hoarding Disorder, as defined in the DSM-5-TR under Obsessive-Compulsive and Related Disorders (p. 277). Her symptoms fluctuate from clear insight to complete delusional beliefs, depending on which DEFCON level she's in.

Her hoarding behaviors have become a reliable indicator of her mental state, particularly when it comes to measuring the level of her depression. The state of Denice's living space has always reflected her internal world. At her baseline, she's disorganized and cluttered. But when her apartment starts getting so messy that she loses things or begins to think someone else moved them—coupled with an overwhelming level of dirt and unsanitary conditions—we know she's struggling to mentally process stress.

When Mom visited Denice's apartment that evening, it was clear we were now in DEFCON 3. As she had done so many times before, Mom began cleaning Denice's apartment in an effort to bring some cleanliness, organization, and order—trying to help Denice deescalate if at all possible. It also gave Mom and me a sense of doing something—anything—to distract ourselves from the crisis that we once again found ourselves in. We hoped the act of cleaning might offer a small semblance of control.

Mom noticed many of Denice's mental medications scattered on the kitchen floor, a clear sign that Denice had reached a point where she could no longer manage her Bipolar Disorder medication on her own. As Mom continued to clean, Denice's scattered thought process became more evident. She began talking tangentially about an old friend from her past, someone who had driven a VW Bug. Denice accused this friend of stealing money from her and taking advantage of her, then abruptly shifted back to the present, discussing plans with this same friend, with no clear connection between the two topics.

It was a classic sign that trouble was brewing.

That night, I received a late call from Mom, clearly worried about Denice's condition after their visit. It was obvious that Denice was rapidly approaching DEFCON 5. After discussing it, we decided to reach out to the after-hours nurse for guidance. The doctor who had seen Denice earlier was on call and returned our call at the nurse's request.

Mom and I explained Denice's current state and shared our concerns. We updated the doctor on Denice's behavior both at work and at home, detailing the mental and emotional disarray she had been exhibiting. The doctor was dismayed by what she was hearing and confirmed that Denice had not tested positive for COVID. She instructed us to remove the Albuterol inhaler from Denice's medications and advised us to try giving her Benadryl to help her sleep. She also agreed that Denice needed to be seen by her first thing Monday morning.

We all agreed that if Denice's condition continued to escalate as we feared, we would need to implement an emergency plan. However, we also held out hope that things might plateau before reaching that critical point.

As Sunday progressed, I received an update that Denice was getting worse. We decided that Mom and Dad should go to her apartment that evening to retrieve her car, in order to prevent her from getting on the road and potentially causing harm to herself or others. At this stage, it wasn't uncommon for Denice to believe she was being followed and feel an overwhelming need to flee.

I called Denice to let her know that I had asked Mom to go get her car. Normally, Denice would have gotten upset, but this time, she simply replied, "Okay," and hung up. I called her back, and she responded with something incoherent before quickly hanging up again. It was clear to me that she was having racing thoughts.

I called again and reprimanded her for constantly hanging up, pointing out her concerning behavior and letting her know I would be intervening. At this point, we decided that

Denice needed to be observed and kept safe, so Mom went to pick her up from her apartment and bring her to our family home.

Dad had already gone to bed, and in Mom's words, "Thank God he did, because he doesn't have any patience for the condition Denice is in." She also added that, "He had the mind to put his earplugs in so he wouldn't be able to hear what took place" on the main floor that night.

Dad's description of Denice's behavior was blunt—he called it childish and said she just needed a spanking. While he wasn't entirely wrong, it wasn't a practical solution. Denice was a fifty-nine-year-old woman, so spanking wasn't a reasonable approach. The truth is, at this stage in her episode, the part of Denice that hijacks her system can often resemble the behavior of a ten-year-old with a five-year-old's temper, trapped in an adult's body.

It's a true conundrum to navigate: protecting her and ourselves from harm while trying to approach the situation with a wise, adult mindset. We aim for as much success as we can on the other side, while minimizing the disastrous aftermath that always seems to follow.

Once again, Mom found herself on the front lines, performing the containment activities. From around 11 p.m. when they arrived home until roughly 5 a.m. the next morning, she spent hours journaling, negotiating, compromising, reprimanding, listening, and commanding—basically, doing everything she could to get Denice to lay down and get some sleep. Mom tried to get her to go upstairs to her childhood room to rest, but Denice refused. Instead, she insisted on laying on the couch, clutching a stuffed animal she treated like a baby.

Denice would lie there for a moment before suddenly springing up and scurrying to the kitchen. Mom managed to get her to sit at the kitchen table to talk, as Denice had plenty to say about everything Mom had done wrong as a parent. Throughout all of this, Denice was still convinced she was "sick with COVID," claiming she needed her emergency inhaler due to her persistent cough and sinus drainage. Any time Mom conflicted with Denice's belief that she was sick, it only made Denice more agitated.

Following the doctor's orders, Mom gave Denice some Benadryl, but Denice, insistent on needing her inhaler, threw a tantrum. She dramatically faked coughing fits, snorted loudly in an exaggerated attempt to produce mucus from her dry throat and chest, and even picked her nose, causing it to bleed. Then, she began pulling tissues from the box one by one, using them and wadding them up to throw on the kitchen floor—each tissue dropped with persistence.

Denice knows, Mom hates messes, and for that matter, so does DeNaughty. Mom describes the scene as the kitchen floor being "littered with dirty and bloody Kleenexes" from Denice going through an entire box during the tantrum. Despite the mess, Mom simply let it happen, choosing not to let Denice's chaos affect her.

Over the course of the evening, Denice's behaviors escalated rapidly. She moved from the kitchen to the family room with swift, dramatic movements. Mom described it as if you could literally see the wheels in Denice's head constantly turning, planning her next move. A few times that night, Mom called me for updates, reaching out for support and to make sure she wasn't alone in this for her sanity's sake. She knew Dad was upstairs if she needed immediate help, but at the same time, she kept hoping to God that he wouldn't wake up and come down. By the way, during this episode, Mom and Dad are elderly—both in their late seventies and early eighties. Mom was tired, and Dad was even more so.

Mom and I had agreed that if she ever felt physically threatened by Denice, as she had in the past, she would directly call 911 for emergency help. Each time she reached out to me during the night, this was our first assessment: "Mom, do you feel you are in physical danger from her right now?" When the answer was "no," we moved on to the next strategy to try to contain Denice. At one point, after Mom administered the Benadryl instead of the emergency inhaler, we learned that the medication had the opposite effect of what we had hoped. Rather than making Denice tired, it made her more energetic and virtually unstoppable.

In case you're unfamiliar, Albuterol is a prescribed bronchial dilator, usually in inhaler form, used to prevent and treat wheezing, difficulty breathing, chest tightness, and coughing caused by lung diseases like asthma and COPD (Medlineplus, 2023). Unfortunately, one of the symptoms of a panic attack is shortness of breath, and Denice's system convinced her she was actually suffering from a lung disease or COVID. As her legal guardian, I had access to all her medical records, and I reviewed each one carefully to stay informed and ensure I could provide the necessary care. There were no current or past medical records or test results indicating she had ever had or currently had COVID.

What Denice did often experience were symptoms of sinusitis, which sometimes developed into bronchitis. I believe this was due to a combination of her genetic makeup, constant exposure to dust and pollution in our state, and her diet, which included foods that tend to increase mucus production, such as dairy. Was Denice experiencing discomfort in her respiratory function? Yes, most likely, the same as she always did. But was this the cause of her shortness of breath? No. That was clearly a sign of her panic attack, exacerbated by the Albuterol misuse. Although Albuterol isn't a steroid, the active ingredient seemed to induce a "high" in Denice, heightening her panic and escalating her to DEFCON 5.

We figured out that by dividing the number displayed on the device counter by the number of days since Denice received the medication, and following the doctor's instructions to use it only for emergencies if she had difficulty breathing, she had been misusing the medication. She was averaging two puffs up to fifteen times an hour, or thirty hits per hour. Remember, too, that the doctor had specifically warned her that this medication could interfere with her mental meds. At that point, she had already passed through DEFCON 1, 2, and 3, and her strategy was to inform her co-workers to let her know if she started acting strangely. When I asked her if anyone had mentioned anything to her, she denied that anyone had expressed concern.

It wasn't until later, when I informed her employer that Denice would be taking some time off, that I learned from them that other employees had expressed worry about her behavior and had raised their concerns to her, just as she had requested. This behavior is indicative of DEFCON 1, where Denice only shares specific information with people she chooses. As the episode escalated, it became clear that Denice had become increasingly disorganized, to the point where she could no longer manage or keep up with handling the information she had received from her co-workers, which she had initially sought out to help manage the episode.

On the world stage, that same weekend in February 2022, Russia invaded Ukraine. In hindsight, this seemed to have triggered Denice's episode, pushing it from DEFCON 3 into full escalation, as the invasion was viewed by her, based on our childhood beliefs, as a sure sign of the "end times"—we had been taught that Russia would start World War III.

The defining signs of DEFCON 2 behaviors observed during this episode included: inconsolable worry about self or others having a terminal illness; exaggerating symptoms in an attempt to justify medical care or an assumed illness; and seeking a "magic pill" or procedure to remedy the symptoms without putting in the necessary effort for self-care to prevent common illnesses.

Chapter 12

Where In the World is Jim?

Before we delve further into defining and understanding DEFCON 4, I want to take a moment to tell you about Denice's husband, Jim, who he was to me, and what he means to me.

At first, Jim was a mystery. I could understand what drew Denice to him—he was intriguing. He came into our lives around 1977, suddenly showing up at church, all alone, with no family. His six-foot-eight to ten-inch stature couldn't go unnoticed. He would sit in the front row pew, closest to the middle aisle on the left side of the pulpit, facing the baptismal. Every Sunday, seemingly without fail, he was there for both morning and evening services. Over time, the first two or three rows became the youth group section, which eventually included Denice sitting next to him. Essentially, she just switched sides from our family's regular spot, which was almost exactly opposite, on the right side of the church.

Mom was the organist, so our family's designated spot allowed her to sneak out during the closing prayer and get to the organ to play the benediction songs.

I'm not sure how long it took, but it seemed like no time at all before Jim started coming over for Sunday family lunch. Mom's traditional spaghetti dinner seemed to be the hook that kept him coming back. From that point on, Jim never missed a Sunday meal. There was a saying in our family: once you're in, you're in. You're welcomed, loved, and cared for as if you were born into the family. It might sound like a perk, but in some ways, it's a bit like the Eagles song "Hotel California," where the lyrics say, "You can check out any time you like, but you can never leave."

No matter the circumstance—whether you divorced, went to jail, committed a crime, or even had a moment of extreme anger—you were always welcome in our family, as long as you were repentant and trying to improve yourself.

Jim carried with him a sealed criminal record, only sharing small details with me about his past before he found Christ. As time went on and he continued to stay faithful to God, that record became something of the past. To me, Jim was living proof of what it means to choose to follow God and change one's life. He fully embraced the forgiveness we receive through Jesus Christ, our Lord.

Personally, Jim was a spiritual leader in my life. I felt a deep spiritual connection with him. I loved listening to him preach, whether around the campfires, in the church bus parked on the side of the road, or at the singspirations held after Sunday night services for the youth group. He was, to me, a true lover of Christ, and I believe we both share our faith in nature and in intellect (Thomas, p. 43-59; p. 207-227).

At Jim's home, there was always the soothing sound of worship music softly playing in the background. He had wired the house so it could be heard in nearly every room—a technology that was pretty cool for the time (I realize I'm revealing my age here). I found it calming until someone else mentioned how strange they thought it was. Enter judgment.

Once it was pointed out, I started feeling weird about it, but I was a young teenager at the time, full of rebellious thoughts, thinking I knew everything.

As I grew into the "black sheep" of the family, Jim was still there for me. He used gentle confrontation techniques, which I now recognize, to help me think logically about my life. He challenged me to consider how I was going to live my life as I fought so hard to break away from my parents' influence—especially my dad—just as I believe many adolescents go through a phase of seeking to understand and claim their own identity in preparation for adulthood.

Despite being a godly man, Jim was still human. He struggled with sin, anger, and sometimes an inability to control his emotions. He didn't always make the best decisions as a husband or parent, and at times, he could be overly passionate when advocating for his beliefs, especially regarding freedom of expression. Communication wasn't always his strength, except when he preached. He would sit and observe, and when he had something to say, it was often loud, terse, and boisterous. That was just Jim. And I learned that we accept people for who they are, as long as they are living according to the family's core values and striving to improve themselves.

I was always fascinated by Jim's ruggedness, his fearlessness in nature. Whenever you saw the old 1970s-style Carryall—whether it was a Dodge or Chevy, it didn't matter—you knew it was Big Jim. For those who may not know, imagine a Chevy Suburban or a GMC-style Ghostbusters car, with 1950s-style police lights on top and a lift package. He carried all the mountain climbing gear and first aid equipment anyone could ever need. Jim was an active member of the State's Search and Rescue team, once spending over three weeks searching for a church member who had gotten lost in the mountains. Thankfully, the young man was found alive and fully recovered.

Jim loved the challenge of 4-wheeling in steep terrain in his Jeeps. If you ever needed a ride during a Rocky Mountain snowstorm—back before the snowplows and technology we have today—Big Jim was there to help. I remember him getting me and Denice safely home during a blizzard one Christmas season, never missing a family Christmas.

Big Jim was a techie, a gadget-lover, a BIG guy with a logical mind and a soft heart. He often found himself misunderstood in many places he went, but he sought acceptance and found it within our family, where he became a protector to me, almost like a big brother.

When I was going through my first divorce, Jim seemed to understand my struggles in a way that other family members couldn't. I couldn't afford the $50 fee to file divorce papers, let alone hire an attorney. Being the first one in the family to go through a divorce, I was already receiving pushback from relatives, including Aunts, Uncles, and Cousins, who couldn't understand why I would "abandon" my husband, especially when he was in jail, alone, and needing help. But Jim never judged me.

One day, without me even asking, Jim came to me and offered to give me the $50 to file my paperwork with the court. I didn't even realize he was aware of what I was going through. But he had been watching, and when he saw a problem I didn't know how to solve, he stepped in. He read through my divorce paperwork, helped with editing, and even printed the documents for me, saving me the extra cost of going to Kinko's.

He helped me file the paperwork, allowing me to move forward with my life without judgment.

Jim showed me what it meant to support someone in a way that wasn't about asking questions or offering opinions, but just quietly doing what was needed.

I always looked forward to Christmas when Jim drew my name. His gift-giving felt personal, like he really understood me. For me, gifts mixed with acts of service were his way of showing love. Every gift he gave was thoughtful, always considering my likes or needs. When I started college in my early twenties, after having my two beautiful babies, he helped me set up my dad's old computer so I could do my homework from home instead of dragging the babies to the library. Whenever I ran into computer trouble, he'd come over to fix it, always patient, teaching me as he worked so I could learn along with him. He spent time with me—not just fixing things, but helping me with my cars when my brother wasn't around.

One time, he heard I needed a filing cabinet to organize my household bills, so he went out, bought one, and brought it to me. And, of course, how could I forget when he went to the Army Surplus store and found me a pair of camo pants in my favorite color—purple! I still have those pants and wear them when I'm tinkering in the garage or working in the yard.

As time went on, Big Jim became just Jim. We became a team, goofing around with each other, laughing, teasing, and learning to enjoy each other's company. I was truly his little sister.

Jim was a Godly man—after he chose to follow Christ. I'll admit, he had a rough past, one that, if we had done the things we did as teenagers today, we would all have criminal records. But Jim left that behind when he chose to follow Christ. He attended a Baptist Bible college and graduated with a bachelor's degree in ministry. That was the first graduation ceremony I attended beyond high school. It was followed by attending my uncle's graduation from one of my two alma maters, where my uncle also earned a degree in ministry. Both of these men, very Godly men, influenced me greatly, inspiring me to pursue my second master's degree from a Christian university with a spiritual foundation.

Jim was a spiritual leader for me, and for many others.

After their first baby was born, I watched Jim carry his newborn son, holding him like a football with pride, even though he hadn't planned on having children. He stepped into his role as a father, doing his best to be better than he had been parented, but like the rest of us, he wasn't perfect. Kids don't come with manuals, and we all struggle to find the balance between giving them the love they need and not always knowing how. Jim worked hard to connect with his boys, trying to understand them, to guide and provide for them. He stood by each one of them through their struggles, never wavered in his faith, and even cried when he couldn't take away their pain or fix the struggles they faced. He prayed for strength and support to endure the agony of life. Through it all, Jim never wavered in his belief in God.

He sold the home he inherited from his parents and bought another, deciding it was finally time to leave the neighborhood he'd lived in for decades. His goal was to provide Denice with a place she could truly call her own. The new house even had a spacious detached garage for his love of mechanics, a passion he shared with his youngest son. He moved in with high hopes and proudly showed me around the home and property, radiating more excitement than usual. It seemed as though this fresh start would bring a renewed sense of joy and happiness to his family's lives.

He handled all the finances, paying bills electronically long before it became the norm for the rest of us. Unfortunately, there were misunderstandings, with some assuming that he wasn't managing everything properly. Piles of unopened mail were often found when any of us went over to help clean the house. Despite his intentions, the new home didn't solve the underlying stressors that led to the hoarding behaviors.

There were also some regrettable decisions, like wearing a banana hammock in public while washing his cars. It was a choice that led to embarrassment he couldn't bear. Years earlier, at the old house, a neighbor had called the police on him for this very thing. Her complaint was much like what we now call "being a Karen." Instead of respectfully approaching Jim about his choice of attire, she called the cops, accusing him of indecent exposure. He chose not to fight the charge, pled guilty, and stopped the behavior. However, as the years passed and crimes against others became more violent, new laws were introduced, requiring anyone convicted of a sex crime, including indecent exposure, to register as a sex offender.

When Jim received that notice, it shattered him. He wasn't a sex offender—he never had been—but the shame was overwhelming. It changed him.

On his sixtieth birthday, the family gathered at Mom's house—Jim, Denice, his oldest son, me, and my kids. Unknown to him, the boys were planning a surprise party for the following weekend. No one could make it the weekend before, so they had to improvise. To keep the surprise intact, everyone acted as if they'd forgotten his birthday. I noticed Jim sitting at the kitchen table, a strange sadness hanging over him. Only Denice knew what he'd been struggling with at the time. I walked over, gently gathered his long gray hair, and lovingly draped it over his shoulder, like a hair stylist would. I placed my hand on his shoulder and whispered, "Happy Birthday, Jim."

He looked at me, his eyes welling with tears. His naturally sad eyes—due to a skin pigmentation condition—softened as he smiled at me the way he always did. "Thank you," he said, his voice thick with emotion. "At least somebody remembered."

Just then, we heard an angry "Gee, thanks a lot" from the end of the table. It was his oldest son, reacting to Jim's emotional moment.

I was preparing to finish my shift at work on Thursday, October 9, 2008, when I received a call from Mom. She told me that Denice had just found Jim dead in the garage and that I needed to get there right away. To be honest, I don't remember the drive—I only vaguely recall that my boss drove me over and dropped me off.

I entered the house to find Denice sitting on the couch with a police officer, who was wrapping up the investigation. The policewoman looked at me and said, "This is an obvious suicide. She's free to go."

I went outside and watched as they removed Jim's body from the garage and placed it in the coroner's van. As more family and friends arrived to offer support, gather information, and grieve, it became clear that Jim had shot himself in the head with his .44 long-barrel revolver, using a hollow-point bullet—likely to ensure that he didn't miss.

My friend. My partner. My protector. My spiritual leader. My brother. He was gone. But where was Jim now? I could feel him still protecting me, guiding me, laughing with me, and loving me from Heaven.

I couldn't help but wonder, "Now what do I do with Denice?" We put her in the car and took her to Mom's house so she wouldn't be alone. Everyone feared that this tragedy might trigger an episode, but, strangely, it didn't.

Chapter 13

That's It! I'm Out!

Moving into 2009, I experienced an awakening. I was turning forty, having spent my entire life giving myself to my family. I was in my second marriage and struggling with relationship difficulties with my husband—a story for another time. I had already lost my brother to ALS when he was just thirty-nine, and now my brother-in-law had taken his own life. I began to question everything: What am I doing with my life? Who am I? What is my purpose?

Was it really to be a caretaker for everyone but myself? My two kids were approaching adulthood, about to transition into independence and start living their own lives, making their own decisions. When they no longer needed me, what would become of me?

OH MY GOD. I was so unhappy. Trapped in a marriage where I had lost respect for my husband and could no longer overlook his mental weaknesses.

I began to believe that God didn't put me on this earth to suffer for everyone else's sake. I started to realize how enmeshed I had become in other people's lives, with no personal boundaries to protect myself—or them—from the chaos. I knew I had to get out. My life needed a change. It *was* changing.

To what, exactly? I didn't know yet, but I knew it had to bring happiness, positivity, and gratitude. I had a career, a family, a master's degree, my own home—but none of it brought me joy. Something was deeply wrong with the formula I'd been following in pursuit of happiness.

Faced with the pushback, the guilt trips, and the disappointed family and friends who didn't understand me or my value, I knew I had to make a drastic change. After helping Denice secure her financial future with the three-quarters of a million dollars she inherited from Jim's death, I left the extended family and divorced my husband. I needed to *get out* of the toxicity.

I became estranged from my family for six years, until I received that call from my sister-in-law, literally begging me to come back and help with Denice. So, what had happened to Denice while I was gone?

Denice had gone from having one episode every three to four years to experiencing about four episodes per year. From what I was told, the family tried to help her, chasing after her, attempting to work with her to manage her behavior. I know of a few episodes when she reached various DEFCON levels, but I'm unaware of any hospitalizations or how she eventually found balance during my time away.

One story I heard was about Denice inviting our sister-in-law to join her on a cruise, sponsored by a Christian radio station Denice had worked for. On this cruise, my sister-in-law recalled Denice being unusually hyper, with flirtatious behaviors and chasing after single men on the ship throughout most of the vacation. During my time away, Denice exhibited other behaviors, like flaunting her money and attracting a crowd of friends, whom she would lavish with gifts. Then, she would turn around and tell family members that she had been stolen from.

Her sons began to believe that she needed a man to settle down with—a companion who would take care of her. They found what they thought was the perfect guy for her: a man who often ate alone at a nearby restaurant the family had frequented for years. Oddly enough, it was the same restaurant where Jim had eaten his last meal just a few years earlier. Success! He liked her, she liked him, and they decided to marry on Valentine's Day, 2014.

About a week before their wedding, I received a voicemail from Denice, completely escalated and obviously in at least DEFCON 1. Her message was urgent: she had discovered something about her fiancé that she didn't think she could live with and needed to talk to me before she got married at the end of the week. She didn't know what to do. By this point, I had been estranged from the family for nearly four years, but I decided to return the call a day or two later.

When Denice answered, her voice was calm and sweet—nothing like the urgency and panic she had expressed just days earlier. I could tell right away that she had entered an episode. When I asked her what had caused her panic a few days prior, she simply replied, "Oh, it was nothing. I talked to Mom, and everything is fine. We'll be married on Friday. Thanks for calling," and then she hung up.

Later, I was told by Mom that the wedding was a chaotic disaster. Denice was an hour late for her own wedding, and nothing had been planned or organized—it was a complete mess. When Denice finally arrived, the vows were exchanged. She was now married for a second time. Her new husband, we'll call him Jack, had vowed to her, to her sons, to Mom and Dad, and to God that he would be with her until death and protect her from harm. They moved into his home to begin their new life, hoping to live "happily ever after."

Jack's property was large enough to have a detached garage, which he turned into an apartment. A couple rented the space, making it a ready-made family for Denice, with others to socialize with. They all, including Denice, started making plans to generate income by launching a business that focused on handiwork projects. Since Denice had the financial backing, she took on the role of financier and finance manager.

Together, they began living the comfortable life. They bought cars, went out to dinner frequently, went on cruises, and had fun. They continued attending church with Mom and Dad, remaining faithful to God, as that was a requirement for Denice in her marriage. Her new husband became another constant family member, always around.

Denice had stopped working after Jim passed, as she didn't feel the need to work due to the benefits she received from his death. Jim had worked hard to establish financial security for her through his working history. Prior to that, Denice had held a variety of jobs. She worked as a "copy lady" at her son's high school and as a bus attendant to help disabled students get on and off the bus for school and during the ride as needed. Growing up and throughout her first marriage, she had odd jobs—she worked at Arby's, a dry cleaner, and even tried being a bank teller. While married to Jim, she also worked at their church bookstore.

I learned from one of my mentors along the way that work can be one of the most rewarding experiences in our lives. It gives us a sense of purpose—not only through helping others but also through fulfilling ourselves with the joy of knowing we've helped someone else. Contributing to the health and welfare of others and making a difference in someone else's life can do wonders for the self if we allow it. Denice certainly exudes this quality, clearly deriving joy from doing things for others. When she is genuinely giving, the recipient can feel her vulnerability and love in an authentic way.

However, when this giving nature collides with uncontained stressors and disrupts her emotional regulation system, her ability to tolerate distress diminishes. This disorganization affects her interpersonal effectiveness skills, and as a result, her capacity for healthy adult executive functioning rapidly decomposes and deteriorates.

During these years, my life was continuing as well. I was in a new marriage, helping my husband raise his three girls, living with my new mother-in-law, and still supporting my two kids who were in their early adulthood, trying to figure out their lives. My daughter had given me two beautiful granddaughters, and I had the wonderful opportunity to have the three of them move in with me in 2013. Having become a single mother, she stayed connected to my family and received help with the girls while she pursued her phlebotomy career (and I proudly add, will be receiving her master's degree this summer). Meemaw's house (the endearing name our children refer to Mom) became the landing point for everyone at any time, and Denice and her new husband frequently landed there. Denice, Mom, and her husband helped with daycare for my daughter. She was becoming a woman, a great mom.

During this time, my son had joined the Army, completing both boot camp and Airborne school. My husband afforded me the opportunity to travel to my son's graduations from both boot camp and Airborne school. As a very proud mom, I watched my son grow up into a soldier, a man. He married and, in 2015, gave me a wonderful, handsome grandson. Now, he had become a dad. He has since remarried to a beautiful woman who also works in the counseling profession. My daughter has since remarried to a handsome, hardworking man who has taken on the responsibility of being a father to my granddaughters, and they have given me my fourth grandbaby, my beautiful boy. All of this, to be introduced much more in another journey. What more could I ask for as a mother? Both my kids are well, pursuing happiness, and are upstanding and responsible citizens.

Well, okay, all HELL broke loose Labor Day weekend, 2016.

ILLUSTRATIONS

Figure 1- Chapter 1 Dad and Mom walking together in Ireland, 2018. They always hold hands lovingly when walking together.

Figure 2- Chapter 1 Dad and Mom's wedding photo 1961

Figure 3 – Chapter 2 Dad and Mom's 60th wedding anniversary 2021

Figure 4 – Chapter 2 Dad re-proposing to Mom at the local Dairy Queen 2021

Figure 5 – Chapter 3 Family of six c. 1969

Figure 6 – Chapter 3 Family of six c. 1979

Figure 7 – Chapter 3 Dan at Battle of the Bands c. 1981

Figure 8 – Chapter 3 Dan at work c. 1988

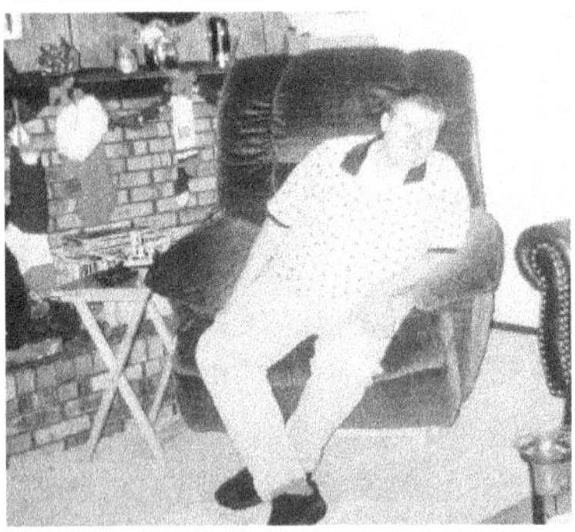

Figure 9 – Chapter 3 Dan enjoying his last Christmas with the family c. 2002

Figure 10 – Chapter 6 Jim and Denice's engagement photo c. 1981

Figure 11 – Jim and Denice got married c. 1982

Figure 12 – Chapter 12 Jim after diabetes diagnosis, working on his health c. 1997

Figure 13 – Chapter 12 Jim and Denice c. 1994

Figure 14 – Chapter 12 Jim and Denice at my second wedding c. 2004

Figure 15 - Chapter 12 Jim working as Santa Claus c. 2000's

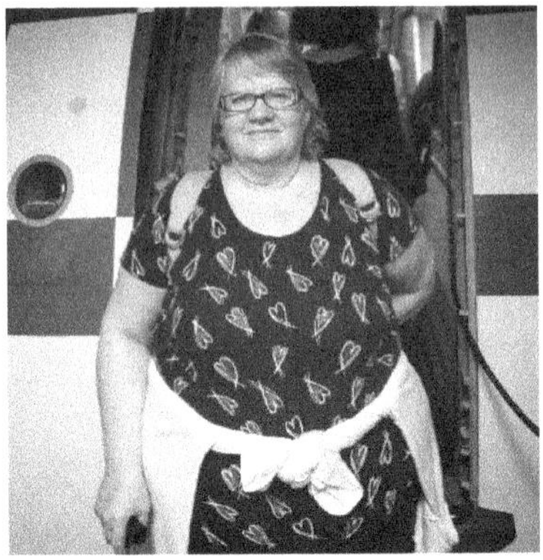

Figure 16 – Chapter 14 Denice boarding the plane to Georgia c. 2016

Figure 17 – Chapter 14 Denice and her youngest son at the hotel in Georgia the night before registration at the residential facility, 2016

Figure 18 – Chapter 14 Denice and her youngest son touring the facility during registration 2016

Figure 19 – Chapter 14 Me and Denice's youngest son after boarding a flight back home from Georgia 2016

Figure 20 – Chapter 14 Denice at her new temporary home at the residential facility 2017

Figure 21 – Chapter 17 Denice at a golfing activity while living at the residential facility in Georgia 2017

Figure 22 - Denice moving into her first Assisted Living Facility post hospitalization 2022

Figure 23 – Chapter 17 Denice, Debbie and April on move in day second Assisted Living Facility 2022

Figure 24 – Chapter 17 Denice and me at her senior care facility for a medical check-up 2023

Figure 25 – Chapter 17 Denice in her room at second Assisted Living Facility 2022

Figure 26 – Chapter 17 "Squirt" the squirrel trying hard to distract Denice and my conversation outside her psychiatrist's office 2021

Figure 27 – Chapter 18 Denice standing in the road the day we took her to the second ER in nine days after being prematurely released from a 72-hour hold 2023

Figure 28 – Chapter 21 Dad, Mom, Sister-in-law and me ready to depart for Georgia to attend the family day to visit Denice. Mom was recovering from the flu virus; my husband took the pictures 2017

Figure 29 – Chapter 21 Residential facility led activity on family day, giving us an opportunity to experience activities Denice participates in during craft time. Dad and Mom "pounding pansies" together 2017

Figure 30 - Chapter 21 Field trip to the Coca--Cola© factory in Georgia. Sister-in-law, me and Denice. 2017

Figure 31 – Chapter 21 Field trip with Denice, visiting the Coca-Cola© factory in Georgia. Denice, my husband, me, Sister-in-law, Mom and Dad and the Coca-Cola© Polar Bear. 2017

Figure 32 – Sisters stick together photo, taken shortly after Dan passed, Denice, Sister-in-law, Debbie and Me 2003

Figure 33 – Sisters still stick together photo, taken at Denice's oldest son's wedding. Denice, Debbie, Sister-in-law, and Me 2019

Figure 34 – Chapter 25 Vase of flowers Denice sent me for my birthday 2025

Chapter 14

Hook, Line and Sinker, TADA, I'm Back

I was stepping into the garage to get in the car on a Saturday before Labor Day in 2016 when the call came out of nowhere. For a long time, I had worked hard to create a life full of adventure—learning what I liked to do, where I liked to go, and how I liked to feel. Living with positivity and gratitude had become second nature to me. Don't get me wrong, my new life wasn't perfect. But it was free from focusing on the negative, expecting the worst, and allowing ruptures to linger. They weren't allowed to take root. I believed this was just a phase in my new relationship, but it was still a necessary one for me.

I can't recall exactly where we were going when my phone rang.

"DeAnna," it was my sister-in-law. "PLEASE come back and HELP US with Denice! She has TOTALLY LOST HER MIND!"

Her voice was frantic. She explained that no one knew where Denice was at that moment. Her husband was in jail for domestic violence, and Denice was in the midst of an episode. All I really heard through the chaos was that everything was a mess and no one knew what to do anymore.

"Please, come help," her voice trembled through the phone.

After speaking with my husband, who gave me his full support, I made my way to Mom and Dad's, arranging an emergency family meeting. I called anyone who could make it, turning what was supposed to be a regular family BBQ for Labor Day into an intervention for Denice. As I thought to myself, "OH GOD, this is eerily familiar, please, not again," I realized this was the moment to set my boundaries.

I demanded that, if they wanted my help, I would be in charge. Anyone willing to help would need to commit fully and follow my rules. Not because I craved control—I wasn't trying to run the show. But I knew that in situations like this, there could only be one Chief in the tribe if there was any hope for success. Since I was the one called in, after everyone realized Denice wasn't doing well on her own, I must have had something they didn't know. My experience made me the one with the knowledge, or at least, the only one they thought might be able to help.

My anger bubbled up, and I wanted to add, "If you're here to help, then damn it, HELP. Don't say you will and then sabotage the entire effort."

If there was ever a time when the phrase "It takes a village to raise a child" was absolutely true, it was now, with Denice.

I briefed everyone who showed up on how the initial meeting was going to unfold. The goal was simple: get Denice to comply and go into a 72-hour mental hold. There was no doubt in my mind that I'd see her in full DEFCON 5 mode when she arrived for the BBQ. Any future involvement would be sorted out later, as we'd define tasks and allocate responsibilities based on what everyone felt they could handle after this meeting. But for now, this was about one thing: getting Denice to agree to voluntary commitment.

Everyone had to sit around her while I talked to her. I was going to gently confront her with what was happening. If anyone had input they felt would help convince her, fine. But if they had anything that could contradict our goal of getting her to voluntarily commit, I told them to keep it to themselves and talk to me later. The LAST thing we needed was Denice sensing any support for her continued DEFCON 5 behavior. I was the brick wall in this, having been called in, and there was no room for wavering.

Dad, Mom, Denice's youngest son and his wife, my son and a friend of his, Debbie, and our sister-in-law—all of them were present at this intervention BBQ. Debbie's wife, April, thankfully took care of Denice's grandkid, who had to be there since both of his parents were. April took him out of the chaos, driving him around town so he could sleep peacefully while the storm raged inside the house. It was also a huge relief to have Denice's daughter-in-law there. When she joined the family, she really stepped up, helping me with Denice's episodes after Jim was gone. She worked so hard, and I deeply appreciated her commitment during this intervention.

As the patriarch, Dad was the one I needed to stamp with his approval. I knew we needed his buy-in for the process to succeed. It was important for him to see and understand what was really happening to Denice. He's logical and authoritative, but in our past conversations about Denice, he still couldn't grasp what was wrong with her. He'd always see it as just a child acting out, needing a "spanking."

"Dad," I'd say, "I get your point, but Denice is an adult woman. Spanking her isn't the solution."

"I understand that, DeAnna. So what do we do?" he replied.

That was the breakthrough moment.

"Dad, I need you to follow my lead. Trust me, observe, and support. But please, don't get all 'Dad' on her like you would have when we were kids," I said.

"Okay," he agreed.

I knew it was crucial to have him involved, but I also had to get him comfortable with the idea of observing and understanding rather than jumping in with his usual "because I said so" approach that often ended in yelling. He needed to be counsel for me, not the enforcer.

I asked someone to video record the escalation that I knew would happen with Denice during the intervention. I also prepared everyone for the two possibilities we might face that evening. First, Denice might be at a DEFCON level where she was still functional enough to carry on after the family event, but taking her to the hospital for evaluation would likely result in her going home anyway. Second, it could end with her being taken to the hospital in an ambulance for a 72-hour hold.

Everyone buckled up for the ride and was ready when Denice arrived. "She's here," I heard someone say as they saw her pulling into the cul-de-sac.

She came in with a heightened, anxious affect that is often confused with elation or excitement. Immediately, I could see she was at DEFCON 5, and I alerted the family team. We had to start right away, getting Denice to sit down at the kitchen table, where I would explain why I was there. She hadn't seen me at a family function for six years, and honestly, in her state, she might not have even realized how much time had passed.

The recording began as soon as I asked her to sit, and everyone took their positions around us—encircling us, but being careful not to crowd us. I began by letting her know that I was aware of the situation that had occurred the day before between her and her husband. As was usual with my interventions, I presented the facts to her about the behaviors being observed, and how they followed patterns from previous episodes. At a DEFCON 5 level, it's much harder to work with her; defensiveness and resistance are much stronger.

What seemed like hours later, Denice finally gave in to the agreed-upon next steps and said she would be willing to go to the hospital in an ambulance for evaluation and rest after what had turned out to be a very long and exhausting few days. I looked at her son and gave him the instruction to call 911.

We dispersed, with most of us leaving the kitchen area while everyone waited. I stayed with Denice, keeping her busy and distracted, answering her questions until the emergency crew arrived.

She appeared defeated and relieved at the same time, trusting me to lead her through a very scary and disturbing state of mind. It was as if she felt betrayed by herself—by parts of herself that had once taken the lead but had now led her back to the place she didn't want to be. Her little girl part was scared but still willing to trust me to guide her out of her nightmare. Only, it seemed to be temporary, as I would soon have to hand her over to the paramedics.

They were let into the house and were made aware of the situation. The EMTs worked to respect Denice's person, safety, and dignity, gently asking if she could walk to the gurney waiting for her on the porch. She agreed that she could and would comply.

But as the group walked her to the front door and opened the screen door to escort her outside, something unexpected happened. Despite her 280-pound, five-foot-one-inch stature, and a chronically injured knee, Denice suddenly took off running down the sidewalk, down the driveway, and toward the streetlight in front of the house. She then started heading up the street.

The EMTs were surprised at first, but they immediately shifted into action, sprinting after her. They had to tackle her and restrain her, administering doses of Propofol, the "milk of amnesia," to calm and sedate her so they could get her onto the gurney. Once she was captured and restrained, Denice began screaming at the top of her lungs, calling for Mom to come help her, crying out that they were hurting her.

We all knew she was in a heightened state, and deep down, we understood that she just needed to go with them—she was now in their hands for her own good. Mom stood and watched for a moment before, in a daze of mental and emotional exhaustion, she shut the door. She allowed them to take Denice, then sat in her chair, overwhelmed by shock, surprise, and the acceptance that we had reached this point once again—DEFCON 5. And in that moment, she wept.

The aftermath for the rest of us was chaos, each of us experiencing it in different ways, with varying levels of emotional intensity. We had all encountered Denice at different points before, but never had we all witnessed an episode like this at the same time. We attempted to debrief and decompress, but with each of us processing through our own unique filters, trying to make sense of the madness, the emotional recovery needs became apparent. It wasn't the time for deep debriefing, but it didn't matter—we were all facing the same devastation, yet we each had to figure out how to cope individually. It was the first time we had all been together, caught in the middle of these overwhelming states of mind. We have learned over time that emotional chaos can hit and take the entire family over when any one of us are vulnerable and try to regulate with or around others in the family. This my friends, speaks to how we all suffer from the mental illness, it is not just our loved ones that experience the deep pain. We experience the pain along with our loved ones and the pain that is causes us each individually. Again, no one is immune from the direct or indirect effects of mental illness.

We all dispersed for the evening, retreating to our respective corners, as we began preparing for Denice's release after at least 72 hours.

Following the usual course, Denice was taken to the ER, observed, and determined to need a mental hold. She was subsequently transferred to the mental facility associated with the ER that night. By this point, she had passed through most of the local mental hospitals in the area, so we were somewhat familiar with this facility.

My husband and I went to visit her, and when we arrived, she was sitting with other patients, watching television. She immediately made it a point to tell me about one of the young women there who had attempted suicide like Jim did. She insisted that I look at one side of the girl's face, which appeared fine, then the other side, where part of her face was missing. Denice kept telling me that seeing this girl reminded her of Jim, never once mentioning her current husband.

Suddenly, Denice shot up from her chair, announcing that she needed to go to her room. After a minute or two of waiting for her to return, something told me I needed to check on her. I told my husband I was going to see what she was doing and went toward her room. I didn't realize at first, but he had followed me a few steps behind.

When I entered and spoke with Denice's roommate, she told me that Denice was in the bathroom. I looked in and was horrified to find Denice completely disrobed, standing naked, telling me she was almost ready to be presented to my husband for sex. "Oh my goodness," I gasped, quickly telling my husband to leave the doorway and wait in the waiting area.

I hurried to get Denice to understand that he wasn't there for that and that she needed to get dressed immediately. I told her that we needed to leave right then, and I went to get my husband so we could leave the visitation.

At that moment, I knew it would be a few weeks before Denice would be able to stabilize enough for release. She would need time in the hospital for them to get her to a baseline, something we all knew was necessary, even if it was painful to watch.

For some, it may be shocking to hear about Denice disrobing and presenting herself to my husband. However, I've found that such behaviors are not uncommon for people in this mental state. I had heard stories from others whose spouses experienced similar mental illnesses—stories of individuals getting naked and going outside to mow the lawn, with no shame about their nakedness. This is very different from a streaking prank. Those with mental illness like Denice seem to lose all inhibition when it comes to covering themselves. It happens in almost every one of Denice's episodes to some extent.

Shedding all judgment and without becoming defensive or offended by this phenomenon, I find it fascinating that there seems to be a connection between this behavior and the story of the Garden of Eden before the Fall of Man. The Bible says that Adam and Eve were naked and unashamed (Genesis 2:25) until they ate the forbidden fruit, at which point they lost their innocence and realized they were naked, feeling ashamed (Genesis 3:7). In some ways, this phase of Denice's mental illness seems like a temporary return to that state of innocence, perhaps a return to pure Self—a mind free of shame and inhibition, much like we all were before we began to carry the burden of knowledge (Schwartz, 2019, March 5).

On a more positive note, with Denice likely needing to be hospitalized for more than 72 hours, we now had more time to meet as a family and figure out a plan to help her unravel the past few years of struggling to manage her life while dealing with this mental illness. The first meeting we had was to research residential treatment facilities that could help Denice learn the skills necessary to understand and cope with her Bipolar disorder. It was clear that we needed to find a place where she could participate in a program that would teach her things we were incapable of teaching her ourselves.

Each of us did our own research, bringing options to the table. Some were within state, and others were out of state. We discussed the pros and cons of each, taking into account cost, benefits, and insurance coverage. After much deliberation, we finally decided on a facility in Georgia.

I began researching the status of Denice's finances, knowing that after Jim died, I had worked closely with her financial advisor to set aside money in long-term, high-risk, high-return investments. These investments carried a penalty for early withdrawal—at least 50% in taxes. Surely, with the guidance of her financial advisor, she would have left that money alone. Additionally, we had set up a medium-risk investment, earmarked for emergencies, and a fun money market account that would grow slowly but would be enough for her to use as she wished.

To my dismay, the money market account dwindled quickly, spent on dinners out and living a somewhat lavish lifestyle. The medium-risk account also saw significant depletion during her second marriage, as it was used to fund cruises and support her husband's friend start up their handyman business. They even used it to purchase new equipment and support vehicles for the neighbor who was also part of their business venture. I soon realized that she, her husband, and their friends had burned through nearly three-quarters of a million dollars in just the past two years. It became obvious that Denice had been taken advantage of, yet within her limited ability to fully understand herself and others, it was still her responsibility to manage.

Anger toward her had to be set aside. At that point, radical acceptance (DBT Skills) had to be deployed to keep my own sanity intact. I was astonished at how recklessly and frivolously the money had been squandered—money that could have been used for her future stability, now gone in what seemed like a blink of an eye.

I needed to get control of Denice's finances and her decision-making, as she had now demonstrated that she was not capable of managing this on her own—whether in a DEFCON state or not. She only had enough funds to self-pay for a very reputable residential rehabilitation center for her care. After that, she could budget enough to live independently on a low-paying job, qualify for low-cost insurance, and make minimal annual withdrawals from her remaining funds to supplement a very basic lifestyle. This was necessary until she would qualify for widow's benefits at the age of sixty.

To manage this for her without resistance from companies, agencies, financial institutions, and medical providers, the logical decision was to file for temporary guardianship and conservatorship—eventually turning into permanent orders. This was a huge responsibility for me to take on, requiring me to testify to the judge about my intentions and my reasons for her needing help. I had to be open and vulnerable for them to review my financial status, character, and undergo a background check before they would grant the orders.

My friends, there is a lengthy manual on how to be a guardian and conservator that must be read and adhered to when you are granted the legal responsibility for someone's care. It is by no means an unregulated or unaccountable action. I was under the microscope of the courts at all times, subject to personal responsibility if I did not comply with every aspect of this manual in caring for Denice. Taking on this responsibility was huge, knowing that, in Denice's episodes, my reputation and freedoms were at stake. The best I could do was to work with her as much as possible to try and avoid a DEFCON 5 disruption in the future. I had to take this responsibility seriously—not only for her but for myself as well.

I also found myself immediately in conflict with my oldest nephew, who was very vocal about my taking on his mother's care. He adamantly believed that his mother was perfectly capable of taking care of herself and didn't need a guardian or conservator. He had not been part of many of her episodes—having spent most of his transition from adolescence to adulthood in prison and on probation for committing a serious felony. This is another journey in itself, and depending on whether or not I feel the need to expound on his story, my experiences, and roles in his life, that will be explored later. At this point in the journey, where I was willing to take on his mother's care, I was very angry with him for not stepping up to care for his own mother. At the same time, I was internally conflicted due to his lack of maturity to have been able to do so, but I also had compassion for his need to experience freedom as an adult and for his denial regarding his mother's mental condition. He had the right to speak his position, and he did so at the hearing.

I was eventually granted permanent orders, which allowed me to move forward with getting Denice applied to and accepted into a remarkable residential treatment program that, for a time, truly changed her life. Part of this preparation included having her fully evaluated by a local psychiatrist, who conducted an extensive psychological assessment. His report—a thirteen-page analysis—outlined her mental state and experiences, both past and present. Among other things, the report confirmed her prior diagnosis of Bipolar Disorder and added a new diagnosis: Cluster B Personality Disorder, Histrionic. I remember thinking, "Okay, what the heck is that?"

The assessment also revealed Denice's intellectual challenges, including difficulties with managing money and an inability to take on financial responsibilities. This report provided valuable insight into some of the stressors that trigger her, often turning what should be simple life tasks into overwhelming hurdles. It clarified why she might struggle more than others with these challenges, making it easier to understand how her reactions can sometimes be disproportionate.

In many ways, the report became a guide—a manual—for everyone involved in her care: the residential facility, the family care team, her parents, her youngest son, and me. It gave us a solid foundation to help Denice navigate her path forward.

Afterward, I arranged travel for Denice, her son, and me to Georgia, where she would be admitted to the treatment facility the day after Christmas in 2016. Oddly enough, the road leading to the facility shared the same name as my son—a very unique name, which being both ironic and calming at the same time, means *Sword Bearer and Protector*. Both Denice's son and I saw this as a hopeful sign. We toured the facility together, becoming familiar with the space where we would eventually leave her. Both of us were confident that this was the right decision, though for Denice, naturally, was a mixture of fear and excitement. Our parting was bittersweet, but her youngest son and I found common ground that day, bonding over the importance of her care and future. I deeply appreciated his willingness to step up, even as a young father with his own family to care for.

I made sure to stay in weekly contact with her therapist, psychiatrist, orderlies, and case managers. Over time, I had learned the importance of a united front in her care. Having legal custody of her was invaluable—it allowed me to bypass privacy restrictions and make decisions that would best serve her.

Looking back, I remember a conversation I had with her husband over that fateful Labor Day weekend. I visited him in jail and agreed to help pay his bail. We talked about their marriage and what he wanted to do moving forward. He expressed that he wanted a divorce, so I agreed to help him facilitate that. He also honored the restraining order, regardless of who was at fault for the incident. A part of me felt sorry for him, but another part of me recognized that his choices were his own to bear.

While Denice was undergoing treatment, she also agreed to the divorce. I filed on her behalf, and the court granted it. Once again, Denice was a single woman.

Chapter 15

Establishment of DEFCON 4: "Oh no, Mom has a boyfriend"

Let's go back in time to when Denice had secured, what I thought to be, the relationship with her first love—a boy from the Senior High church youth group. She was on cloud nine, completely in love with him. I'm not sure how long they "went together," but to me, it felt like years—or at least long enough for her to have planned her wedding. She was so happy, always singing, always smiling. She seemed almost "high" whenever she was getting ready to go on a date with him, which likely meant a youth group activity. Oh, and that Valentine's Day banquet—she was practically oozing love leading up to it. It seemed like she started planning what to wear for that Valentine's Day the minute Christmas was over.

What I saw and thought was love, I now believe was likely puppy love that blossomed quickly, maybe too quickly for him. Perhaps it became overwhelming, and he broke it off. I'm not sure I ever got the full story, but I did see it all from Denice's perspective. She was heartbroken for a while but eventually got back up and started looking for another boyfriend. I remember riding in the car with Mom and her, taking her over to some boy's house or sometimes picking this boy up after a youth group activity he'd attended.

But there's one memory I have that I know for a fact traumatized Denice, and became a part of her DEFCON signs. It was when she was working at a bookbinding company. I remember that night so clearly. Mom and I went looking for Denice late. It was dark, and I think she was supposed to be off work around 8:00 or 9:00 p.m. She still wasn't home, and it was well past the time she should've been. Mom was frantic. Let me mention—there were no cell phones back then, so it wasn't as if Mom could call or track her location. The only thing to do was get in the car, drive to where she was supposed to be, and hope to find her car—and her.

We took that short ten- to fifteen-minute drive, and thank goodness, there was her car. But as soon as we saw the car, the calm was gone. We found her car, but she wasn't there. The company she worked for was closed, locked up, and dark. Panic resurfaced in Mom. Where in the world was Denice?

Mom is so smart. I have to tell you, I've gained so many useful skills from her, especially when it came to raising my kids. I truly believe she learned a lot during her Valley Girl hoodlum days—chasing after her sister, who was always testing the waters on the "other side of the tracks," as they called it back then. They did things like "dragging the gut" down Main Street—drag racing in their small town. Thanks, Mom!

Instead of letting the panic and fear consume her that night while searching for Denice, I remember us just sitting there, trying to think through where Denice might be. Maybe she ran out of gas, or her '65 Mustang wouldn't start. Or maybe she'd caught a ride with someone else and would be home safe.

As we left the parking lot to check a few places—like the local Pizza Hut to see if she'd decided to meet friends there—Mom noticed another car still parked. Being as stealthy and nosy as she is (again, thanks, Mom!), she slowly drove over to check if anyone was inside. I remember her turning off the headlights while moving toward the car and then shining them on it once we were close. She got out to peek inside, and there she found two people—an older Black man and a young white woman—engaged in sexual activity in the car.

Oh shit, it was Denice. I swear, I remember Mom's pointer finger cocking into her "Shame on you" position. From the car, I could see her shouting, her top and bottom teeth barely separated, "YOU GET IN YOUR CAR NOW AND GET YOUR FANNY HOME, RIGHT NOW!" Mom was *Moses Stick* mad—something I coined when I made her that mad in my teenage years. She came after me with a walking stick made from a tree branch that looked like Moses' staff. She literally shoved it through my bedroom door once, but that's a story for another time.

She was furious, likely from the shock of seeing what she saw, but also from the fear of not knowing where Denice was. Then, the anger of finding her—alive and well—without a care for the worry she'd put Mom through by not being home on time. To be fair, I honestly think kids have no idea what it's like for a parent to go from the panic of wondering if their child is alive or dead, to the anger of finding them safe and sound—and suddenly wishing they were dead instead because dealing with a parent's wrath feels like the worst punishment. Why or how could we ever understand that shift in emotion until we experience it ourselves as parents? I truly believe it's one of God's jokes—making us wait until we have kids to get the punchline. There's nothing else like that shift of feelings. I can say now, after raising my own children, I've been there—going from utter fear to straight-up anger. Not funny, God.

I don't recall being part of the fallout when Denice came home that night. My memory picks up months later, when she had been misdiagnosed with V.D.—what we called sexually transmitted diseases back then. She was drowning in shame of Mom's accusations continually begging for Mom's forgiveness while clinging to God, the church, and the Bible like they were lifelines. Looking back, it's possible Denice was in an episodic mental health crisis without realizing it—and Mom, like so many parents then, could only act on what she knew. Her mission was simple: keep us safe, steer us toward righteousness, and mend our fractured bonds with God.

Now, let's talk about sex.

Each of us girls received a set of hardback books—skinny encyclopedias with clinical diagrams of male and female anatomy, the reproductive system, and... well, that was it. I was a reluctant reader, so I mostly flipped through the pictures. They confirmed a hazy memory from when I was five: sneaking into my parents' room at night, terrified to see Daddy "jumping" on Mommy while she screamed. When I told Mom what I'd seen, she must've explained they were having sex. So at five years old, armed with nothing but toddler logic and toys that fit together, I decided a penis must go into a vagina, and after a man "peed" inside, a baby happened. I carried that theory straight into sixth grade, when I finally brought home the holy grail of permission slips—the one allowing me to attend sex ed. My parents signed it without hesitation; they'd done the same for all my older siblings.

I pitied my church friends who attended Christian schools where these classes didn't exist. Turns out, I was almost right about the mechanics—just swap "pee" for semen, a cocktail of ingredients ready to mix with a woman's egg. By seventh-grade Human Growth and Development, our crown jewel of lessons arrived the day before winter break: the teacher demonstrating how to roll a condom onto a banana. God bless those educators who endure the giggles, the heckling, and the sheer chaos of teaching teens about sex.

Sex. Everything else, I learned through experience. When I first had sex at a young age, I shared it with Denice. I don't remember why I did, but I know it was around the time she was dating Jim and struggling with her own guilt about not saving herself for marriage. We were in the "blue room"—a space we had named after the colors of the rooms in our house. The blue room was the quiet, "to be kept nice" living room, unlike the "red" family room, which was more casual. I told her, and she passed it on to Mom.

Regardless of whether what I did was right or wrong, that was the moment I felt Denice broke my confidence. It felt like she had drawn me in, gotten me to share something personal, and then turned around and told Mom, almost as if to absolve herself of her own guilt for not being a virgin at marriage. It felt like she had turned the blue room into a place of repentance, where I was expected to confess my "sin" for having sex before marriage. She prayed with me, asking for forgiveness, and I promised to never make that mistake again. Then, she said, "Maybe Jesus will restore your virginity."

I was detached from myself in that moment, as though I was an observer, watching what was unfolding between me and Denice. It felt like the first time I experienced ego-dissociation—perhaps it was the beginning of my development of a "wise mind," a way of separating myself from the illogical and strange guidance I was being given. Looking back, it marked the beginning of a new journey for me: learning who I could truly trust with my most personal thoughts and experiences.

Debbie had already violated that trust with other experiences, but that's another story for another time. From this point on, I grew closer to my brother. He became my confidant, my best sibling friend—the one I could trust and turn to from then on. I rejected the drama of girls and their emotions, starting to lean into masculine logic over feminine feelings. "Screw this dramatic girly crap. Girls are just back-stabbing bitches," I thought.

Denice, on the other hand, pursued a few guys, living out the fairy tale dream of marrying her prince charming. She attended friends' weddings, some where she was an attendant, and others where she simply went as a plus-one. It seemed like there was a wedding every weekend—a new couple from the youth group tying the knot. They were all beautiful ceremonies, and I know this because Denice took me along to the ones she wasn't in the bridal party for, and our family attended those where she was. Like so many other girls, Denice dreamed of her own knight in shining armor coming to claim her as his bride. For her, that knight was Jim. Jack, her second husband, was different, but still, he vowed to be her partner.

Outside of her two committed relationships, whenever Denice was a single adult, there was always reason to question when she began to consistently talk about any particular male. As much as we wanted her to have a companion—a partner to fulfill her basic human desire for a relationship—those desires had to be measured against some serious caution. It quickly became clear that Denice had difficulty processing the difference between someone being cordial and respectful, simply acknowledging her as a person, and believing that their interest in her was Love. If that person was male, the situation became emotionally dangerous for him very quickly—and he would most likely have no idea until it was too late.

So, what should one do in such a situation? Is it fair for someone to follow Denice around, warning the men she meets about how they need to be careful because she means them no harm? Absolutely not. It's unfair to both Denice and the men involved. Besides, who would ever expect sweet De"Nice" to be anything but nice? She presents herself as a genuinely kind person, just like the rest of us—empathetic and compassionate to others. But that's not always the case. It's almost as if a switch flips inside her when there's something or someone she desires so deeply. Her internal dialogue begins working overtime, strategizing how to obtain that thing or person.

In DEFCON 4, that person can seem to transform into a "thing" or an "object" for Denice to acquire. Over time, I've come to fully believe that Denice's personality, particularly her Histrionic traits, comes to the forefront in DEFCON 4, overshadowing the other levels. Let me explain why, using the diagnostic criteria for Histrionic Personality Disorder (DSM-5-TR, p. 757). For the diagnosis to be made, a person must exhibit five or more of the following characteristics:

Is uncomfortable in situations in which he or she is not the center of attention.

Interactions with others is often characterized by inappropriate sexually seductive or provocative behavior.

Displays rapidly shifting and shallow expression of emotions.

Consistently uses physical appearance to draw attention to self.

Has a style of speech that is excessively impressionistic and lacking in detail.

Shows self-dramatization, theatricality, and exaggerated expression of emotion.

Is suggestible (i.e. easily influenced by others or circumstances).

Considers relationships to be more intimate than they actually are (DMT-5-TR, p. 757).

In DEFCON 4, every one of these traits manifests in Denice. She acknowledges that she expresses each of these behaviors and understands when they emerge. Up until DEFCON 4 is reached, it's a matter of helping Denice recognize these behaviors as they appear, and hoping she can understand which levels of each are normal for her to manage and keep under control within her system. To illustrate this, let's look at some examples of how it plays out when she's in DEFCON 4, rapidly approaching DEFCON 5.

It usually starts with Denice disclosing that she has interest in someone specific. This disclosure often happens with Mom, I believe, because Mom has traditionally been more closed off when it comes to talking about relationships and sex. In a way, this can be seen as secret-keeping. Over time, especially as family holiday parties approach, we start hearing that this person of interest will be attending the gathering. This scenario is reminiscent of how Jim began to become part of the family. Denice is able to become the center of attention both within the family and with her guest, if they attend as her plus-one.

When we hear over several events that this person is supposed to come but doesn't, it's time to start questioning the level of intimacy Denice has disclosed about the relationship. Her conversations become filled with an overabundance of details, as if she's trying to convince us of the depth of their connection. Additionally, we begin to see rapid shifts in her emotions, particularly if anyone contradicts her view of the relationship.

It also becomes evident that Denice starts spending more time "gussying up" for occasions where she hopes or believes this person will be. She dresses more flamboyantly, wearing bold colors and matching accessories, and applies more makeup than usual—indicators of exaggerated self-expression. Coupled with a more jubilant mood, she uses a more impressionistic vocabulary, raising her voice louder and drawing out her syllables. All these behaviors are signals of heightened activity in DEFCON 4.

The most striking behavior, however, is the shift toward more seductive actions. These may include seductive smiles, lingering looks, winks, and a physical closeness that invades another person's personal space—where you might hear someone make statements like, "You're in my personal bubble, please back up," without seeming to notice how uncomfortable she's making the other person. The culmination of these behaviors often leads to a collision with DEFCON 2, manifested in an overwhelming difficulty with urinary tract infections due to excessive masturbation.

When DEFCON 4 collides with DEFCON 3, Denice exhibits over-judgmental behaviors toward other people's relationships. She adopts a savior-like complex, believing it's her duty to "right the wrongs" in others' relationships. She becomes deeply enmeshed in the roles of being cheated on or controlled by a dominant partner, often embodying the drama that she perceives in others' relationships, seemingly preparing for the final scenes of DEFCON 5.

Pause. It's a good time for an intermission. As I'm writing this for you, I'm feeling a sense of mental clutter with so many scenarios that have been in play over the years with DEFCON 4. If you're with me in this moment of spinning chaos, trying to unravel and understand what you're reading, take a moment too. This shit is confusing. When people become objects to someone who is mentally ill, it really takes mindfulness to re-center and not get caught up as a pawn in the game or start thinking you're the "insane" one, questioning your own reality. Breathe and count to four, hold for four, and exhale counting to four.

There were four men to mention who became objects of Denice's affection during various episodes after Jim died, aside from the one she married. Because we are a family that values laughter as a mechanism for balancing out the tragedies we have experienced, I will take author's privilege here and use the names "Tom, Dick, and Harry" and "Sam" for this segment. By the way, Debbie recently pointed out that all of us kids were named with "L. Augh" in our names. Good one, Debbie, that helps to justify the use of laughter in such difficulty as a coping mechanism.

The first man was someone Denice became friends with at her job when she was a school bus attendant, whom we'll call Tom. We began hearing about Tom more frequently as he became increasingly part of Denice's conversations with us. They went on activities together, like attending drag races and going to movies—it all seemed normal. But once it became the narrative that he was coming to family BBQs, holiday gatherings, dinners, etc., and then never showing up, it started becoming clear to me that the level of intimacy she was describing wasn't quite as she believed. Now, it very well may have been reciprocal at a friendship level, but little indicators from Denice, like "Tom likes this other woman too" or "He can't come today because he has plans with someone else," began to show that things weren't what Denice thought or wanted them to be with Tom. Tom eventually filed a restraining order against Denice as she had began to demonstrate stalking behaviors toward him.

The second man, whom we'll call Dick, was younger than Denice and attended the same church. He was a very good carpenter and did some work for Mom and Dad, replacing their older kitchen cabinets and sink. Dick was easy for Denice because he went to church, and she would be seeing him regularly, just like when she met Jim. Because he also knew Mom and Dad, when invited to join family holiday activities, he was more likely to attend. I personally only saw him at one Thanksgiving or Christmas dinner—I can't remember which—but he did come, at least once. As time went on, though, Dick realized the strangeness of the situation he was in and sought counseling and guidance from the church pastor. Since the pastor knew of Denice's mental health history, he approached Mom and Dad to let them know what was happening from Dick's perspective. Apparently, the pastor advised Dick to distance himself from Denice. Dick was also pursuing a relationship with another young lady he was interested in, and he eventually married her shortly after. Mom told Denice to let go of Dick as a love interest because it was clearly not reciprocated.

Harry, the third man in this story, was the only Black man among the four, and I must say, a very good-looking one at that. I could easily understand what Denice saw in him—he was kind, compassionate, and undeniably attractive. His race is pertinent only to enhance Denice's observed heightening of internal satisfaction by challenging the religious teachings that do not allow for being unequally yoked (*Holy Bible, 2 Corinthians 6:14*).

Denice met Harry at the residential treatment program we enrolled her in, in Georgia. Harry worked at the facility, sitting behind the front desk of a building that Denice regularly visited for her classes. Over time, Denice developed an infatuation with him, and the Histrionic personality traits began to take over her behavior.

As her guardian and someone involved in her treatment, it quickly became clear that she had reached DEFCON 4 in her obsession with Harry. I had to step in and literally try to save his job. Denice believed she was in a relationship with him, putting both his career and livelihood at risk.

The fourth man, whom we'll call Sam, was an old love interest of Denice's from high school—one that never came to fruition for her, either. This dynamic was strange for me. Not only had Sam never dated or shown any interest in Denice back in high school, but he had also dated Debbie and had been in a serious relationship with Debbie's best friend for a time. Sam was someone who had been a part of our household for many years during my teenage years, only to resurface four decades later. For at least a year, if not two, Denice would always announce that Sam was "gonna come over" for family gatherings—yet he never showed up.

In one of the rare occasions when Denice's oldest son was involved in the conversation to debrief the situation, he simply and matter-of-factly said, "If mom has a boyfriend, we are at DEFCON 4." And with these four men, his statement couldn't have been more accurate.

The behaviors observed during this episode became the defining signs of DEFCON 4: fantasy relationships, hyper-flirtatious behavior, an unrealistic self-image, and hyper-sexuality, as evidenced by the somatic symptom of frequent and untreatable urinary tract infections (UTIs).

Chapter 16

Establishment of DEFCON 5 - It's Time!

Shortly after reaching DEFCON 5, it's only a matter of time before all hell breaks loose. But DEFCON 5 is also a waiting game—an unpredictable limbo where the tipping point for calling for help is never clear. If the call is made too early, Denice has the uncanny ability to say exactly what she knows needs to be said to medical staff, turning the entire ordeal into a waste of energy, resources, and money for everyone involved.

The other component of DEFCON 5, for those of us on alert, includes a desperate kind of prayer: that she doesn't hurt herself or anyone else, that she doesn't disappear, and that we can summon enough patience to keep her stable as she rapidly unravels right in front of us.

Much like the incident described earlier, Denice developed an overwhelming urge to flee. It was similar to the time she was found in a woman's garage, claiming she was being followed. In this particular episode, it began with the sixth anniversary of her oldest son's accident—a date that carried a painful emotional charge. She had stopped taking her medication, was growing increasingly paranoid about money, even though Jim was managing the family's finances. That night, it all came to a head.

Local police were dispatched to respond to a domestic call about a woman who had wandered into a man's home around midnight, claiming people were after her.

Denice had left the house in the middle of the night wearing only a tank top and flannel pajama bottoms. It was January 2nd—icy cold, with frigid winter temperatures. She slipped away while Jim wasn't watching, running down the street toward the creek behind their home. In her mind, if she could cross the water, the bloodhounds searching for her would lose her scent.

On the other side of the creek, she stumbled into a stranger's backyard, panicked and disoriented, pounding on his back door. Seeing the distress she was in, the man let her inside, gave her warm clothes, and called the police. Denice told the officers that her husband was abusing her, hoping they wouldn't return her home. While one unit kept her safe, another was dispatched to Jim and Denice's house to investigate her claims.

Jim hadn't even realized Denice had left the house. Their youngest son—who was still living at home and about to turn twenty-one—was dumbfounded when the police began recounting Denice's claims of spousal abuse. It just hadn't happened. No way. And their son would have known if anything even remotely close to what she was alleging had taken place. Nope.

Jim calmly explained Denice's mental condition and the patterns that typically unfold during her episodes. Though unsurprised by her behavior, he was clearly hurt by the accusation. Accusing him of physical abuse? That was a line he never thought she'd cross. Still, he simply asked the officers to take her to the hospital for a mental evaluation. He knew—with one hundred and fifty percent certainty—she would be placed on a 72-hour psychiatric hold.

As you know, when Denice hits a DEFCON 5 state, she often needs to be physically restrained. Trained professionals know how to do this safely. But when a family member is the one trying to intervene, the line between necessary restraint and perceived abuse can easily blur—especially from the distorted lens of someone in the middle of a psychotic break.

She was admitted to a local mental health facility via the ER of a partnering hospital. Jim called me the next day. His voice was heavy. "Denice has gone off her rocker again," he said. "And I'm done." Done with her. Done with the marriage. Just... done.

He was devastated that things had escalated to the point where she'd accused him of physical abuse. Yes, abuse happens in relationships—of course it does. But this wasn't that. There's also a different kind of moment, one that exists specifically in Denice's DEFCON 5 world, where someone has to physically protect themselves or others. You'll recall—Denice once punched Mom during one of those episodes.

When she's in that state, Denice genuinely believes she's in danger. She fights—hard—convinced that everyone around her is the aggressor. But in truth, it's her. She becomes the threat.

Later, Denice would describe these moments as feeling "superhuman," saying she turns into "Mrs. Hulk." And honestly? She's not exaggerating. Her strength becomes surreal—unbelievable, unless you've seen it for yourself.

That night, during the "anniversary" episode, Jim said he tried to hold her—tried to calm her down the way he usually did when she became agitated. She eventually seemed to settle, went to bed, and he went to shower. He had no idea she'd left the house.

His account of the incident was nothing close to what would typically be flagged as a domestic violence case. And yet, here they were.

Jim told me he was ready for a divorce. He couldn't—wouldn't—let her destroy his reputation with false accusations. Being labeled an abuser? That was his breaking point. She had crossed the line.

And honestly, I couldn't blame him.

Still, I begged him not to follow through with the divorce. I pleaded with him to let me intervene—to try to help Denice understand what was happening to her marriage. But I knew that wouldn't be possible until she was stabilized—until her thinking returned to clarity again.

We agreed to let Denice settle in at the mental hospital for a few days before I visited. After waiting about two or three days, I finally went to see her. The staff seemed relieved—genuinely happy—to have someone show up who actually knew her. Since she'd been transferred from the ER after police involvement, they had no personal information, no contact details, no real sense of who she was.

When I signed in, they showed me the visitor list she'd filled out. It was heartbreaking. The approved names included people from her distant past... along with Humpty Dumpty, Pinocchio, Santa, and Dumbo. She'd been admitted under the belief that she was a Jane Doe, terrified that someone was hunting her down. She hadn't given the hospital any accurate information about her identity or significant others. So my visit wasn't just welcomed—it was needed.

When I approached her in the common area, she was sitting quietly, coloring. At first, she looked content. But the moment she recognized me, her entire face changed. Fear. Panic. And a flash of "Oh shit, I'm in trouble." It was like she suddenly realized someone had found her.

The first thing I did was assure her she was safe with me. That she didn't need to be afraid. Slowly, she started opening up. She told me she believed the Italian mafia was going to kill her and Jim, and the only way she could save herself was to run. Her hallucinations were still active, but the hospital gave her a sense of protection—no one inside knew her, and, more importantly to her, no one on the outside knew where she was.

She insisted Jim would be safe because he could take care of himself. But she kept glancing nervously over her shoulder toward the window that looked out onto the courtyard. As the sky darkened, her fear intensified. She was convinced her oldest son was out there, watching her, waiting to kill her too.

The hallucinations made it clear—the anniversary of her son's car accident had triggered this episode. In her disordered, overwhelmed mind, she was certain the man killed in the accident—someone who had been a prominent figure in the Italian community—was the reason the mafia now wanted revenge. Her fear was real to her. And even though her son was serving time in the youth offender system, she was convinced he was lurking outside the facility.

I kept reminding her where he actually was, trying to use that fact to calm her.

Once her condition stabilized—thanks to time and medication—discharge planning became complicated. Denice had falsely accused her husband of abuse, and this time, Jim had reached the end of his patience. The escalation of her behavior into accusations of spousal violence had driven him to consult a divorce attorney.

I worked with both of them, trying to bring them to a place of reconciliation so Denice could return home after her discharge. At a point when she was calm and thinking clearly, I asked her to sign a statement affirming the truth: that Jim had never physically abused her. That if he had ever restrained her, it was only in an effort to prevent her from hurting herself—or him—during an episode of paranoid hallucinations.

Jim was satisfied with the statement. He believed Denice was sincere in her admission and willing to acknowledge what had really happened. They both agreed to work on their relationship, to rebuild trust, and to better understand how her disorder impacted both of them. The goal was for Denice to feel cared for—not controlled. Protected, not attacked.

The HELL that broke loose when my sister-in-law called me to come back and help during DEFCON 5, 2016, was exactly that—Hell. It was Labor Day weekend. All I knew at the time was that her husband was in jail, and she was out running about town—operating at a minimum of DEFCON 3, though no one truly realized it. Everyone around her could only describe, piece by piece, their individual interactions with her leading up to the weekend. I organized the meeting, just as I'd explained earlier. She showed up to the party already deep in DEFCON 5, took off running, and had to be medicated just to get her into the ambulance.

What her husband revealed a few days later, after I posted his bond, was eerily similar to the circumstances surrounding Denice's prior claims that Jim had abused her. Husband number two—Jack—described a scene that took place in their bedroom. Denice was acting out of sorts and became very upset during a sexual encounter. She began yelling at him to get off her. As he moved to comply, they both fell from the bed, with him landing on top of her. He claimed he was trying to do exactly what she asked, but in her agitated state, she kept fighting him while he attempted to calm her down.

"There was nothing I could do to get her to calm down. Nothing at all," he said.

The next thing he remembered was Denice, in a full-blown screaming tirade, calling the police.

In our state, when there's a domestic violence call, someone has to leave—usually the accused aggressor—and Jack was the one arrested. To complicate things further, they were living in a completely different, major metro city and county where the local police had no history or prior contact with Denice or her mental health crises.

So, unfortunately for Jack, he was the one who got hauled off. Denice, in her DEFCON state—the place where she becomes adept at saying or doing *whatever* it takes to redirect attention away from herself and onto someone else—was able to "win" the who's-right-who's-wrong contest. That power struggle, which typically begins at DEFCON 1, escalates quickly through the process.

To be fair to Denice, this was also very real to her. From her perspective, she *was* being abused. As tragic as that is, when she is in a DEFCON state, her perception becomes her reality. She genuinely felt violated—just as she had before with Jim.

Trauma begets trauma. No one is immune.

This situation was especially difficult to unravel. As much as I didn't believe Jack was intentionally abusive, or that he deserved to be charged with domestic violence, Denice's recollection—however muddled by her mania—was that she had been abused. And as she came down from the manic state during her nearly thirty-day hospitalization, she continued to respond as someone deeply traumatized.

It no longer mattered who was telling the truth. It didn't even matter what I believed. In her mind, she had been assaulted and victimized, and she needed support to process what she'd experienced.

And if I'm being honest, it didn't help that I didn't particularly like Jack. I later learned he had a criminal history that was kept from our family until *much* later. That revelation is its own journey entirely, but I'll say this: the charges he carried—and how that information was eventually disclosed—caused a great deal of pain and trauma, especially for my daughter.

What really connected the dots for me was remembering a strange phone call I'd received from Denice just days before her wedding to Jack. The call, I would later realize, came in the middle of a panic episode—triggered by her discovering Jack's criminal past. She left a voicemail first, sounding distressed, but followed up within twenty-four hours to say, "Everything is fine. I talked to mom about it and what I was worried about isn't a big deal anymore. We'll be married on Friday."

There is *no doubt* in my mind—Denice was in DEFCON 5 when she said "I do."

Chapter 17

DEFCON 5 – The Rise of De"Naughty"

As you may have noticed throughout my story, I've chosen to use Denice's real name, with her full permission. You'll also see that I present her name in two different ways: sometimes using standard proper case, and other times capitalizing the "N" to emphasize the "Nice." That is not a mistake. That is intentional.

Dad was very specific about how he spelled all of our names. I always thought that was something really cool and special, giving meaning to each of our names as though he was setting intention for who we were meant to become. Denice, in her journey, has embraced not just the name she was given but also the many names her internal parts have been given. Some were chosen by her, and others were seemingly adopted to help bring order and purpose to the roles they play within her system.

In the IFS (Internal Family Systems) therapeutic model, it's common to name our internal parts. This is often done through the 6F's process: Finding them, Focusing on them, Fleshing them out, identifying how we Feel toward them, Befriending them, and lastly, asking them what they Fear. In other words, what they are afraid might happen if they are not allowed to take over the system (Riemersma et al., pp. 466–467).

For Denice, the "Nice" in her name reflects her core Self. I capitalize Self here intentionally, following the IFS definition Jenna Riemersma, LPC, uses. She defines Self as "our central core that is who we truly are. The Self is the seat of our authentic spiritual connection to the divine. This reflects the Christian understanding that humans are made in the image of God (Genesis 1:27)." She continues, "The God image is undamaged in all people and reflects qualities of the divine such as the fruit of the Spirit or the Eight C qualities [of IFS]" (p. 207).

Denice's *imago Dei,* her God-like image, is truly who she is at her core. That is my sister.

I remember moments that made this so clear to me. Like when she taught me childhood songs such as *Bringing Home My Baby Bumblebee* during our long car rides. Sometimes they lasted four hours as we drove to our extended family's farm or to our grandparents' home nearby. We played games in the backseat like *Popeye* and *Slug Bug,* and we laughed until our bellies hurt while listening to the *Free to Be... You and Me* record.

At home, we had endless fun in the blue room playing *Simon Says, Red Light, Green Light,* or just spinning in circles on a blanket until we got so dizzy we would collapse in giggles. That continued until Dad would call from the other room, "Settle down in there before someone gets hurt!" Denice helped me study and memorize Bible verses for our AWANA's club at church, encouraging me to earn those "Word Perfect" ribbons. That is who she has always been: nurturing, playful, smart, and deeply kind.

Denice's inner Self, the Nice in her name, is loving, compassionate, and genuine. And I honestly believe that anyone who has met her or knows her well would say the same. In fact, whenever I had to call people in her life to let them know she had been hospitalized, I could always count on hearing the same reaction—utter surprise and disbelief.

"This can't be the same Denice," they would say. "She's so sweet. So put-together. So... Nice."

And she is.

When you hear the word *Bipolar*, clinically, it refers to the diagnostic characteristics outlined in the DSM-5-TR, which spans eight pages. In layman's terms, it might be understood as an abnormally escalated mood presentation, sometimes changing rapidly, and other times more slowly over time. For Denice, however, it also presents in how her IFS parts hijack her system, each part fighting for control. As she escalates into DEFCON 5, De"Naughty" takes over.

I would like to add here that DeNaughty is born out of Trauma—severe Trauma—and represents her "emotional response to an event that threatens, causes harm, and increases negative emotions" (Riemersma et al., 2023, pp. 167–168). When DeNaughty loses control of the system, the reaction triggers the appearance of what Denice has named Mrs. Hulk. This part has one main job within her system: to protect and destroy anything or anyone in her path, all in the effort of fulfilling DeNice's needs. Whether she needs to get "out" or escape from being trapped in the Hell she is experiencing while triggered in her mentally ill state, Mrs. Hulk makes it her mission to clear the way.

The DEFCON 5 incident that transitioned Denice from independent living to assisted living occurred in February 2022 but began brewing much earlier, in September 2021. Since her last DEFCON 5 hospitalization in 2016, Denice had been doing well on her own, with me as her legal guardian and conservator. My role during this five-year period began in a way that helped her achieve independence. She worked hard at adulting, another term used in the mental health field to describe someone managing responsibilities. With my assistance in decision-making, and using the money she had left over from Jim's death benefits, Denice lived in her own apartment. She held jobs at a dry cleaner's and then at three different daycare facilities. She even had her own car and regularly attended church. She was really doing well.

Until, of course, De"Naughty" started wanting more than Denice could afford and became jealous of what others had—things Denice no longer had or could not afford. DeNaughty longed for the frivolous and luxurious life they had before, when I was estranged from the family.

There were times during the years of guardianship and conservatorship when Denice and I had conflicts. One such conflict arose when she wanted to move from the third-floor apartment we had leased for her after she returned from residential treatment in June 2017, to a ground-floor apartment. Due to a knee injury she sustained in high school, her knee had deteriorated to the point of bone-on-bone contact, making it incredibly painful for her to walk.

We worked together to help her understand and navigate how to lose weight, as the orthopedic surgeon who would eventually perform her knee replacement surgery made it clear he wouldn't proceed until she lost eighty pounds. At just five feet tall, the weight was far too much for her body. The surgeon explained that even with a knee replacement, her bones, which he described as "chalk-like" would disintegrate under the strain. She had a lot of work to do if she wanted any relief from her chronic pain.

Losing that amount of weight is overwhelming for anyone, but for Denice, dealing with all her internal conflicts made the task even more daunting. Together, we attended nutrition appointments where she learned about portion control and how to shop for healthy food. We set small, manageable goals for her with the nutritionist and established accountability measures.

I took more of a backseat role in this process, often battling my own internal frustrations. There were times when I found myself sighing, thinking, "We've done this so many times before," or reminding myself, "She has to take control of her own weight loss if she wants that knee replacement." I was also perplexed because, after her time at the residential treatment center in Georgia, Denice had been at a healthy weight. When she came home, I didn't understand why she couldn't or wouldn't maintain it or work to get back to that healthy weight so she could get the surgery and finally be free of the chronic pain.

Managing my own emotions and frustrations while supporting her through this process took incredible internal control, but I knew that if she wanted to find relief, she had to be the one to take charge of her health.

She and I had talked many times about her desire to move to a first-floor apartment because of the stairs. Each time, we'd both come to the same conclusion: the stairs were actually a positive when it came to weight loss. It was, after all, the only real exercise she got on a daily basis. She admitted to herself that she wasn't exactly active and had no real motivation to exercise. But this time, something was different. It was the first time in all those years that I realized she had activated DEFCON 1 and was using Dad to get me to help her move to a first-floor apartment. Here's how it played out:

When we worked through the problem together, she would eventually arrive at the logical conclusion that the stairs were essential for her weight loss. I know it doesn't sound glamorous or sophisticated, but she really tried to think of other solutions. "What if I join the gym? It's only $10 a month," she'd suggest. It seemed like a cheap and doable option, right? But unfortunately, Denice's tight budget made even that small expense a challenge. Even at $10 a month, she'd need to cut something else from her spending. And there weren't many, if any, frivolous expenses to trim.

So, we came up with a plan together to see if she could find a way to fit that $10 into her budget.

I should pause here to give a bit more context on her financial situation. When Jim passed, she received nearly $1 million in benefit payouts. As you may recall, I helped her divvy it up to cover immediate, short-term, and long-term needs. Looking back, I'm so grateful I stepped in at that time. I was involved in some of the discussions with her and her two sons—both in their early twenties, one still living at home. Listening to them talk about how they wanted to use the money, including Denice, sounded like something straight out of a dream: new cars, motorcycles, vacations, cruises. It's hard not to dream big when you're presented with an unexpected windfall, right?

But, as much as they dreamed about these things, I knew it was my responsibility to make sure that the money would be used wisely. After securing her funds for long-term stability, I left her some to enjoy as she saw fit. She was able to buy a brand-new Ford Taurus SHO with her portion, and I believe she gave some money to each of her sons, though I don't recall the exact details. At the time, I didn't feel it was my place to dictate how she should spend the money she set aside for fun.

Fast forward to 2016. When I was called back to the family, I had to research Denice's money situation to provide the court with a financial plan I was required to propose as her Conservator, a plan I would subsequently have to adhere to. I discovered that within the two years from 2014 to 2016, when she was married to Jack, she, they, whoever was involved with Denice, had spent most of the three-quarters of that $1M we, and her financial advisor, had strategically placed in funds to earn enough interest over time. Denice was set so she would be financially secured for the rest of her life, and after turning sixty-five, she could start withdrawing money without penalties. Let me restate: in two years, close to $750,000.00 was GONE! "OMG! WTF happened here?" was my initial reaction—a reaction that continued to hit me many times over the next few years, like a slap in the face of reality, reminding me of why I became her Conservator.

Okay, what did Denice have to show for any of this money that was spent? She must have some kind of assets that could be of value. She just has to! NOPE! When accounting for her assets for this financial plan and report I had to complete as I filed to become her legal Conservator, she had two vehicles: one she still had from when Jim was alive, so it didn't count against this spending spree. And she still had the Ford Taurus SHO she purchased. Technically though, it was also purchased before she married Jack. Therefore, there were no properties, no stocks, no jewelry—other than her new wedding ring from

"Jared's"—nothing. The only things to explain the spending were, one, accounts from others who would tell of how they saw Denice and Jack always going on vacations, getaways, cruises, and being "flashy" as if they were wealthy. I also talked to her financial advisor, who told me about a time when she, Jack, and the people who lived in the converted garage on Jack's property came in for a meeting about a business proposal. Denice withdrew some money to start their new handyman business. The advisor told me the original amount of money they asked for was way too much, and he was able to talk some sense into Denice, getting her to only take a little bit—although still against his recommendations. Thank God for him because that actually left about $250,000.00 for me to work with to create a budget as strictly as I could for Denice to afford to live independently, combining an annual withdrawal with her less-than-living wages earned at her part-time jobs.

I strategized a strict but reasonable budget for her to live on until she would be qualified for widow's benefits at the age of sixty. More of this in the chapter about legal guardianship and conservatorship, but I think you get the picture: Denice had absolutely no financial wiggle room for spending any longer. Her system had trouble appreciating and remembering the experiences she had when she was spending all her money. Rather, she was good at seeing what others had and what she didn't have, which seemed to activate DeNaughty's jealousy and envy of others.

Back to the third-floor apartment with stairs to help her lose weight. As I mentioned, Denice was able to use Socratic questioning with me to come to her own logical conclusions. After some back-and-forth, Denice concluded that she would continue using the stairs and also utilize the workout facilities at her apartment clubhouse—part of her rent—every day for a set period of time, working toward an intermittent weight loss goal and showing her persistence in the process. Her ultimate goal was to lose weight to qualify for a knee replacement. These goals seemed more than reasonable for her physically; the difficulty would be in overcoming her mental barriers—her innate lack of motivation and her self-defeating mentality. Not to mention, there was the envy of others having what she didn't have. These were all normal human struggles, things everyone deals with. But, DeNaughty didn't like the outcome of the agreement Denice and I had made. And so, here begins DeNaughty's efforts to divide the united front, where I became the enemy, and through her passive-aggressive tactics, she would try to get what she wanted.

Dad, too, was suffering from knee issues and needed his second knee replacement around the same time as Denice. She began to get his sympathy for her pain, as he was actively fighting his own, with the exact same struggles. One day, he called me with his authoritarian tone, wanting to discuss Denice's need to use the stairs at her apartment.

"I'm hearing from her that you won't entertain the option of her moving to a first-floor apartment so she doesn't have to go up and down the stairs every day," he said, using his 'Board Member Parental' approach.

"Okay?" I replied.

He continued, "I can't help but empathize with her. I understand her pain. The thought of having to do that every day is just too much for me. I can't fathom what that's like for her."

"Okay?" I repeated.

"So, what do we need to do to get her into a first-floor apartment to give her some relief from this issue?" he asked.

"Well, Dad, would you like me to tell you what has already been done toward this, which by the way, Denice has already agreed to, or would you prefer I just tell you when it could happen?" I gave him the choice, respecting his position as her parent, who was essentially opposing me as her legal guardian, and also respecting him as my parent, advocating for me to help him help her. He opted to have me provide the details—"Hmmm, gee whiz, what a surprise," my internal voice remarked—information he clearly hadn't gotten from Denice or Mom, or both.

After explaining the plan and the effort Denice had agreed she needed to show, he seemed a bit dumbfounded. He backed off a little from his authoritative stance and moved into the more familiar dad role, saying, "Okay, please just do what you can to get her into a first-floor apartment as soon as possible. It's hurting me to see her struggle with this."

"Okay, Dad, I will do that. Just please be patient with me because it will take some time to budget her funds for another move, and we have to wait for a first-floor apartment to open up in the complex," I responded.

"Okay," he said. "Thank you for listening to me. Your mom and I really appreciate what you're doing for her."

That was it. DeNaughty won this battle, but not against me—against Denice. About a month later, I was able to arrange her move to a first-floor apartment that became available. This was now the close to twentieth time I had helped her clean her "hoarder" living space or moved her completely from one place to another in my lifetime. It was definitely something that required a lot of planning, time, and energy taken away from my daily life and responsibilities, as well as significant mental preparation and recovery each time. And unfortunately, it wouldn't be the last time I'd do this for her.

DeNaughty existed at this point but wasn't named until the episode when Denice transitioned from independent living to assisted living. This was an absolute nightmare for me, and it all began with DeNaughty using Dad to get her moved. It ended with DeNaughty using Debbie and April in an attempt to divide the united team. Unbeknownst to me, Denice had been working on getting Debbie and April's sympathy for a while. She had them buying things she couldn't afford but seemed to have a righteous reason for "needing." DeNaughty was manipulating them to get what she wanted, and the items kept increasing in both quantity, variety, and cost.

I found out by happenstance on September 13, 2021, what had been going on and how deeply she was using them. My parts inside were furious at Debbie for letting Denice manipulate her. I felt they all, including Mom, had violated the agreed-upon rule of transparency. I had to exercise incredible self-control as Denice and I had a "come to Jesus" meeting.

We had just left one of her psychiatry appointments, and as usual, we sat on a bench outside the office building, enjoying nature and the very friendly squirrel playing with us while debriefing the appointment. I happened to notice something odd. Somehow, Denice had acquired brand new, very nice, and high-end tires for her car.

"Hmmm," I said, "where did those new tires come from, Denice? Didn't we just put some very good condition used tires on your car that would get you through the winter and probably into the next one, with the amount of driving you do?"

"Umm, whelll, yeeaaah," she started, not realizing that I was well aware of her behavioral tell—stretching out her words, which never worked on me.

"Well, I hit a pothole the other day," she said, "you know, they're all over the place, and the one I hit was really, really big."

"So?" I said, already feeling my irritation rising.

"I didn't want to bother you with it," she continued, "so I called Mom." There it was, another tell again. It never worked on me.

"And she called Debbie to see if she could help, because you were probably too busy."

"OH MY GOD," my internal parts were literally screaming, but outside, I kept calm, listening to this dramatic presentation rapidly inflating.

"Um-huh, please continue," I said.

"Well, you know, it takes so long for AAA to respond. Sometimes I have to wait for an hour for them to get to me," she said, as my internal parts were imagining throwing my head back, rolling my eyes into the back of my head, and letting out a growling sigh.

"Go on," I replied.

"Well, you see, those used tires really weren't in that good of condition."

"YOU LIAR," my internal parts silently yelled, but I calmly responded, "Well, I have to disagree, but please continue."

Starting to escalate her voice, she used bigger, more convincing words, because DeNaughty was taking over the fight. She kept arguing her logic, eventually saying, and I'm not kidding, "Well, my car drives on the road differently than any other car out there. The asphalt changes when my car is driving on it and then changes back when other cars are on it. And my car makes itself find the potholes, so it needs the most expensive tires to hug the road in the right places so it doesn't veer off toward the potholes on the side of the road. So, I needed the tires that Debbie and April bought me," all in one breath.

"Wow," I said aloud. "I'm sorry, Denice, but here's what really happened."

"You weren't paying attention when you were driving, like so many other times in the past—like when you stopped at the stop sign one night coming home from church. When I asked you why you weren't going, you looked at me and said you were waiting for it to turn green."

I continued, "Not to mention, this is now the fourth time just this year you've needed pothole repairs on your car. That's why we just spent the money Mom gave you to get you very nice used tires to prepare you for the winter."

I went on, "So, no, your car didn't need brand new tires. What happened was you wanted new tires and didn't have the money to pay for them yourself, so you had Mom help you get Debbie and April to buy you brand new tires, by playing on their sympathy."

She sighed, "Okay, yes, you're right."

I continued, "Okay, so what else have you been getting them to buy you?"

She went on to list so many things she'd been acquiring from them over I don't know how long.

After getting my Self in order and calming my parts, I had to call Debbie. Oh boy, it wasn't going to be fun, nor would it resolve as swiftly as it did with Dad. Debbie is, by nature, just as stubborn and headstrong as the rest of us, with a need to be right. Her values and motivations are very different from mine, and it wasn't easy to want to begin this battle with her. But for Denice's sake, it was a battle I needed to win and get her back as an ally, rather than an enemy aligned with DeNaughty. This battle was won in February 2022 when Denice reached DEFCON 5. I had to call in the troops for assistance because I wasn't doing this by myself. It got to the point where Mom had called Debbie and told her that she needed to come help the way I needed her to help, rather than the way she felt was right. She said, "We will end up losing DeAnna this time, and we can't afford for that to happen." Debbie fell right in line with the united front and joined the forces. Realizing she had been used and manipulated by DeNaughty, Debbie finally woke up.

From that day in September 2021, I began the battle with Debbie, pleading with her to please stop providing Denice with all the amenities that were consistently increasing in perceived need, quantities, and cost. Denice continued to slowly decompensate over the next five months, and though it was difficult to detect, I knew deep down we were heading for chaos—I just didn't know when. She grew smarter at playing the game and had Debbie on her side. Denice began talking about Sam, her old friend from high school, about how he would be coming to Thanksgiving. She eventually started weaving him into every conversation she had with anyone. Thanksgiving came and went—no Sam. Christmas festivities came and went—no Sam.

We ended up at DEFCON 5 stage, with me in Phoenix, helping Mom get her to the ER. It got to the point where everyone seemed to go on edge whenever I would announce my travel plans. My sister-in-law would say, "It's like clockwork. Whether or not you tell her you're going out of town or not, it's like Denice can sense you're gone and she starts up."

After being at Mom's and subsequently taken to the ER, Denice was transferred to the same facility she was in for her very first episode, over twenty years ago. I had done my now-routine introduction by calling to inform them I was her legal guardian and conservator and sent all my court documents. I got in contact with the attending psychiatrist early in her stay and gave him the rundown of Denice's patterns. He seemed to receive it all well and was very grateful for the information so he could provide her care. He ended the call with me, actually stating, "I promise that she will not be released from care until I talk to you and let you know." It comforted me that he fully understood, and this would give me and the family time to unspin and wind down from the psychologically violent behavior we, mostly Mom again, had just had to deal with before we had to jump back in.

Throughout Denice's stay, her behavior remained consistent with her previous DEFCON 5—an inpatient state. Mom, Debbie, or anyone she could get a hold of in her contacts were constantly receiving calls at all hours—day or night. These calls were scattered in thought and speech, sometimes whispered, sometimes shouted, and often filled with instructions followed by paranoid delusions. There were sidebar conversations with people who obviously couldn't have been with her. Denice was still in a severely ill psychological state, and this continued for the entire duration of her inpatient hold.

I hadn't heard from the doctor, which I took as a sign that he felt she wasn't improving. Ugh. Joke's on me.

Late Thursday morning—about 72 hours after she was admitted to the ER—I finally got a call from her attending psychiatrist. I'll cut to the punchline: he was completely and utterly hoodwinked by DeNaughty. This was the moment I truly learned about the standards for treating inpatient psychiatric patients in our state. It was also the moment I realized I needed to become more educated. I've since pursued becoming a Licensed Professional Counselor, and I've been blessed with the chance to work at local inpatient hospital facilities, so I've gained a deeper understanding of the system.

But at that time, before I had the knowledge I do now, the experience was traumatic. It blindsided me and continued to wreak psychological havoc on all of us. Denice, a very mentally ill family member, was being released from care—and she needed a ride home "TODAY."

I was livid. I kept my cool for most of the conversation with the doctor, but the more he spoke, the more it sank in: Denice was no longer exhibiting the need for psychological care. She was doing her Adult Daily Living (ADL) skills at "baseline," and had declined voluntary admittance. Her 72-hour hold was set to expire that afternoon.

I learned that the 72-hour hold is actually "up to 72 hours." If the patient reaches baseline before that, they can be released. As her guardian, I could make decisions for Denice—except in mental health matters. So, I had no control over whether she stayed inpatient. But once she was discharged, my responsibility kicked in.

I pleaded with the doctor to keep her because of her continued psychotic behavior, which was clear to all of us on the outside. But he flatly denied what I was telling him. In the few sessions he had with Denice, she was acting at baseline, and he didn't see any medical reason to keep her. BULLSHIT! That was it. I finally lost it when I felt a direct threat from him. He said, "She WILL be discharged today, and if you're not here to pick her up, I'll put her in a taxi to her home and turn you in for neglecting to care for an at-risk adult."

I snapped back, "Okay, I've already contacted my attorney, and today ends at 11:59 p.m. If she's released before I can get there, I'll turn you in for releasing a patient who is in active psychosis, and is at risk of harming herself or others. You will be held responsible for that."

Internally, my emotions exploded—anger, disgust, fear—along with all the secondary emotions that followed. Baseline? WTF does that even mean? DeNaughty may have been at baseline, but Denice was far from it.

I had to take a moment to gather myself—though really, that was all the time I had—before I got on the phone with the rest of the team. I needed to let them know that the tornado of chaos was back in our hands to manage. I arranged to pick her up from the hospital, and there was no way I was dealing with this on my own. There was no way I could trust DeNaughty in this state to be at my home without others there to protect me from her—or her from me, for that matter. I couldn't risk her making false accusations about my husband, especially after what happened during the first episode when she disrobed and was about to be presented to him in the hospital. She'd already accused two of her own husbands of assault—what would stop her from doing the same to mine?

In her state of mind and with her history of making false claims, she could easily fabricate something about either of us. There was no way she could go back to her apartment alone and risk decompensating further.

I called every family member, setting the rules: "Be here tonight for a family meeting because I need everyone's support for her to stay at my house." There was NO way she was going to mom and dad's again. My mom was still recovering from the trauma of three days ago when Denice had been strapped to a gurney, screaming for my mom to help her. No, not happening.

I had no choice but to bring Denice into my home and care for her until she became regulated enough to be safe. Despite my lack of trust in her, her safety had to be my primary concern for now.

I called Denice's oldest son, straight up, and told him I needed him to come to the hospital with me to pick up his mother. He drove himself there and met me and my son, who drove me, in the parking lot. Denice's oldest knew there was a family meeting scheduled at my house after we picked her up. We walked into the hospital together, with not much conversation among us, just the shared understanding of the situation. A hospital orderly escorted Denice to join us, smiling and saying, "I'm so touched to see you boys here for me."

We all made our way to my son's truck. I helped Denice into the back seat, where I had the child locks activated on the truck doors. Her son gave her a superficial hug, then walked to his car. As he was leaving, I asked him if I was going to see him at my house. His response, typical of him, was "Probably not. I have better things to do." That response wasn't unusual, as he had remained largely absent during most of Denice's DEFCON states, only hearing about them from his brother and his dad over time. Denice's youngest son had moved out of state with his wife and kids, so he wasn't available to join the meeting in person—but maybe he was there via speakerphone. Honestly, I don't recall.

Denice worked hard in the back seat of the truck to try and control the ride home. She demanded my son change the music on the radio, insisting that's what she needed to be happy right now. Nope. Right or wrong, I wasn't playing that game with DeNaughty. She proceeded to sing her songs louder and louder, drowning out the radio and our conversation about how my son's day had gone. This was behavior directly attributed to her Histrionic Personality Disorder, still very active at DeNaughty's baseline.

Ignoring the theatrics, we arrived at my house, where everyone who could and wanted to attend the family meeting was already there. DeNaughty saw it as a "welcome home" party just for her. She was once again, dramatically "touched" by the attention she was receiving. She was so excited to be able to "stay at DeAnna's Spa," as I came to realize she imagined my house. On the way out of the parking lot, she had described her stay at the hospital: "It was so nice, like being at a spa. It was peaceful, and now I get to go to DeAnna's spa to continue my recovery."

Internally, my parts were screaming: "Oh no she didn't just say that. Oh God, she has a rude awakening coming." My house was not a resort for her to take advantage of, and there was no way she was going to take advantage of me during her stay.

Once the initial "welcoming celebration" wore off, I began with, "Denice, look around at everyone here for you." She took about ten minutes, carefully studying each person, as if trying to send mental messages. It was as though she was silently assigning duties and tasks to each person. She saw

Debbie and April sitting at the kitchen table, Mom sitting near them, our sister-in-law standing by the sink, my husband sitting in his usual spot on the couch, with Dad sitting right next to him. My son and his wife sat just adjacent to them. Denice positioned herself on the other end of the couch by the fireplace, where she could see all of us. I sat in a kitchen chair, placed between her and Mom, who was visibly shaken and weary, struggling to stay strong.

I continued, "Because you hoodwinked the doctor and got yourself prematurely released, and because you are still in a very dangerous state, you will be staying at my house until your scheduled therapy session on Tuesday." I went on to tell her that, since she was in my home, she would need to comply with my rules. I wasn't about to let her disrupt my life while I was protecting her from herself. Normally, when people are guests in someone's home, there's an initial discomfort as they adjust to the host's routine. But with Denice, in the mental state she arrived in, I knew I had to set clear instructions and boundaries. I'd already heard what she thought staying with me would be like, and she was in for a rude awakening. I wasn't providing her with a paid spa service package. I'd been taken advantage of enough in the past—I wasn't about to let her do it again.

The open bedroom for her was the one in our very nice finished basement, which had previously been used by my husband's mother when she lived with us. It was also the suite where my daughter and her kids stayed when they lived with us. Given Denice's active mental illness, she needed to follow a routine, including eight hours of sleep. This would be tough for someone in active mania, but it was non-negotiable. No eating in my home, except in the kitchen. And there would be no open flames unless they were attended to at all times. Candles would not just be left to burn. I also made it clear that someone had to be here with me and her at all times, for my psychological safety.

Debbie and April signed up for the day shifts, and my son and his wife stayed for the overnights, taking the main floor master suite, which was big enough for all three of them, as they had my grandson with them during their parenting time. My husband and I regularly use the upstairs suite, so the arrangement worked perfectly.

We proceeded with the family meeting, starting with Dad, who wanted to understand why we were at this stage and still couldn't grasp how we got here. He just didn't understand why his fifty-nine-year-old daughter was behaving this way, saying, "This is not the DeNice little girl I had. As far as I'm concerned, this is DeNaughty, and she's acting like a five-year-old child who just needs a spanking. I just don't understand what I'm seeing here."

He was right in what he was witnessing. DeNaughty was definitely active, exhibiting extreme and rapid mood changes. She switched from a calm adult tone to a childlike voice and gibberish instantly. Boisterous sighs, tongue clicking, rolling her eyes, slamming her hands onto her thighs, stomping her feet—behaviors typical of a two- to five-year-old throwing a temper tantrum. She did, however, comply with my rule: she could sit there and throw her tantrums as long as she didn't throw anything, get up from her chair, hurt herself, or anyone else.

As she exhibited these behaviors, I directed everyone to ignore her until I spoke, asking if she was ready to continue. At times, it would take minutes for her to gain control of herself, but it felt like hours. She seemed to feel some sense of control by being allowed to throw her Kleenex on the floor as hard as she could. I noticed a little giggle from behind me. It was Mom, recalling that this was exactly where Denice had been the previous Sunday night, when Mom's kitchen floor had been littered with dirty, bloody Kleenexes. I heard her whisper, "I'm so glad you're all here to see this. I'm not crazy, it really did happen."

We helped Denice regain control as best we could, and when Dad couldn't take anymore, he and Mom left to go home. Debbie, April, and our sister-in-law helped get Denice settled in her room at "DeAnna's spa" before they left, allowing my son and daughter-in-law to do what they needed to do to stay overnight until Tuesday morning.

For my own sense of safety in my home with DeNaughty staying with me, I set the expectation that she was not to come up from the basement until 8:00 a.m. the next morning. She agreed to stay downstairs. While helping her wind down for the evening, we provided her with a clock, as she was trying to justify needing her phone to wake up in the morning. But I knew this was just an excuse to keep her phone so she could stay up all night on Facebook, calling her friends and disturbing them from their sleep. She still had no concept of time.

By the way, mental health assessments measure for thought and orientation, and a person should be oriented 4x: to time, place, person, and situation. Denice was clearly disoriented 4x—unable to sleep, constantly calling friends at all hours, and fully believing she was at "DeAnna's spa," expecting to be pampered and treated specially, remaining firmly in her DeNaughty state. She didn't understand why the world wasn't revolving around her.

And remember when the doctor said he had no medical or legal reason to hold her because she was fine and refused to voluntarily remain at the hospital? I call BULLSHIT.

I woke up Friday morning hoping and trusting that she had complied with staying in her basement suite until 8:00 a.m., using the time for activities like Bible study, watching TV, taking a warm, cleansing shower, using the workout equipment down there, or even reading a book—things she could do and had access to in my finished garden-level basement. But no. I came downstairs to find her "cleaning" my kitchen, which, by the way, wasn't dirty in the first place. Our daily routine was to clean up our living space every night before bed. More than cleaning, she had completely rearranged my kitchen appliances, moving my coffee machine and toaster oven to different counters. She had also lit candles and put an arrangement in the center of the kitchen table as a decoration, expecting me to be thankful and happy for what she had done.

Now, you might say she was trying to do something nice, and if it had been Denice, maybe I'd see it that way. But Denice would have also complied with the activities I had set for her to do downstairs and would have respected the 8:00 a.m. rule, understanding that I had good reasons for wanting to feel safe in my own home. But no. This was DeNaughty, who believed she was an adult and could do what she wanted, when she wanted, using other people's things without regard for them. In this case, without regard for me or my home.

She even tried to justify her actions by claiming that my daughter-in-law and son needed to wake up and get ready for their workday, as they had to leave at 8:00 a.m. That's why I had set this specific time—so I could take over DeNaughty-sitting at that time. Needless to say, I did not respond with the appreciation she was hoping for. I was well beyond playing into her manipulations.

I reprimanded her, feeling like this was a strategic attempt to take over my home. I reiterated to her why candles were not allowed, why I had everything in my kitchen where I needed it, and why we didn't have centerpieces on our kitchen table. This is my home, and she was a guest—not a paying consumer at a spa. I explained that she had no right to change or disregard our house rules, something a host should never have to tell a guest, especially within the first twelve hours of their visit.

This did not sit well with DeNaughty, starting the day with discord. I reached out to Debbie and April to find out when they would be coming over to help with their shift. Debbie had an appointment to attend, and after that, she and her daughter came over to assist for the day, taking DeNaughty out to do things while I got a break to prepare for Denice's second night staying with us.

Once my son and daughter-in-law were able to return after their workday and picked up my grandson, we ate the dinner my husband went out and bought. He prepared a plate for Denice and gave it to her, letting her sit in his spot on the couch, wanting to make sure she was comfortable. He showed compassion for her condition, trying to understand what he was observing but unable to fully comprehend what it would be like to have bipolar disorder. He was empathetic to her mental distress and wanted to do what he could to help. I felt his compassion and appreciated his effort immensely.

However, I somehow knew that his kindness would not be received well by Denice.

I decided it was best for him to do what he felt was right. He had opened up our home to her, allowing her to stay and recover since she had been prematurely released from inpatient care and clearly needed help. He had seen her in this condition only once before, back in 2016, and he had been there for me every step of the way as her legal guardian and conservator, supporting me through the previous six years as we navigated this tumultuous situation.

We got through Friday, but Denice soon started complaining to Debbie that being forced to stay in the basement wasn't fair. Debbie came to me and said Denice was claiming that the bedding and towels were smelly and that I "wouldn't let her have clean linens and towels." Having absolutely no patience left for these kinds of communication games, I responded to Debbie, "If Denice thinks she's at a spa, what would she have done in this situation? Called housekeeping to bring new towels? I showed her where the laundry room is, and she's allowed to wash the bed linens and towels if she wants to."

Apparently, that wasn't what Denice had in mind as a "guest" at "DeAnna's spa." Despite it being made very clear to her that she wasn't here on vacation, nor was I responsible for doing everything for her, she seemed to think otherwise. She was allowed to stay in my home for her protection, and for the safety of others—but I wasn't her employee or servant. I know I came off as harsh, but I had reached my limit. I felt like the least she could do was take care of herself within the boundaries of my home rules, just like everyone else who had lived here had done. Each person, including Denice, was expected to contribute, respect my husband's and my routine, and manage their own needs.

I had already bent as far as I could by bringing her here for shelter. There was so much to do for her in the coming days, weeks, and months. I had nothing left to coddle her. This was about her safety, yes, but it was also about setting boundaries. That's why I insisted on others being here to help with her; I simply couldn't handle it on my own anymore.

We got to Saturday, and when Debbie and April arrived for their day shift, all hell broke loose. Denice (DeNaughty) took one too many liberties with my husband around lunchtime. He had made sandwiches for everyone, which, if you know my husband, was a huge deal—he doesn't cook for himself, so the fact that he made sandwiches for everyone, including Denice, was a significant gesture on his part.

Then came the fatal statement from DeNaughty: "Get me a glass of milk." I could feel the tension building in the room. Debbie, April, and I froze, waiting to see how my husband would respond. Everyone knows that no one commands my husband to do anything, especially not when he has been so kind to someone in need. He looked at her squarely and, in a firm voice, said, "You got legs? Get up and get your own milk."

That was the tipping point. From there, it all went downhill. DeNaughty accused him of saying things he never said and then tried to manipulate Debbie and April into siding with her against him. My husband, however, wasn't having it. He called her a liar, and she responded as though he had mortally wounded her, trying to draw him into an argument to prove herself right and him wrong.

Oh shit, she had just crossed the line.

He took control of the conversation, reminding her how he had opened his home to help her, and told her she would not be allowed to disrespect him. He promptly disengaged from her and went to his study. Then, he summoned me to join him immediately.

I knew what was coming. He told me flat out—DeNaughty had to go. He had had enough of her disrespect and manipulation, and he wasn't going to allow it in his home any longer. I had no choice but to respect his decision.

The process of getting her out by nightfall began. I needed a moment, so I went to my study and then called Debbie to join me. I explained to her that Denice needed to leave, and we immediately called Denice's youngest son to let him know what had happened. We then called my parents, my son and daughter-in-law, and our sister-in-law to keep everyone informed.

Debbie went downstairs to sit with Denice while I updated April. Everyone's first concern was for me as her guardian—everyone was afraid of what might happen to me if Denice was left on her own. "What if she ends up killing someone before we get her to her doctor appointments on Tuesday?" Debbie asked, her voice full of concern.

I had to accept, with radical honesty, that if something like that happened, I would have to deal with it when and if it happened. There was nothing more I could do. My loyalty was to my husband, and I knew I had to stand by him. It was a chance I had to take.

Chapter 18

DEFCON 5 – The Reign of DeNaughty

"For by grace are ye saved, through faith, and that not of yourselves, it is the gift of God, not of works, lest any man should boast" (Holy Bible, NIV Ephesians 2:8-9).

It is by my faith in God and *only* by the grace of God that we got from that Saturday evening to the following Tuesday morning without any loss of life or Denice being arrested. It certainly felt like it required more faith than a mustard seed *(Holy Bible, NIV Matthew 17:20),* but I knew I had to let go of control—not only for myself, but for DeNaughty to have her reign and to be an example to the rest of the team on how to disconnect from the outcome.

Debbie and April took Denice to her own apartment that evening. When she got settled in the car and they began driving away, DeNaughty said to them, "Thank God I am out of DeAnna's Hell hole," as it had not turned out to be the "spa" experience she had expected. Stopping by the grocery store, DeNaughty told them that she had no food in the house, and they chose to comply with her stated needs so there would be nothing she could say she needed over the next few days. Turns out it was yet another lie to manipulate them into doing her bidding. They parked in the parking lot, leaving the car running for Debbie to stay with her, knowing DeNaughty was in no condition to be in a public space. Besides, why should she have to get out and use the energy to do her own grocery shopping when she has "staff" to do it for her, as she had begun to refer to us as when she was at DeAnna's spa turned hell hole?

April reached back and asked for Denice's debit card to pay for the groceries DeNaughty so desperately needed. Receiving a very nasty response at the thought of April expecting Denice to pay for her own groceries, she eventually handed April her debit card. After leaving the car, Debbie, who was left to sit with DeNaughty, tells about the wait as being the most terrifying experience she has ever had.

Just like when my son and I were transporting Denice from the last hospital stay to my house, DeNaughty began instructing Debbie to change the radio station to Denice's gospel station. "No," Debbie replied, "this music is the best music for me for calming, so we are just going to leave it here." Not getting her way with Debbie, DeNaughty, like clockwork, began singing the gospel music loudly to drown out Debbie's calming music. Next, Debbie witnessed the next level that only few people have ever seen, and tells her experience as follows:

"I can't explain it but I can describe it. I heard this deep growling noise coming from the back seat, where only Denice's body was sitting. I took my mirror to move it where I could watch her without turning around but could see her plain as day. This growling was like a wild animal sounding a warning that it is contemplating an attack and then the growling voice said out loud 'should we kill this one?'. When I looked at her eyes, they were totally black, no color, no white, no nothing, just black as night. All I could do was hope that April was hurrying in the store to get back, it was terrifying."

April returned to the car, and they drove to Denice's apartment, got her settled, and then went home. Debbie called me to check in, letting me know what had transpired and confirming that Denice was at home. "Okay, here we go," I thought—DeNaughty was on her own now. I prayed and went to bed.

Sunday morning, crickets. Sunday afternoon, crickets. Sunday evening, Denice called Mom, totally confused. "I don't know what is happening, Mom. The family has abandoned me. I'm here all alone. I have no food. I don't understand why everyone has left me. At least I have my church family that loves me," and then she hung up. Mom called to relay the report to me. Crickets.

Monday morning, I called Denice's new church to find out what had happened on Sunday afternoon, based on her statement about having her church family to help her. I narrowed it down to finding the leader of the Ladies' Sunday School group and reached out to her. She was relieved to hear from me because, she explained, she and some other ladies from the group had been over at Denice's all afternoon the previous day. They had been deeply worried about Denice because she had told them her family had abandoned her, presenting herself as alone, discarded, and victimized by us.

I explained the situation to her—what had occurred and what I predicted would happen. I suggested that she and the other ladies offer only prayers for Denice, as anything else done for her would likely be taken advantage of by DeNaughty. She was grateful for the explanation, though devastated by the reality that she and the others wouldn't be able to do anything more for Denice.

Monday night, crickets.

Tuesday morning. Here we go. Debbie and I had already made arrangements to meet at Denice's apartment to pick her up and take her to her 9:00 a.m. follow-up doctor appointment from when she got her albuterol prescription. We stopped at the gas station just diagonally from Denice's apartment to fuel up. Before getting out to pump the gas, Denice asked me to pick her up some snacks from the convenience store. After putting the fuel nozzle in my tank and starting the pump, I got back into the truck when she said, "I have it all planned out what you are going to do to sue that doctor from the mental hospital who let me out still being in this manic state."

I simply said, "Nope, not going to buy you anything. You should have eaten what you needed to before I picked you up," delaying a response to the other statement. Shaking my head, I shut the door and continued filling the tank, having no idea what the conversation was between her and Debbie while I was out. After the tank was filled, I got back into the truck, and before starting it, I turned to her and said, "What happened with the doctor is for me to handle. I do not need anything from you to deal with it."

Surprised by my response, DeNaughty deflated her stance on the issue and said, "Okay." We drove to the doctor appointment with me and Debbie just talking about normal everyday things in our own lives. We kept the conversation superficial, not saying anything DeNaughty could latch onto and mentally ingest, turning it into Denice's life rather than ours or using it against us later.

By now, the doctor had been fully educated about what was happening and was not going to be blindsided by DeNaughty's presentation at the appointment. I parked the truck in a space that fit and had fewer cars for me to navigate, as it was an extra-long bed. The three of us got out and walked across the parking lot to the doctor's office building. Denice checked in and was called back for the nurse to prep her for the visit. One of the tests she had to do was to check her breathing with a spirometer. Right away, DeNaughty became resistant, refusing to do the test. The nurses—yes, more than one—worked with her to get her to do it, but she insisted, "I'm ONLY doing it ONE time and THAT IS ALL!" she said loudly.

They managed to get the first reading and worked with her for about twenty minutes to get a second reading because she refused to do it correctly the first time. DeNaughty knew what was wrong with her—she has COVID, lung disease, and now "going to have a heart attack if you keep insisting that I do these stupid tests!" she exclaimed.

The doctor finally came in to do the exam, and DeNaughty began to tell her what a terrible person I was because I wouldn't allow her to have her "emergency inhaler" of albuterol after that nice doctor prescribed it for her. This presentation was obviously DeNaughty's attempt to align others against me, manipulating them into seeing her reality, where I am controlling her and not letting her live her own life.

This two-sided presentation is exactly what had been happening since at least the previous September. Waiting patiently for DeNaughty to finish her monologue at the doctor, and allowing the theatrics and drama to simmer down enough for me to respond, the doctor looked squarely at Denice and said, "I am the one who told your sister and your mom to take it away from you and stop the use immediately; it sounds like they followed doctor's orders."

DeNaughty was stunned and dumbfounded, realizing she was no longer controlling the doctor or the situation. The doctor gave the aftercare instructions, confirmed that Denice was totally healthy in every area except for being overweight, and advised her to continue working to lose weight before leaving the room.

This appointment, which reasonably should have taken about fifteen minutes for a follow-up, ended up lasting close to two hours. Now, by "ended," I mean DeNaughty finally left the exam room. We still needed to get her out of the exam room, to the car, and on to her next appointment with her therapist at 11:00 a.m.

DeNaughty continued with her dramatic behavior, and it was still working—at least a little bit—on one of the nurses, bless her caregiving heart. The nurse made the fatal suggestion of having Denice taken out of the office in a wheelchair to avoid exerting energy because she was feeling so sick and having trouble breathing. Internally, I was screaming, *What? With her entirely healthy body that needs to lose weight, you are suggesting she be taken to the car by someone else?!*

I immediately said, "Absolutely not, she will not be taken out in a wheelchair. She will walk herself from here to my car and get herself in for me to take her to her therapy appointment."

The nurse responded that, for their liability, it would be better if they took Denice to the lobby in the wheelchair, but they would only be able to get her there. Denice would then need to walk to the pick-up area in front of the building, under the awning. This pick-up area was large enough for two-way traffic and had a crosswalk for people to get to their cars in the parking lot.

"Fine," I said. "Take her ass to the lobby. Debbie and I will meet you down there. Then, Denice, you will get up out of that chair and walk your happy ass to my car. I WILL NOT go get the truck and bring it to you. You walked yourself into the doctor's office from where I parked. You have a healthy report from your doctor, so you will walk yourself back to my car, just like Debbie and I have to do."

We met the elevator in the lobby, and the nurse wheeled DeNaughty out. DeNaughty refused to get out of the wheelchair until I went to get the car. *Nope, no way. Not happening.* I guess you could say here, DeNaughty, meet DeAdamant.

The poor nurse, really, God bless her soul, told Denice she needed to get up and go back to the office. She explained that if Denice would get out of the wheelchair and go outside, the nurse would wait inside to ensure Denice made it safely to my car. Yes, I had parked further from the door to provide an opportunity for Denice, Debbie, and me to get some walking in—however, this wasn't out of my normal routine. I had implemented this parking rule in my life years ago. I'm not one to drive endlessly or wait for an empty spot in the front row to open.

Also, keep in mind that Denice had already had knee replacement surgery three years prior, so there was no sympathy from me for her claiming to have a bad knee in this scenario. As the doctor had just said, "She only needs to focus on losing weight, as morbid obesity seems to be her only health issue."

Finally, DeNaughty succumbed to the nurse's suggestion, rising slowly and dramatically from the wheelchair. She shuffled toward the glass doors, every step deliberate, all the while being cheered on by the nurse. As she exited the building, she glanced back forlornly, but the reflective glass prevented her from seeing inside. From within, we faintly heard the nurse's voice, "I am still here, I can still see you."

Standing there like Eeyore, pathetically burdened with her own paperwork and purse, DeNaughty took a deep breath. She turned and made her way to the two-way traffic sidewalk beneath the awning, stopping in the middle. She looked both ways—then stood there. And stood there. And stood there.

Debbie, ever the cheerleader, urged her to keep moving. DeNaughty remained frozen. Frustration set in as Debbie's patience wore thin, watching DeNaughty refuse to budge from the center of the road. Another car approached, forcing it to swerve around her, DeNaughty didn't move. A second car followed suit, swerving to avoid her. Still, DeNaughty stood there.

At this point, Debbie had lost all patience. I calmly suggested, "Come join me on the curb on the other side. We'll wait there." Debbie, clearly stunned by the scene, shook her head. "I don't know how you do it, DeAnna. Putting up with this kind of stuff—has it always been like this for you?"

"Yes," I replied simply. "We're just going to sit here and wait."

"What if someone hits her?" she asked.

"Well, we're at a doctor's office," I said with a half-smile. "If that happens, at least we'll have plenty of help right away."

Debbie just shook her head again. "She looks like a goose in the road, just standing there."

We both chuckled. It was our way of coping, our family's defense mechanism against the overwhelming sadness. "I've already planned what to do if the sheriff is called," I added. "So don't worry about that."

After about thirty minutes of this, with people coming in and out of the building, already having completed their business, I turned to Denice. "I need your phone to call your therapist. We've missed her time slot now, and you need to explain why."

She refused to use her own phone, so I called the therapist on mine, holding it on speaker so Denice could talk. As I held out the phone close to her to talk, she lunged for it, not moving her feet from their spot. "Nope," I said, pulling it away. "This is my phone. Since you refused to handle your own business, you'll talk to her on speaker while I hold it."

I'd learned from past experiences that if I let her hold the phone, it might end up in pieces on the asphalt. By this point, it seemed she had either forgotten about or let go of her protective watch from the nurse, though I was sure they were still observing us from their second-floor office windows.

I got Denice's therapist on the phone and explained the situation: we were stuck at the doctor's office with Denice refusing to move from the middle of the drop-off road section for the past thirty minutes. The therapist, already aware that Denice had been in the hospital, understood the context and was grateful that I'd kept her informed about everything since Denice's premature release. With the therapist on the line, she was able to coax DeNaughty into walking to the car, all the while staying on speakerphone as Denice murmured, "I only feel safe with you."

We got her into my truck, and the therapist continued to work with Denice through calming exercises over the phone as I drove us to her house, where the office was. We all participated in the exercises—even me, though I was driving. Thank God it didn't put me to sleep, but it really came close.

When we arrived at the therapist's house, we got Denice settled for the session, and all three of us participated. Debbie and I let Denice tell her side, and of course, it was all about how terrible I was—how I tried to control her, put her in danger, and didn't let her make decisions for herself. According to Denice, I was the enemy, the sole cause of all her behaviors.

It was obvious Denice was severely dysregulated, evidenced by her rapid, tangential speech. She was in full psychosis, convinced that someone, particularly me, was out to harm her. She even asked the therapist if she could "please go upstairs" to "take a shower." Inside, my mind raced. I thought, *Oh God, this is where she disrobes and prepares herself to be used by whatever man is available—knowing the therapist's husband is often home in another room during sessions.*

Thankfully, the therapist declined Denice's request but did go to the freezer and retrieved an ice tray—something she often used to help clients deescalate through sensory techniques. Denice eagerly accepted the ice, stood up abruptly, and proceeded to shove the entire tray of ice down the front and back of her pants.

Once again, Debbie was in shock and disbelief at what she was witnessing.

The therapist asked Denice who she felt safe with. Without hesitation, Denice answered, "Debbie."

"Okay, Denice," the therapist said, clearly recognizing that Denice was in full-on mania, at DEFCON 5, "I'm going to recommend that you allow Debbie and DeAnna to take you to the ER—a different one this time—and get you evaluated. In my opinion, you need to be hospitalized again, so you can get the help you need to rest and regain control of yourself."

Tears welled up in Denice's eyes as she replied, defeated, "Really? That's what I need?"

"Yes, Denice," the therapist said gently. "You're in a state where you need more help than I or your sisters can offer. I really recommend that you go with them voluntarily, and let them take you to the ER for the help you need."

"Okay," Denice agreed, and we left the therapist's office. We got into the truck and headed to another ER, this time the one associated with the mental hospital where Denice had received much better care in the past.

As I merged onto the highway, Denice's voice came from the back seat. "I really am sick, aren't I? I really do need help, huh?"

I struggled to hold back the tears, but they came anyway. "Yes, Denice. You are really sick, and we are here to help you get the help you need."

For the first time in a while, Denice seemed to relent, riding quietly to the hospital without issue. It was a brief reprieve for both Debbie and me before what awaited us at the hospital. I took a moment to regain my emotional balance and soften inside, seeing Denice's wounded child parts—hurt and defeated—and finally, compliantly riding with us.

At the hospital, we checked in at registration. I stood behind Denice, watching as she checked herself in. We all headed to the waiting room, where we sat quietly. When her name was called for registration and triage, Denice went up freely, though she spoke in a jumble of gibberish to the staff. I provided the necessary information and insurance card, and helped her with the I.D. bracelet.

We settled back into the waiting room. Debbie recalled how cold it was, and we realized we hadn't eaten all day. For me, eating didn't cross my mind, but I was thirsty. I grabbed a bottle of water from the vending machine, and Debbie followed suit, getting herself a drink and a snack. We sat down.

Then, DeNaughty reappeared, turning to me and demanding, "Where's MINE?"

"No one can read minds, Denice," I replied, keeping my cool. "If you want something to eat or drink, you're an adult. You can get it yourself."

She hesitated for a moment before saying, "Okay, get me a water and a candy bar."

I got out her debit card and handed it to her. "You're an adult. You can get whatever you want from that machine."

Her face twisted in a mixture of surprise and disdain as she grabbed the card, spun on her heels, and stormed off toward the vending machine. We could hear her grumbling loudly as she muttered, "Three dollars for a tiny bag with a few nuts in it. That's ridiculous!"

She returned to her seat, her snack and drink in hand, and I asked her to give me back the debit card so I could put it back in her wallet. With a huff, Denice threw the card toward me, letting it land on the floor in front of me, forcing me to get up and pick it up.

We had already moved to another part of the waiting room to avoid disturbing the other patients. In Denice's world, the reasons others were there didn't matter—everything revolved around her.

Living in DeNaughty's world is surreal. There's no sense of time, only a sense of urgency whenever she experiences moments of panic. There's no sense of self—I truly believe she doesn't know who she is or how she's behaving. It's simply not her. There's no sense of place, either. Sure, she knows she's at the hospital, but it seems like only so she can manipulate the situation to get what she thinks she needs. And there's no sense of the situation—she has been in this state before, but it's as if she doesn't really understand that she's headed for days, maybe weeks, in a locked facility where she'll receive care to help her get back to baseline. Therapeutically speaking, she is not oriented 4X at this phase; she's hit the DEFCON 5 tipping point again, for the second time in just nine days.

"Denice," they called. It was time for her to go back to the exam room. Debbie and I followed, exhausted but trying to stay focused. The staff began their routine questioning, asking her what had brought her to the ER. DeNaughty quickly started to decompose, telling them flatly, "I'm hearing voices telling me to do things, and I need mental help."

Debbie and I briefed them on how we had ended up there—following the recommendation of Denice's therapist, hoping to speed up the process. We were all running on empty, having been at this for over ten hours. The staff left the room, and we were left waiting. And waiting.

To pass the time, Debbie and I started chatting, reminiscing about things we used to do as kids—just small talk to keep some semblance of normalcy in the situation. But then we heard it—the unmistakable low yet boisterous laughter from DeNaughty. Her face had that look again, the one that told us she was in her own world, conversing with the voices in her head, plotting something sinister.

We were right. The hammer hit the nail on the head.

"What's going on in there, Denice? What are you thinking about?" Debbie asked, trying to keep her calm.

Without acknowledging who had asked, DeNaughty began to carry out her plan. "Oh, God just told me to kill myself when I get home. To get a knife from the kitchen drawer and slice my throat."

Debbie, ever the pragmatist, turned on her phone recorder, capturing the conversation. I let Debbie take the lead in the discussion, only chiming in occasionally, knowing she was recording everything. The conversation continued for about fifteen minutes—DeNaughty ranting, trying to get a reaction, while Debbie tried to keep her grounded.

Then, DeNaughty gave me a firm instruction: "GO OPEN THE DOOR so they can hear what you guys are doing to me in here."

I replied coolly, "You want the door open? Get up and open it yourself."

Without moving, DeNaughty yelled, "I AM GOING TO KILL MYSELF!"

Still, no one from the outside came in. It was as though no one was paying attention to her cries for help. Her attempt to grab the attention of the staff had failed, and we waited to see what the next move would be.

A few minutes later, DeNaughty got off the ER gurney, shuffled toward the sliding glass door, cracked it open, and stood in the hallway between her room and the nurse's station. With her hands intertwined behind her back, she stood there, in what could only be described as "goose mode," scanning left, then right. After a moment, a nurse walked by and asked if she needed anything.

The ER was bustling with caregivers, all rushing around with patients needing emergent care. Our room, however, seemed to be ignored—clearly, Denice wasn't the priority. But that didn't stop her from creating a crisis. As the nurse paused to help her, Denice suddenly declared, "I am being abused in here, and I'm going to kill myself."

The nurse, visibly stunned, quickly ushered DeNaughty back into the room. She turned to look at Debbie and me, her gaze sharp. "What's going on here? She says you're abusing her and that she wants to kill herself."

In that moment, it felt as if DeNaughty had reverted to being a child, tattling to get her sisters into trouble, smirking and giggling as she watched the drama unfold as she crawled back up onto the hospital bed like a little child.

I took a deep breath, trying to keep my voice steady. "Excuse me," I began, "I am fully aware of how busy this ER is. The reason we are here is because Denice is in active manic psychosis. We've been patiently waiting for her to be evaluated for a 72-hour hold. What you just saw is exactly what we've been dealing with—and it's why she's here."

The nurse looked at me for a moment, then left the room. Seconds later, she returned with an orderly, who introduced himself and said, "We're moving her to another room now. It's in a secure area for mental health emergencies." He looked at Debbie and me. "You two should wait in the waiting room. I'll follow up as soon as I can."

They took DeNaughty away, and Debbie and I made our way back to the waiting room, unsure of what would come next. We knew the drill, but we still weren't certain if she would be admitted or if we would be sent home with her.

We waited for what felt like hours, though it was only about fifteen minutes. Finally, they came out to tell us they were keeping her until a bed opened up in their mental health inpatient unit.

"Free," I whispered, my voice barely above a breath. "Thank God, we're free at last." I looked at Debbie, and we shared a moment of silent understanding. The words of Martin Luther King echoed in my mind, "Freedom." For us, it meant that we had won this battle—for now—but the war was far from over.

I called my husband and told him I was taking Debbie to her car and would be home soon.

Chapter 19

DEFCON 5 – Meet Mrs. Hulk

"If I hadn't seen it with my own eyes..." "I was terrified. I've never seen anything like that before..." "It's like superhuman strength..." These are just a few of the comments from those of us who have witnessed Denice's "Mrs. Hulk" side—the part of her that she both fears and, at times, cannot control. You've already read about some of the moments when Mrs. Hulk has surfaced.

Recently, Denice, Debbie, and I had a brutally honest meeting with her social worker. The topic: Denice's "Mrs. Hulk" persona. How do I know it was Denice who was present in the meeting, not DeNaughty? Because this was an honest conversation. Denice was vulnerable—open in a way we rarely see her. What she shared came from her heart, from her true Self: calm, clear, compassionate, connected, creative, confident, and courageous (Riemersma et al., p. 169). When we are in this foundation of Self, we are in our truest state.

Denice spoke about her experiences with Mrs. Hulk, describing how she has learned to recognize when this part of her is starting to emerge. "It feels like my muscles inflate—like my entire body is swelling up so much that my clothes tear off. My arms and legs double in size," she said. As she continued, her voice grew soft, almost fearful. "It's like I'm trying to stay small, hoping she won't notice me, and I'm watching her from somewhere else." Here, Denice was describing a dissociative state.

Her voice quivered with raw emotion as she went on, the fear and shame evident. "I'm so afraid of her. But when she comes out, I've lost control. There's nothing I can do to stop her. All I can do is sit and wait for her to finish her destruction, and hope she calms down."

This is Denice. The real Denice. The sister I've been searching for my entire life. I'm not looking for someone weak, vulnerable, or someone I can control. Absolutely not. What I've longed for is a real connection with my sister—the one who is willing to be honest, imperfect, and human. The one who doesn't see me as a plaything or a tool to manipulate.

This, my friends, is the Denice we were speaking to in that moment—the Denice I've always known she could be. This is my sister, DeNice.

Understanding Mrs. Hulk, her role, and when she is summoned to perform within Denice's system is essential to recognizing the complex dynamics at play. When DeNaughty manages to hijack Denice's system, she works tirelessly to weave a narrative that serves her needs. But when things go awry, when roadblocks arise—like me, for instance—everything DeNaughty has carefully stitched into her story begins to unravel faster than she can repair it. When that narrative starts to collapse, DeNaughty feels controlled and trapped within the psychosis she's created, unable to break free.

This is akin to the time Denice punched mom and then ran, "clearing an eight-foot fence like a gazelle," as mom described it. "I couldn't believe my eyes," she said. "She's overweight, with her knee the way it is, and yet there she was, leaping over the fence as if nothing was wrong." DeNaughty's narrative often includes the belief that someone is after her, even though she's not oriented to the situation. Like when she told the woman whose house she entered, "I think I just killed my mother-in-law," completely unaware that she was referring to our mom.

Mrs. Hulk makes an appearance whenever Denice feels cornered or trapped, as she did when the EMTs asked if she could walk to the gurney at mom and dad's house. Denice said "yes," but the moment the door opened, she sprinted away, despite her knee and being morbidly obese. She almost outran two healthy young men, covering a surprising distance before they could catch up and sedate her enough to restrain her for the ambulance ride.

Mrs. Hulk brings with her an extraordinary surge of energy—energy that Denice channels in an attempt to escape what DeNaughty perceives as a dangerous situation. Denice has shared how Mrs. Hulk will "break restraints on the beds, in the ambulance." "She does everything in her power not to be trapped," Denice says, her voice cracking. "She's so strong, and it scares me so bad. She scares me" as real tears stream down her cheeks, obviously in true and real vulnerability.

Watching Mrs. Hulk scream out in fear while tied to a bed for her own safety—and the safety of others—is gut-wrenching. For mom, who's had to witness this most frequently, it's heartbreaking. Each time, it weakens her heart, and at the same time, it makes her stronger and more resilient. Over the years, mom has learned to understand the parts of all her children, acknowledging that we all have our adult "monsters"—not just Denice. We all have our battles to face, and in our family, we're learning to navigate them together.

There is a phase Denice goes through before Mrs. Hulk fully expresses herself, right before she hijacks Denice's system. This phase is terrifying for those who have witnessed it, as Denice can appear possessed, with her eyes turning completely black, as I've mentioned previously. I have seen it, Jim has seen it, mom has seen it, and Debbie has witnessed it. One other person who described this phenomenon after Denice's last major episode was her caretaker at the assisted living facility where Denice had been placed to live.

Following the 2022 episode, medical professionals and our team agreed that Denice had decompensated further with each episode, making it evident she was becoming less able to manage her mental health medications on her own. Without the ability to consistently adhere to her medication regimen—critical for preventing the severe Bipolar episodes that often accompany her Histrionic Personality Disorder—Denice qualified for assisted living care. The general belief among the team was that 24-hour care would be sufficient to prevent any further episodes. I wanted to believe this as well. After all, having someone there to ensure Denice was taking her meds at the right times, in the right dosages, seemed like the perfect solution. But I knew better.

There is a false comfort in thinking that with someone constantly monitoring Denice's medication, no more episodes would occur. In a perfect world, this might be possible. But the reality is that humans are not perfect, and there's always room for error. We can set all the aviation safety rules we want, but even then, a series of mistakes could lead to a catastrophic outcome. This is the reality with Denice and those responsible for her care as well.

In 2022, on Mother's Day, despite being in assisted living, Denice started attending a church created for individuals striving to live better lives after incarceration. It was a positive and supportive environment for those looking to make a fresh start, and Denice genuinely wanted to help others walk with Christ. However, even with her medication administered regularly and appropriately, Denice still struggled to make sound decisions without falling into DEFCON 3, using DEFCON 1 logic. This, combined with the fact that one of her caretakers was connected to the church and had become vulnerable to Denice's extensive knowledge of the Bible, created a volatile situation. This caretaker began trusting Denice and even leaned on her for biblical guidance, sparking jealousy and envy in DeNaughty. This emotional turmoil pushed Denice into DEFCON 4.

As DeNaughty's jealousy grew, she began fantasizing about a relationship with another member of the church. At the same time, she began passing judgment on others, especially when she discovered, according to her own account, that "the preacher was having relations with another woman, despite being married." We don't know the actual truth of the situation, as it came solely from DeNaughty's perspective. But what truly matters is how Denice and DeNaughty believed the events were unfolding. This distorted view created the perfect storm once again.

After finding out what was happening, and after trying to talk Denice down from DEFCON status, it seemed like she was beginning to trust the assessment that Debbie and I had worked on together. Denice agreed to stop attending that particular church, and we thought she was doing better, able to redirect herself and focus on her mental health balance. She managed okay for a while, but unfortunately, in October 2022, things began to shift again. Denice started talking about going on double dates with someone from her home and another man she had met at a different church she began attending off-site.

As November approached, and with Thanksgiving coming up, Denice began speaking about recurring rashes that needed cream applied to areas she "couldn't reach." She began describing how it felt when the caretaker applied the cream to her private areas, saying it made her feel pleasure. She went on to explain, "It feels like when I was a baby, and mom would put butt cream on me after changing my diaper. It feels so good." Then came the recurring urinary tract infections (UTIs), which seemed to escalate quickly, with conversations confirming the growing concerns during team meetings. We were definitely in DEFCON 2, with occasional flashes of DEFCON 4.

After Thanksgiving, during the weekend when everything was closed due to the holiday, Denice told us that the night caretaker had informed her, "The state came in and audited our med cart and said your prescription had expired, so you don't have your meds to take. We have to wait till Monday to get your meds refilled." This caretaker handed over Denice, on the verge of being hijacked by Mrs. Hulk, to the day shift team. The perfect storm had begun.

Through what seemed like an endless series of conversations with the nurse line, the caretaker, Debbie, and Mom, everything spiraled into yet another controlled chaos. The tipping point was reached. Denice would soon be back in an ambulance, strapped to a gurney, with Mrs. Hulk ripping her way out, on her way to yet another new ER, associated with another new mental hospital, where Denice would be cared for until she could return to her baseline—rather than DeNaughty's baseline. It was like seeing a MAC truck coming toward us from miles down the road, knowing we were going to get hit head-on once again.

Around mid-afternoon on Saturday, I received the final call from her caretaker. Denice was doing well enough to handle herself, or so it seemed—at least for the moment. But the caretaker could feel it too: DeNaughty was about to summon Mrs. Hulk to take control of the situation. The conversation with the caretaker went like this:

"I don't know what to do anymore here. I have other elderly people who need care, and Denice just wouldn't accept that she needed to wait a few minutes for me to help another housemate. Denice's need is not a priority over the other person's at this time; that's how we have to prioritize care. Denice was not having that. I've never seen her like this—so adamant, so aggressive. She's being a bully. I was in the community bathroom, getting something for the other housemate when Denice came in behind me, locked us in the bathroom, and stood at the door so I couldn't leave. Then, she got really close to me and said, 'You will get me what I need right now, or else.' I was terrified. When she was staring at me and telling me this, her eyes were totally black. I've never been so scared in my life. I just told her, 'Ok, Denice, I will,' and then she let me leave. I immediately called you. What should I do? I have so many people here to take care of, but I'm afraid to death of her right now."

"Ok. It's time. I will call her on her phone, and after we hang up, you call 911 and tell them what happened. Give them strict instructions that she has been known to flee despite appearing to verbally cooperate. Make sure they understand the urgency and know that you and others may be in physical danger."

The caretaker followed the instructions. Debbie and I conference-called Denice to gently, but firmly, let her know that "the jig is up" and that she had crossed the line. Timing was key when working to get her to the ER from afar. By the way, the assisted living facility where she had been moved was an hour and a half drive from where I lived. It was the only facility associated with the company she had moved to after her 2022 episode, and at the time, it was the only one that would accept her Medicaid.

I had told the caretaker to inform me when the ambulance and police arrived, so I could be the one to tell Denice she would be going with them, once they had entered the home and secured the other housemates. I think Debbie then got on her wife's phone with the caretaker at the same time the caretaker, police, and EMTs were with Denice. I was still on the phone in conference mode with Debbie. The circle of communication was tight, and Denice went with the EMTs without issue and complied—this time.

There were a few calls after Denice left, over the next few days, to debrief and decompress with the caretaker. She was now initiated into the "terrifying black eyes" group. "What the heck is happening with this?" I began to explore. We now know that it's a stage reached during DEFCON 5, between DeNaughty losing control of the narrative and just before Mrs. Hulk is summoned to "get the hell outta here" through fight or flight. Is it a religious possession occurring? Is there a physiological explanation for this? We are beyond questioning whether it happens. It does, and there is no denying it. Now, the question is: what the hell is it?

There are many thoughts, ideas, and judgments that could be used to explain what happens to Denice during this stage of a bipolar episode. There are two different—perhaps opposing, depending on one's belief system—perspectives that I lean into for understanding. Beyond disbelief and into acceptance without judgment lies a space I tend to occupy when seeking understanding from God. It is my nature-based, analytical Gethsemane. For me, this space balances biology, physiology, and spirituality, and I can't help but say, it is a heavenly place for me. As I dig into research, what may seem to be polar opposite forces, I begin with the Bible.

There are factual accounts of demonic possessions written about in the Gospels of Matthew and Mark. Accounts describe Mary Magdalene being possessed by seven demons (Luke 8:2). Other accounts include unusual, sometimes violent outbursts, speaking in strange voices, and superhuman strength (Luke 4:33-36; Mark 5:1-20). Some scholars, through their research, believe that people in the Bible, such as Ezekiel, were possessed and suffered from what today is known as schizophrenia (Bagwasi, 2011). For my peace that passes all understanding, I find it foundational to my research that in accounts throughout history, the common signs described in ancient biblical times of someone behaving abnormally are the same signs observed in present-day situations, including my own story. There are also other ancient cultures—Japanese, Chinese, East Indian—who follow different religious paths but have similar accounts of these behaviors in humans as well.

There is growing scientific evidence emerging from research that seeks to explain why the body does things such as protect us or communicate on our behalf, particularly when our minds want to act or speak in ways that don't align with the body's actions. As Charlotte Brontë once said, "The soul, fortunately, has an interpreter… the eyes" (Parker, Coroneo & Spoelma, 2023). To specifically address the phenomenon of the eyes turning black during a particular stage in Denice's DEFCON cycle, there have been studies published about this very occurrence. Thank God, because not long ago, it felt like we were alone in witnessing this, and there was great internal turmoil within us—individually and as a team—trying to find a reason behind it that wasn't simply demonic or socially taboo.

What is now being referred to as "Bipolar Eyes" has caught the attention of researchers. One study explains that when a person is in manic, hypomanic, or depressive states with increasing levels of the neurotransmitters dopamine and norepinephrine, it triggers sympathetic discharge in the retina and surrounding areas, resulting in pupillary dilation. When the pupils over-dilate, they push the color of the iris, and in rare cases, even the sclera, causing the eyes to appear black in dysphoric and mixed states (Parker, Coroneo & Spoelma, 2023). In layman's terms, Denice appears to have a rare case where her eyes are signaling that she is severely chemically imbalanced during her mania, actively dysphoric, and experiencing psychosis. Her soul is crying out for help because she is unable to control her inner demons. As she has said, "The only thing I can do at that point is to hide... I get so scared."

These "Bipolar Eyes" appear in Denice during DEFCON 5, when the behaviors of mania and depression collide, which is termed dysphoric mania. For those of us who have had the opportunity to peer into Denice's eyes, the window to her soul reveals intense sadness and fear. It's a soul that is deeply struggling, losing the battle with herself and her inner parts, desperately trying to cling to a failing goal of proving that there is nothing wrong. I've said it before: it's as though you can look into her eyes and see the gears of her thoughts turning to keep the machine running. You watch her restless, impulsive movements, jumping around so quickly she can't keep up with herself. Suddenly, her system seems to realize what's happening and flashes the warning sign—those blackened eyes—to alert us to her struggle. Those who have witnessed it have felt as though their lives were in danger, terrified for their safety. It's almost as if Denice has somehow transmitted and projected her true inner feelings outward, allowing someone else to speak her message through their own mouth on her behalf.

Thank God for the majestic and phenomenal ways He has designed our human bodies—complete with a dashboard of warning lights for us and others to notice, so long as we choose to listen and seek to understand what His message is with an open mind. Whether one sees it as demonic possession, scientific physiology, or simply an adult throwing an unregulated temper tantrum, the important thing is to look beyond what we think it is and seek to understand why. If you have the capacity to understand, great; if not, that's okay too. As long as you can remove judgment, which often leads to criticism of others just to make yourself feel better. I choose to believe the blackened eyes are both a spiritual miracle and a scientific phenomenon—good and evil in one. Accepting this without judgment is what brings me peace and understanding, helping me move beyond the fear.

Chapter 20

Legally Obtaining Custody - Guardianship

In 2016, when I was called back to the family in desperation to help fix what seemed to be an internal mirror of Denice's external hoarding disorder, it became crystal clear that Denice had no ability to manage her own life, make major decisions, or handle her finances. Having squandered away most of her financial security with nothing to show for it, marrying a convicted pedophile while in a DEFCON 5 state, and going from one major bipolar episode every four to five years to having four to five episodes per year, the situation was dire. How does someone called in to rescue her and the family do what needs to be done, efficiently and effectively?

For me, the answer was to find a way to help Denice re-parent the internal parts of herself that had hijacked her system, gaining control over her adult body but with the emotional and mental age of whichever part had matured to that state. This was evident in her behaviors, which were not consistent with her physical age. "How can this be done?" I began to internally dialogue with my parts.

I researched and discovered the option of seeking a legal guardianship for at-risk adults, which I could file with the court. If granted, this would give me the authority to make decisions on Denice's behalf. It sounded like a powerful and straightforward solution, but there were important considerations. First, I only recommend this action if someone is truly able to set aside their personal desires completely, detach fully from the outcome of any decisions made on the loved one's behalf, and be steadfast in teaching, guiding, and leading them to learn the process of decision-making. It's crucial not to simply make every decision for them. Just like in parenting, the person under your care—whether a child or, in this case, the protected party—will, not might, will blame you for making them do things they don't want to do. They will fight you every step of the way and will try to push you out of the position you hold, much like an adolescent striving for independence from their parents before they come of legal age to become their own adult.

This situation was particularly difficult because Denice is the oldest sibling, and I am the youngest, making it challenging for her to take my lead, simply due to the natural roles and expectations we each carry within the family dynamic. It wasn't easy, and it certainly wasn't a power I wanted to have over her. Additionally, you may recall that the decision-making authority I had only extended to everything except psychological and mental health-related decisions. Once Denice was placed on a 72-hour hold, my decision-making authority ceased. Even after that time expired, she retained the authority to decide whether to stay inpatient voluntarily or to discharge herself from care. I had no authority over that decision; I could only offer suggestions and try to help her make the best decision to stay in care voluntarily. My decision-making power was only reinstated after she discharged, regardless of her state at the time. It seems almost ironic that the mental health condition preventing her from functioning with self-leadership was the very reason she needed a legal guardian in the first place.

With the support and agreement of everyone in the family, except for Denice's oldest son, I filed for emergency guardianship and conservatorship over Denice. The goal was to help her manage and regain control of her life while still maintaining my own. At that time, I had been remarried, was a stepmother to three girls, and a grandmother to three grandchildren from my daughter and son. I was also beginning to reintegrate with my family, whom I had been estranged from for six years. On top of that, I was two years into running a new start-up software business with my husband. This wasn't just one full-time job, but two. I had to be willing to take on not just the responsibility for Denice, but also for my aging parents. Both Mom and Dad were in their seventies, quickly becoming at-risk elderly adults. Ironically, Denice, as an at-risk adult with her own severe mental health diagnoses, had already, and would continue to, violate the boundaries of my parents. I felt a strong responsibility to protect them, knowing that protecting her from herself would, in turn, protect them from her. There was no other option—I was the only one qualified for the job at that time.

In 2016, since Denice was temporarily living with Mom and Dad after discharging from the mental health facility following her separation from her husband, I filed the necessary forms with the county where they lived. Having filed papers for various matters in the past, this was a relatively simple first step to take without an attorney. The court set a date and time for the emergency hearing, and we were off to the races. I informed everyone about the date and time of the hearing, asking that they appear if they were able to.

I vividly remember getting up in the witness box, speaking into the microphone, and explaining why I was seeking guardianship and conservatorship over Denice. I tried to be as clear and concise as possible, describing the situation I had returned to within the family and what I had already discovered about Denice's financial state. The judge granted me temporary status for her decision-making and finances, and I was scheduled to appear again in thirty days if I wanted to pursue permanent status. I retained an attorney who specialized in mental health cases and immediately got to work digging deeper into Denice's past six years. I began developing a plan for her recovery, with the intention of helping her re-parent her internal family system with my support.

The further I dug, the more was revealed, and the more I became convinced that I was doing the right thing. Through interviewing family members and piecing together the jigsaw puzzle, I discovered that Denice had, in fact, been in DEFCON 5 when she married Jack. Her adult sons had matched her with him, hoping to find a partner who could and would take care of her. It worked—for two years, well, kind of.

I figured out the reason she called me in apparent DEFCON status just two days before her wedding was because she had found out that her husband-to-be had been convicted of pedophilia, specifically for actions against his under-aged teenage niece. Learning this sent her into DEFCON status, but, despite the revelation, she justified moving forward with the marriage. Later, Denice told me that she had "talked to mom, and mom made it okay by telling me that God was in charge of forgiving him for what he did. She probably was at fault for it happening because she flirted with him, and he just couldn't help himself." So, years later, after all the damage had been done, it became "mom's fault" that Denice married him.

Further digging into this DEFCON episode revealed how Denice continued to spread significant emotional and mental damage to others in the family. As the jigsaw puzzle image became clearer, I began to see the extent of the fallout. From my daughter's perspective during this time, she was a single mom relying on my mom's help to care for her daughters while she worked and went to school to become a phlebotomist. Since Denice and Jack were always at Mom's house, living a life of luxury on Denice's bank account, they were often available to help with the babies. Mom was also at the time, recovering from surgery on both her shoulders and it seemed convenient to have Denice and Jack to help. But when my daughter learned that Denice had known all along about Jack's charges, and that the secret had been kept from her, her trust in them—was shattered. This betrayal left my daughter feeling intense self-doubt and profound emotional damage. Although my daughter has continued to heal, she remains protected from the devastation she experienced and carries the shame of feeling like she didn't protect her children from harm. She had been misled into believing she was leaving her baby girls in safe hands.

Mom has also been affected by this incident feeling blamed for others believing she knew about Jack's charges, therefore thought to have condoned his behavior. In talking with her about what she knew and didn't know, she has suffered devastatingly emotional blows for being accused of allowing her great-granddaughters to be potentially exposed to harm. It is her narrative that Denice did not fully disclose to her the charges Jack had been convicted of, during the conversation she had with Denice prior to them getting married. Mom recalls that it was not until a later episode that had taken place where Jack came clean to Dad about what he had done and Mom overheard the conversation between them. For Mom, that was her awakening to the potential harm my granddaughters were exposed to, leaving her in overwhelming panic, worried if something could have happened to them.

What a mess. A chaotic, devastating emotional storm of destruction for so many loved ones was left in the wake of Denice's thought processes and behavioral patterns. Denice consistently demonstrated an inability to make sound decisions for herself, usually commencing with the irresponsible decision to stop taking her medication—medication that helped regulate her bipolar symptoms and gave her some control over her personality disorder. This simple, reckless decision set in motion the very chaos that has been described here, impacting not just her, but everyone around her.

Let me be clear: the process of becoming legally responsible for Denice required me to undergo a thorough forensic investigation. This included a criminal background check, a review of my financial records and history to demonstrate my ability to manage my own finances, and an effort to ensure my petition wasn't a way for me to financially exploit Denice while holding a legally granted position. The court investigated my character by interviewing my friends and coworkers, checking my employment and education history, and scrutinizing every aspect of my life to ensure I was fit for the responsibility.

Denice was also assigned a guardian ad litem to represent her interests, essentially opposing my decisions if she ever felt I was acting against her wishes. On top of that, I was required to report annually (and sometimes more frequently if needed) to the court and other interested parties identified by the court. These reports covered her progress, daily living experiences, and financial accounting of how her money was used.

The interested parties included Jack (until the divorce was finalized), Mom, Dad, and her two sons. Her older son was strongly opposed from the start, refusing to believe that Denice needed a legal guardian or conservator. He made his opinions known and remained vocal throughout the process, but as time went on, he became increasingly distant, stonewalling and even sabotaging efforts to establish the guardianship. His stance was clear: Denice was fully capable of taking care of herself, and whatever happened as a result of her actions was her responsibility to handle, period.

My husband insisted I include in my story how the annual court reporting process affected me. Writing these guardian reports was emotionally difficult, particularly during the years when multiple DEFCON states had to be documented. The financial reporting, as many of my friends who are CPAs and Denice's financial advisor pointed out, was complex and confusing. I often found myself frustrated by the tedious requirements. The report was due every January 7th, right after the holiday season, which also coincided with my grandson's birthday. To make matters worse, I am not an accountant. Even with the help of CPAs who offered assistance pro bono because Denice couldn't afford a professional conservator, I was reassured that the reporting format and instructions were far from optimal.

Each year, I experienced rising anxiety, not because I had anything to hide—as Denice's oldest son accused me of—

but because I knew the court would inevitably identify a mathematical error in my filing, requiring immediate correction under a tight deadline. This only added to my stress. In 2017, I was audited by the court, which significantly increased the workload for that year. Despite the added pressure, I'm proud to say I completed the audit with an A+ grade. That success bolstered my confidence, reaffirming that I was the right person for this responsibility and that I was managing Denice's finances in a fiscally responsible manner.

Unfortunately, all of this effort didn't solve the deeper issues. Despite my best attempts to bring order and accountability to Denice's life, her internal chaos only intensified. My role as her guardian did little to stem the tide of her rebelliousness and internal struggle. It was as if Denice was stuck in a perpetual battle to gain control over herself, like a teenager fighting her parents for independence before she was capable of understanding the consequences of her actions.

Chapter 21

Obtaining Legal Fiduciary Control - Managing the Money

As for the legal conservatorship over Denice's finances, I felt that aspect had already been established. At that point, she only had a quarter of her benefits left to support her financially for the rest of her life. She needed someone to manage her spending and budget while helping her apply for any benefits she could qualify for, particularly government disability support. The process of applying for these benefits is overwhelming for anyone, but for someone already dealing with significant mental health challenges, it would have been nearly impossible to navigate alone.

Money management was straightforward in some ways. I put her on a budget that allowed her to live independently for as long as possible before she became eligible for federal benefits like food stamps or Section 8 housing assistance. With some of her financial savings remaining, she was placed on a spend-down budget designed to stretch her resources over the next eight years. This budget, though limited, gave her the financial stability she needed for that time, essentially providing a window during which we could focus on re-parenting her internal system. The goal was to help her mature enough so that when it was time to terminate my guardianship, she would be in a better position to manage her life independently.

As you recall, nearly all the family team members concluded that Denice required intensive residential treatment upon discharging from the hospital in 2016. We all agreed that she needed a facility to teach her skills in emotional regulation, interpersonal effectiveness, and distress tolerance. I tasked each team member with researching a facility that could meet her needs. The chosen facility would need to be residential, requiring a stay of at least three to six months, and provide the necessary skills for living independently.

Debbie found a facility about forty miles west of us that was within the budget I had allocated from Denice's funds. However, the program was only six to ten weeks long, which didn't seem like enough time for Denice to make the kind of progress we hoped for. Other team members suggested options, but at that time, our state lacked the resources to provide the intensity of care she truly needed. We had already exhausted attempts to get her outpatient help, and mental health services in our state were insufficient to meet her needs.

I found a well-regarded program in Georgia that met all of Denice's mental health needs, but it was located fourteen hundred miles away from home. After much discussion and collaboration with the team—including Denice—we agreed that she would apply to the program. If accepted, she would register and move away for the treatment she required.

The pros of this decision were significant. Moving to Georgia would allow Denice to experience independence, similar to a teenager leaving home for their first college experience. It was far enough away that she couldn't easily return to her parents if things got tough, but it also gave her the opportunity to travel and meet new people.

The cons, however, were also substantial. Denice would be far away from her family for an extended period, which caused anxiety for both her and for Mom. It was an entirely new experience for Denice, and the distance was a source of stress for everyone involved.

To prepare for this opportunity, the facility required Denice to undergo a full psychological evaluation, which took about three days to complete. I found a reputable psychiatrist who specializes in these kinds of assessments. The results were fascinating and eventually became something of a manual for Denice. Her diagnoses of bipolar disorder and histrionic personality disorder were confirmed, and the report also detailed her emotional and intellectual levels, helping to explain why she had struggled so much with managing her finances. The evaluation provided valuable insight into Denice's baseline functioning, highlighting areas where she excelled and others where improvement was needed. It also identified tasks she would likely never be able to manage on her own without some form of assistance.

With the test results in hand, we completed all the necessary medical check-ups. On the day after Christmas 2016, Denice's youngest son and I helped her pack up, and we flew her out to the facility. The moment was reminiscent of what parents experience when sending their eighteen-year-old child off to their first college dorm—both a farewell and a new beginning for her. It was an emotional family send-off, with everyone hugging, kissing, and crying as we left Mom and Dad's house.

Once we arrived at the hotel, Denice's son and I helped her get settled. The following day, we had an intake appointment, a tour of the facility, and then our emotional goodbyes. I also wrote the largest check I'd ever written—$90,000—covering the cost of her "mental health education" experience. This included room and board, meals, nutrition counseling, weight management, exercise facilities, group classes, individual therapy, psychiatric appointments, gene typing for medication matching, activity fees, transportation, and everything else she would need for the next five months. It was a lot of money, but the care, guidance, and psychoeducational training she received were invaluable, and it was well worth the expense, as it was an investment in her future.

While she was inpatient, we stayed involved by participating in family telehealth meetings. These helped Mom and Dad understand what Denice was learning and allowed us to hear about her progress. In February 2017, the facility hosted a family day, where we could visit in person and engage in hands-on learning with her care team. We met the staff and were given a detailed explanation of the individual progress she had made during her stay. During that visit, we were also able to take Denice on a field trip, which provided us with a firsthand opportunity to interact with her and observe the improvements she had made. The program was led by people who genuinely cared about her, and it had a profound positive impact on her.

Denice and I had a disagreement when she graduated from phases one and two of her program, as she wanted to come home and move directly into her own apartment. However, I didn't believe that either of those phases provided the independent living experience she needed to be truly successful once she returned. As disappointing as it was for her, I insisted that she stay and complete phase three, which focused on independent living. This phase was crucial for her to demonstrate she could live on her own, with me only stepping in for major decisions and helping her manage her finances. It also included learning how to properly adhere to her prescribed medication regimen, which was essential for managing her bipolar episodes.

She stayed for a total of six months, learning vital life skills and fulfilling the requirements for graduation. When she returned home, she was a more mature and different woman.

I had already rented her an apartment, bought her furniture, and helped establish a monthly budget to cover her food, medical insurance, transportation, and a small allowance for occasional spending. We set up Uber and Lyft accounts so she could get to and from her job at a local dry cleaners, which she secured quickly after returning home. Later, we purchased a car for her, added auto insurance to her renter's policy, and budgeted for gas and maintenance once she started earning money from her job.

To manage her finances, I opened a checking account in my name for her, keeping her funds separate from mine. Since this account was linked to my credit, I had to ensure it was kept clean and balanced. I also got her a prepaid Visa card, which she could use for grocery shopping. I funded this card using her money from the separate account, and we set up a process to ensure it was topped off monthly. This gave her a sense of control and financial responsibility while still allowing me to manage her funds.

We established a strict but reasonable budget for her groceries and dining out, also helping her stay on track with her health goals and weight management. It wasn't a luxurious lifestyle, but it met her needs and kept her within her means, ensuring she could cover her basic needs—food, shelter, and clothing—without going without.

I created an annual budget and had to withdraw enough money from her IRA to cover her expenses. This included a large sum to set aside for the hefty tax penalty she incurred each year. My goal was always to leave as much as possible in her IRA to allow it to earn interest, so we could repeat the same process the following year. In addition, I had to track every penny she spent, earned, received, and was gifted. This meticulous record-keeping was necessary for her conservatorship report, which had to demonstrate that none of her money was being misused, spent unwisely, or stolen. I had to maintain extremely clean and organized records, knowing that the next report deadline—January 7th—was always just around the corner.

I took Denice to her physical health and mental health appointments, ensuring she received both the psychiatric care and therapy she needed. She attended her own therapy sessions to maintain a sense of autonomy, working directly with her therapist on her mental health. I helped her prepare for her knee replacement surgery, assisting her in losing the weight the doctor required before the procedure. However, at some point, I realized I wanted the surgery for her more than she wanted it for herself, and that was when I had to step back.

Her doctor, sympathetic to her situation, decided to proceed with the surgery, despite her not meeting the full weight loss goal. He justified it by noting that she had lost over half the required weight before reaching a plateau. I arranged for her to move to a rehabilitation facility after the surgery, ensuring she received proper care, rather than allowing her to move home or go back to living with mom and dad for recovery, as she desperately wanted. As her recovery progressed, however, she grew increasingly disturbed with me, feeling more and more that I was controlling her life.

This process went on for eight years, and the situation became progressively stressful. As expected, Denice's finances continued to dwindle over time, and she became increasingly frustrated and jealous about being on such a tight budget. She focused more on what she didn't have and what others seemed to possess, feeling constrained by my management of her finances.

This marked a turning point in 2021, when a significant episode ended her independent living status and led to her moving into assisted living. Fortunately, she had just enough money left to move into a decent facility, which allowed her to have some options. The timing of this situation was impeccable, as, had she run out of money before this episode, she would have had fewer options for assisted living, and neither her mom nor her sons would have been in a position to take her in. Looking back, it's clear that God's timing was at work, guiding us through each step, ensuring Denice's shifting needs were met at just the right time.

Chapter 22

Therapy

Over the years, Denice had seen a number of therapists trying to figure out how to deal with her emotional issues. Our family wasn't particularly invested in therapy during the '80s, especially with the social stigma surrounding it. Denice always had medical coverage, so finding a psychiatrist was never an issue. Once she was diagnosed with something that could be treated with medication, getting what she needed was easy. However, there seemed to be a prevailing assumption in our culture that medication was a cure-all, as if a magic pill could solve anything. This belief extended to weight loss and any other problem associated with pain or aging. Many people, it seemed, had been hooked by marketing schemes that sold pills for almost everything. While this wasn't unique to Denice, it became especially problematic for her when her system became deregulated.

There was a time when both she and Jim became severely depressed and were both prescribed lithium. I had never, in my life, seen anyone—especially them, who had regularly gone to the gym, attended church activities, or spent time at Mom and Dad's—become literal walking zombies. I had seen *One Flew Over the Cuckoo's Nest* and understood that people sometimes end up heavily medicated, but I'd always associated that with hospitals, not people driving cars and trying to live their lives.

One day, while I was cutting Jim's hair at Mom's, I paused and looked him in the eye as I worked on his bangs and sides. I said, "Dude, I'm really worried about you and how you're acting." He told me that he and Denice had just started the new medication. "You're not yourself," I said. "I feel like this either isn't enough or it's too much. Please, go back to the doctor and make sure this isn't just... you."

"Okay," he responded, tilting his head in that uniquely pure and curious way of his.

It wasn't long after that brief interaction when I saw Jim and Denice back at Mom's. He was acting like himself again and told me he had switched medications, which seemed to be working better. Around the same time, Denice started taking medications specifically for her bipolar disorder. She had been diagnosed with bipolar disorder by her psychiatrist, but it wasn't until much later—after Jim died—that I realized she had held on to something her psychiatrist had told her years earlier.

"We really don't know if it's bipolar disorder, but we're going to put you on meds to try and help you, whether it's bipolar or not," she recalled the doctor saying.

Looking back at her medical records, which I had to dig through in order to piece together her puzzle, I found a physician's note referencing the statement she had recalled. It was dated 1994, after her first major episode when she was flown home from Chicago. Yes, they were trying to find a diagnosis and were leaning toward bipolar disorder. As an LPC today, I understand the process of diagnosing mental illness. It's far different than diagnosing a broken bone or cancer. There's no blood test or X-ray to diagnose bipolar disorder. It requires observing a pattern of behaviors over time to make an accurate diagnosis.

I realized Denice had latched onto the uncertainty of the diagnosis process back then and never truly believed she was struggling with bipolar disorder.

When I recognized how she was thinking, I knew from my deep dive into her records that I had seen a note with a clear diagnosis established in later documents, well past the time she had clung to in her mind. I showed her that, in fact, she had been diagnosed with bipolar disorder. Whether it was type I or type II didn't matter at this point. What mattered was that she accepted the diagnosis into her system. She needed to stop using the doctor's earlier uncertainty as an excuse to say, "Well, it could be bipolar, but we're not sure, sooo…" with her DEFCON 1 approach.

For these parts of her system, the "jig" was up. What she had done by accepting the reality of her diagnosis was part of Acceptance and Commitment Therapy (ACT), intertwined with Dialectical Behavioral Therapy (DBT) and Cognitive Behavioral Therapy (CBT). She had radically accepted what she had long been denying. She also came to terms with it by using tools like Socratic Questioning to shift her internal belief system, moving from emotional desire to evidence-based understanding.

By the way, this revelation for her came long after she had gone to and graduated from residential treatment, and after we had received the report from the psychiatrist necessary for her acceptance into this facility. My system was dumbfounded when I realized she had, even years later, been operating her internal family system under the very incorrect and outdated foundational disbelief and denial of what she had been fighting against for decades.

I learned the skill of meeting her where she was, rather than where I thought she should be or even where I believed she thought she was. I know, confusing, right? Basically, it describes true empathy: seeking to understand what it is like for another person to be in their experience, while at the same time compartmentalizing your own filters and experiences. You apply similarities, not as facts, but as possible ways to understand how she may have been feeling through her experiences. I know, still complicated—especially when it involves a loved one or close family member. This is one reason why it's unethical for a therapist to treat a family member: we're just too close, making it that much harder to detach from the outcome and remain empathetic.

Denice did learn a significant amount of skills in residential treatment. She became an expert at CBT and DBT, actively implementing what she had learned, and was able to explain these skills and how they worked for her. She was very proud of herself—and rightly so. She truly did an excellent job of learning and applying what they taught her, working tirelessly to change her life based on what she had absorbed. Honestly, it became a double-edged sword for me that she had become so knowledgeable about DBT. After hearing so much about it, and how it changed her life ad nauseum, the acronym itself later caused a visceral reaction in my system. This happened well after I had started my internship and was asked to teach DBT to clients. I definitely had some parts work to do—to unblend, figure out, and reintegrate into my own system, learning to overcome my own triggers.

Anyway, Denice had made significant progress from her treatment experience. However, she still endorsed not functioning emotionally, mentally, or intellectually in a way that was equivalent to her physical age. She was not yet able to make major life decisions or manage her own finances independently.

Upon discharge from the residential program, she was required to secure a licensed therapist and have at least three sessions already scheduled. She also had to have a psychiatrist selected for a warm transfer of care, so her records and medications could be uninterrupted. She chose a female therapist, similar to her in age, and a Christian, in order to incorporate spirituality as a therapeutic foundation.

At her request, I attended the first therapy appointment so that we could help the therapist understand the situation and the connection I had with Denice, and to begin aligning on her goals. This dynamic had to be different from the family dynamic of transparency and no secrets. Denice's therapeutic environment needed to respect her confidentiality, providing her with a safe space to work through her inner demons with her professional therapist.

The plan was quickly established: I would attend sessions periodically for check-ins on Denice's progress, and I would have permission to contact the therapist anytime if I had concerns about Denice's behavior or condition. This allowed the therapist to address any issues directly and promptly. Over time, Denice grew in her relationship with her therapist, and the need for check-ins and calls about concerns became fewer and farther between. This was further evidence of Denice's progress and mental health growth, showing a diminishing need for my level of involvement, while still maintaining foundational support for major life decision-making and financial management.

Don't get me wrong—there were still plenty of frustrating moments and events that literally pissed me off. For example, I would go to her apartment to monitor her living space as we had agreed. This was mainly because my name was primary on the lease, and I was responsible for any damages. Her living in an apartment with my name on it required me to trust her to live independently, maintain her space, and act responsibly, just as any other adult would be expected to do when living on their own.

It was imperative for me to exercise self-control and compartmentalization so I could separate my standards from what I considered reasonable for her in terms of maintaining the apartment. After all the times I'd already cleaned out her hoarded homes, I had developed an internal aversion to clutter. On top of that, I had a mother-in-law with a hoarding disorder, and I had lived in my first marriage with a husband whom my mom endearingly described as someone "you cannot even drop an eyelash on the counter without him finding it"—a description of his Obsessive Compulsive Disorder (OCD) tendencies, which he had developed from living with his mother. My system was well-acquainted with the polarized behaviors between hoarding disorder and OCD.

Denice and I had an agreement about what would be acceptable between these two extremes, and I used this as the basis for monitoring her living areas. This is where my responsibility for my own emotional regulation began. When I became frustrated by her clutter, it was my emotion to handle. But when it went beyond our agreement—like seeing the same pile of clothes on the same chair for the third monitoring visit, or the same dust bunnies in the same corner of the kitchen floor, or recurring issues with the toilet or faucet for the third visit—I began to see a pattern. The repetition of not seeing things cleaned signaled to me that she was slipping out of positive behaviors and needed to be redirected.

This redirection was like setting boundaries and, when necessary, enforcing consequences—much like you would see in a healthy parent-adolescent relationship, where the adolescent is learning responsibility and preparing for adult independence. And yes, you can imagine, Denice would get pissed off at me too.

This is where the skills of effective communication, interpersonal effectiveness, and emotional regulation—central to DBT—came into play. "Wow, there really is something to this stuff Denice learned, and I'm now learning vicariously," my pre-mental health educated system parts were thinking, while at the same time, my post-parenting of adolescents parts were being reactivated.

Denice and I worked tirelessly together for a long time in this complex and multifaceted relationship dynamic—sister to sister, guardian and conservator to protected person, parent to child, adolescent, and adult-child, woman to woman, adult to adult, and whatever else applied at any given moment. I always had to stay alert, constantly assessing whether she was learning, practicing, implementing, strategizing, or manipulating—whatever she was doing—so I could continue to protect her from others, protect her from herself, and protect myself and others from her in DEFCON states. To manage this, I had to rely on her therapist to help me, help us. She was a critical and positive factor in Denice's growth and mental health progress.

A word to the wise for professionals: there are no guarantees, ever. Disconnecting from the outcome of the work we do with clients is often most clearly understood in situations like this one.

Despite the desire to believe in a magic pill or a quick-fix therapy, personal responsibility and accountability are the only ways we, as adults, can truly demonstrate and prove that we are capable of managing our own systems. When this system becomes dysregulated, disorganized, and dysfunctional due to an individual's inability to maintain or nurture it, there's no magic pill or person who can fix it. The responsibility lies with the individual.

When someone becomes dysregulated and crosses boundaries—especially in Denice's case—she has to be restrained and detained in a mental health facility, where she and others are physically safe, until she becomes regulated again. Over the years, and with increased episodic events, the time needed for Denice to regulate herself grew from about seven days to almost sixty days during her most recent episodes. It has only been by the grace of God that, each time, she was taken to a mental health facility instead of being arrested, incarcerated, or even killed during these events. Despite the consequences of her actions—harassment, stalking, home invasion, or driving while mentally unstable (which is akin to driving under the influence)—she has been blessed and fortunate not to have ended up in a much darker place when her system became hijacked by one of her parts.

Now, I feel it's the right moment to explain the therapeutic method of Internal Family Systems (IFS), developed by Richard Schwartz. I must say, he is a genius, a guru, an answer to all my prayers. This man, in all his wisdom, created a way for me to understand what I had been dealing with in Denice for decades, and in my professional opinion, his method works for every person alive who is trying to heal, organize, and understand why we act and behave the way we do as adults. IFS provides an opportunity for each of us to love and nurture our inner child—the one we all carry within us, the child who may not have received enough love and nurturing from our parents. No matter how much a parent does for their child, it will never seem enough for that child, and IFS allows us to begin healing that wound.

IFS provides a pathway for each person to understand why we can be so critical and harsh with ourselves, continuing to shake that "finger of shame" at ourselves long after the time when our parents, teachers, pastors, or other figures have passed. It offers a way to reparent those difficult, rebellious, yet incredibly intelligent adaptive teenage parts with love and what another guru, answer to my prayers named Terry Real calls "carefrontation." This method teaches us to put the adaptive child part into the back seat to protect them from external attacks and, in turn, protect the person we feel is attacking us from that part. We are reminded to "take their sticky hands off the steering wheel" because they don't know how to drive the car without crashing it, leaving destruction in their wake after taking over and running the system (Real, 2022, p. 76).

Furthermore, IFS helps re-task the internal "firefighters," shifting them from merely responding to fires that have already engulfed the internal building to developing fire prevention skills (Riemersma, 2020, p. 206). For instance, it teaches healthy ways to respond to triggers and activating experiences, instead of reacting impulsively by reaching for that bottle, illicit drugs, sex, shopping, gambling—whatever the system has used to numb the emotional pain. IFS provides an effective approach to managing a disorganized and dysregulated internal system, allowing us to overhaul and reorganize it by building love, trust, confidence, and self-worth without firing any of the players from the team.

I believe this methodology is as close to a magic pill as there is for helping people manage their inner demons, regardless of the mental illness, diagnosis, or difficulty they may be facing. While it is not the end-all-be-all, I believe it works and can work for everyone. Therapeutically speaking, it has formed the foundation of my approach with most of my clients. It creates an internal roadmap that I, alongside my clients, can follow, applying other therapeutic methods when a particular part is identified as needing additional skills to mature within the client's system. This, my friends, is my understanding of and how I have learned to apply Integrated Psychotherapy, perhaps also Eclectic methodology, to help my clients today.

"Thank you, God, for blessing this profession with Richard Schwartz and Terry Real, helping me help others by organizing my experiences, like with my sister, throughout the years. Amen."

Chapter 23

Transitioning from Independence to Assisted Living

Let me bring you back now to the 2022 episode—the day Denice was resisting both me and Debbie, standing defiantly in the middle of the road. It took her therapist, on speakerphone, coaxing and guiding her just to get across the parking lot and into my truck so I could take her to her therapy appointment. This therapist, who had done so much *with* and *for* Denice over the years, came to a critical realization that day: Denice's condition had evolved in a way that allowed her Parts to become increasingly skilled at masking or disguising their true intentions—even within the safe, confidential, and trusting space of the therapy setting.

The therapist had been receiving periodic updates from me over the course of the day, and she was slowly beginning to grasp the severity of the episode that was unfolding. Over time, the pieces she'd been given came together, and it became clear that the therapeutic relationship had, in fact, become detrimental rather than helpful for Denice.

In the middle of the therapy session, with Denice fully active in DEFCON 5, she turned to her therapist and said, "Come on, you're my BFF—you're supposed to help me here."

She pressed on, "We worked on this plan together. You're the one who's supposed to help me accomplish it. Remember? We're BFFs, right?"

As a therapist myself, I found even greater respect and appreciation for this woman in that moment—for her professionalism, her tact, and her ability to compassionately disconnect from the outcome. She had the clarity and courage to recognize she had reached the end of her professional capacity to support Denice.

She responded to Denice, "You and I have always had a *professional* relationship, and that is all it has ever been." She added, "Yes, we are both Christian women with shared beliefs, and we've built a strong connection through our therapeutic work—but that connection has never been, and could never be, considered a 'BFF' relationship, Denice."

With grace, she shifted gears and began strategizing, trying to determine who Denice might still trust and follow in that moment. Because it certainly wasn't me—and now, it wasn't her either.

Denice said, "I trust Debbie."

And that was all we needed to hear.

With that, the motion was set into action. Debbie led the way, and Denice followed. We swiftly got her back into my truck, and from there, straight to the second emergency room in just nine days.

During this inpatient hospitalization, as Denice worked to recover and rebalance, our family team once again regrouped to confront the reality of her declining ability to live independently. Nearing sixty years old, her physical age was beginning to work against her—despite being generally healthy aside from her morbid obesity. The time it took for her to regulate and return to baseline had grown substantially—this time, it took thirty-five days.

From a practical standpoint, the prospect of future employment was bleak. While her most recent employer had graciously kept the door open for her return, Denice herself began to doubt her capacity to handle the job. The triggers and emotional activations she had experienced during the episode left an imprint too deep to ignore, even once she reached a regulated state. With both sadness and wisdom, Denice made the decision to resign. It was bittersweet, but ultimately the right choice.

She also came to another difficult realization: despite her intentions and efforts, she could no longer reliably manage her medications on her own. Even missing a single dose could—and often did—lead to major disruptions, setting her and her Parts on a turbulent course that was increasingly hard to recover from.

During the escalation leading up to her hospitalization, our mother had gone to check on her before bringing her to my house. Later, Mom recalled finding and sweeping up a bunch of pills scattered across the kitchen floor, tangled in dust bunnies. Given Denice's challenges with maintaining cleanliness and organization, it became impossible to know how long she had been off her meds—or how many doses she had missed.

As her guardian, I was limited in how much I could intervene. For Denice to live independently, there needed to be a foundation of mutual trust: trust that I wouldn't overstep or smother her autonomy, and trust that she would stay on task with her daily living activities. But that delicate balance was becoming harder and harder to maintain.

In an effort to foster spiritual healing, Denice had recently branched out to a new church community that seemed to meet her spiritual needs. But during the escalation of this episode, she broke trust and connection with those she was fellowshipping with. Through no fault of their own, they didn't understand what was happening. They had no training or knowledge to guide them—only prayer.

On the Sunday after Denice left my home, she called on her women's group for help. She told them that her family had abandoned her, that we refused to help her, and that she had no food. She presented as alone, desperate, and destitute.

Not knowing the full picture, and being kind-hearted Christian women, they responded the only way they knew how—through compassion, support, and prayer. But in doing so, they became unintentionally and vicariously traumatized by Denice's dysregulated, manic state.

Once again, Denice had lost friends. Lost community. Lost trust. What would she come back to this time?

A life that required rebuilding—again. Finding employment. Making new friends. Finding a new church. Repairing and restoring broken family ties.

It's exhausting just writing that list. I can't even imagine having to *live* it—as a sixty-year-old, vulnerable, mentally ill woman who is already tired.

During this hospitalization, I received a call from Denice's hospital social worker, who sounded genuinely concerned. "Denice's fiancé isn't responding to her calls," she said, "and he hasn't reached out to the hospital at all to check on how she's doing." Her tone shifted instantly when I gently corrected the record.

"Denice isn't engaged," I said. "She's been fantasizing a relationship with an old high school friend—one she's been harassing and stalking while spinning a false narrative that they're in love and planning to be married."

This conversation happened during the Valentine's Day weekend—the same time of year Denice had married Jack eight years earlier. Coincidentally, we had just celebrated a family engagement party for my son and his soon-to-be bride on February 12th—just as Denice's DEFCON 5 state began to unfold. The timing wasn't lost on me. It never was.

The social worker was surprised, but not shocked. Given what she had witnessed of Denice's behavior, the possibility of such a delusion made a sad kind of sense. She admitted that in her professional career, she had never worked with someone as fragmented in thought and belligerent in defending a false reality as Denice. And yet, this social worker was one of the most attuned professionals I'd ever worked with in any of Denice's episodes. She didn't just see the surface behavior—she saw into the inner system, the brokenness beneath the chaos. From her perspective, Denice was no longer able to maintain a baseline stable enough for independent living.

She recommended that we begin preparing for a transition into assisted living—primarily for medication management, but also for help with daily living tasks. The goal was to reduce the overall strain on Denice's aging system, giving her a chance to preserve quality of life with supportive structure.

Glory, glory, hallelujah. In that moment, I felt God had answered a prayer. He brought someone into our team—someone on the inside—who could advocate for Denice's best interest while I worked on the outside to manage her discharge plan. For the first time in a long time, I had professional confirmation of what I had already been sensing in my heart: that it was time to pursue a new path for Denice.

This time, her pre-DEFCON 5 state had created so much disruption, so much loss. Starting over again would be overwhelming. In addition to the friendships and community she had painstakingly built over the last eight years, she now also faced the reality of losing her therapist, who, with professionalism and compassion, had reached the necessary conclusion to terminate treatment.

The thought of Denice having to rebuild her life from scratch yet again—without the safety net of her therapist, her job, or her church community—was daunting even for *me* to consider. I couldn't imagine how heavy that burden must feel for *her*.

I spoke individually with each of our core family members—Mom, Dad, Debbie, her youngest son, and our sister-in-law. I asked them to put themselves in Denice's shoes and give me their honest thoughts about the possibility of assisted living. Every single one of them agreed: the emotional toll, the mental instability, the losses—this was too much. Trying to start over again would be impossible.

Assisted living was no longer just an option. It was the best path forward—for Denice's safety, stability, and dignity.

Ok, we all agree. Now what?

How do we go about getting someone into an assisted living facility who, on paper, doesn't fit the mold?

Denice wasn't physically old enough. She appeared relatively healthy—aside from being significantly overweight—and she wasn't ready to accept that she'd have a better quality of life with support than continuing to live independently. The road ahead felt impossible.

Once again, I found myself staring up at *Mount Everest.* Only this time, I had no gear. No oxygen. No guide. And I wasn't climbing alone. I had to carry Denice—every piece of her—on my back to the other side of that mountain. And to make matters worse?

I had ten days to reach the summit.

Step one? Pray. Hard. Desperate. Heart-open prayer. The kind of prayer that's both surrender and plea. Because I knew, without divine intervention and a little earthly favor, this next stretch was going to take everything I had left—and then some.

"Dear Lord, Thank you for bringing this social worker to our situation, she has done so much already for Denice and for us. Please dear God, lead us down the path we are meant to go for what is best for Denice. Help her heal and help us help her heal. Be with us as we embark on this journey, and help me listen to your messages so I do your bidding and thy will for her. In Jesus name, Amen."

I went to bed.

The next day, I received a call from the social worker, who gave me the name and number of someone who could help guide us through the assisted living process. He was a man who had once been in the same situation—searching for a facility for his own mother without the slightest idea of where to start or what to do. That experience led him to start a company designed to help families like ours navigate the process. His services came at no cost to us, as he received compensation from the facility chosen by the client. Importantly, he only partnered with places he would feel confident placing his own loved ones in, and he arranged appointments for family tours himself.

After speaking with him, I called Mom, then conferenced in the rest of the team.

"God has just dropped a man in my lap," I said. "I know it sounds too good to be true, but I believe we need to take what he's offering seriously. If we all agree on his recommendation, we should move forward—diligently and swiftly."

Once everyone had shaken off their initial shock, it didn't take long before we had unanimous agreement. There was a collective deep breath, both to cleanse and to prepare ourselves for the sprint ahead of the long marathon that awaited.

Within twenty-four hours, our newest teammate and friend had set up a video call to meet the rest of the family and explain his services directly. Everyone joined—except for Denice's youngest son, who lived out of state and had work obligations. We all gathered at Mom and Dad's house, each with a laptop, sitting in different rooms so that Mom and Dad could clearly see everyone on screen. This was their first experience joining a virtual meeting like that.

By the end of the call, our new partner had already secured a confirmed appointment for us to tour one assisted living facility and was waiting on a second confirmation. He mentioned having a favorite between the two but chose not to share which one, not wanting to influence our decision before we had the chance to see them for ourselves.

After ending the call, we debriefed briefly as a team. For the first time in a while, there was a sense of hope in the air.

Mom turned to me and said, "You were right, DeAnna. God dropped this man in your lap for a reason. Let's follow his lead and see where it takes us for Denice."

Dad added softly, "Amen."

Later that afternoon, I got another call from our new friend—who already felt like family. The second facility had confirmed, and the owner herself wanted to lead the tour, having been given a thorough background on Denice and our family dynamic.

Both appointments were scheduled for the next day: one in the morning and the other in the afternoon. I confirmed with the team who would be able to attend, and together, we began preparing for the journey ahead.

We converged at Mom and Dad's house early that Tuesday morning. Dad was walking from the family room toward the kitchen, and Mom was coming down the stairs—both of them dressed, put together, and carrying uplifted spirits. It was a day of exploration. The house felt bright, the air smelled fresh like a spring morning, with just a hint of lingering chill. Outside, birds sang beyond the walls, adding a soft, natural soundtrack to our morning. The gloom had lifted, if only for the day, and there was a shared happiness in the air, despite everything.

We were a team—united, present, and ready to represent Denice. Each of us wanted nothing but the best for her once she was discharged from inpatient care. We loaded into Mom and Dad's van. Naturally, I drove, and off we went to our first appointment, each of us mentally preparing to explore the experience through Denice's eyes as best we could.

When we arrived at the first facility, we each began taking in the surroundings from our own perspectives, while also trying to imagine how Denice might feel if she were here. We had agreed to remain open, absorb everything we could, and reserve our thoughts and decisions until we had completed both visits.

Here is what I experienced:

The first facility reminded me of a renovated Super 8 hotel. The moment we walked in, the scent hit me—old meatloaf. I hate meatloaf. ICK! But then I thought, *Maybe Denice doesn't,* I told that internal part of me that lives in my nose.

We were greeted by an older, heavy-set woman with gray hair, who led us to a room I quickly realized served as both the library and community room. The space was dark, and the furniture was stiff and uncomfortable. We sat at a table while she began speaking with Debbie, asking what Denice's needs were so she could explain how the facility might meet them.

A few minutes in, it became clear that she thought Debbie *was* Denice. After a brief, strange chuckle, we corrected her and steered the conversation back to Denice's actual needs.

She walked us through the rest of the hotel-like building, pointing out the amenities that would be available to Denice. As we moved through the halls, I began to notice a multitude of Catholic symbols hanging on the walls. I thought, *Well, at least there's some spiritual guidance here. That's good.*

The tour ended in her office, where she shared that she was a retired nun who had been managing the facility for some time. I noticed a sign on her desk that mentioned something about being addicted to chocolate. I smiled and commented on it.

At that point, we all felt we had gathered the information we needed. No one had further questions, and we were ready to move on. We climbed back into the van, grabbed some lunch, and set our course for the next appointment.

When we arrived at the second facility, we signed in and were greeted by the owner of the property. She was about Debbie's age—fit, spunky, and full of energy. She began leading us through the community family room, which was spacious and welcoming, featuring a gas fireplace, a television, and a piano at its center. A few residents were enjoying their day there, and she stopped to greet them warmly. She introduced us, letting them know we were touring the facility.

She then guided us down a hallway to one of the rooms available for Denice. It was located right next to a cozy sitting area with a television and a reading nook. From there, we took the elevator up to the second floor, which opened into another lively space complete with a pool table and a second television. After observing all the potential activity in that area, she led us down another hallway to a second room available for Denice. This one was slightly larger, though it would be a shared space.

We made our way back downstairs, passing once again through the first family room, then into the dining area. The ambiance there felt like a nice restaurant. Several residents were seated, enjoying coffee and tea, chatting with one another. We stopped to say hello, enjoying the warmth and sense of community in the room.

From there, we continued through a small walkway that passed a beauty salon and entered the craft and activities room. We paused to chat with the owner and learned that she had attended the same Christian school many of our church friends had gone to growing up. As we exchanged names and stories, we realized we knew many of the same people through shared connections.

Was this another sign from God? I wondered silently.

We thought the tour had come to an end—until Dad pointed out the small houses nearby and asked, "Those little houses out there next to us, what are they?"

The owner explained that they were independent living cottages and part of the same property. However, the people living there didn't receive medication management or daily medical care like the residents in the main building. They were welcome to eat all their meals at the facility if they wished, though their homes were fully equipped with kitchens for cooking independently. Medical staff could see them if needed, but these residents had to schedule appointments in advance, since priority was given to those living in the main building. Housekeeping services were also available to them, but at an additional cost.

"Wow," Dad said. "Can we go look at one? Maybe I want to move in there."

We all turned to look at him in disbelief. Dad had always been adamant, repeating for years, *"I'm not moving. I will die in my home."*

We finished the tour and gathered briefly in a smaller community meeting room to go over the final details and discuss the move-in requirements.

We all loaded into the van. As we left the property, Mom said, "I know we were holding our opinions about what we saw, and we haven't heard from the third option yet—but is it time to state our position soon?"

I turned to everyone and said, "We're on a very short timeline here, so I think we should debrief sooner rather than later."

"Oh good," she replied. "I can't hold my opinion in any longer."

She went on to say that for Denice, the second place was definitely her pick. Dad chimed in with the same opinion, noting how he felt happier and more alive at the second facility. He said it was a stark contrast to the gloom he had felt during the darker, less lively first tour. He also appreciated the biblical foundation of the owner, which aligned with our family's values. For Denice, he felt that would support her spiritual well-being.

Mom nodded in agreement and added how she could easily imagine Denice enjoying the craft room, joining in the activities, chatting with other residents at the dining table, and reading in the quiet areas—all the things Denice really loved. Debbie agreed and emphasized how the availability of an exercise and nutrition program, tailored to Denice's dietary needs, would be a vital part of her care plan.

"I think God gave us this place as an answered prayer," Mom said with quiet conviction.

I agreed wholeheartedly. Since the third place hadn't responded by the end of the day, and after updating Denice's youngest son, it felt clear to all of us that it was time to inform our consultant of our decision. The second facility was the one.

We began the lease agreement process the very next day. Thankfully, that was another part of the service our consultant offered. He drew up the paperwork and negotiated the placement based on Denice's income. We reviewed everything carefully, signed it, and just like that—Denice had a place secured with a move-in date.

A big sigh escaped me. One that carried both relief and the weight of everything still ahead. It was time to take in a breath of fresh energy, because the break was over.

While the consultant worked on finalizing the lease, I had to begin the process of moving Denice out of her apartment. I'd already spoken to the property manager, letting her know Denice would be transitioning to assisted living following her discharge from the hospital. She was incredibly understanding and kind, though saddened to lose Denice as a resident after six years. She reassured me there would be no penalty for breaking the lease, since the move was for medical reasons—saving Denice a significant amount of money.

By this time, I was already on day three of my ten-day deadline. Seven days remained to clean out Denice's apartment and pare her belongings down to what would fit in her new space. She was allowed to bring a bed, dresser, chair, and two trash-bag-sized bundles of personal belongings.

Inside, my internal "manager parts" were activating quickly. Some of them began complaining: *Oh no, here we go again—cleaning up after Denice for what, the tenth time?* I could feel them throwing their heads back in exasperation, preparing to groan their way through another round.

Then my "Coach manager" stepped in. *Come on,* she said with clarity and determination. *Let's push through like we always do. Time to get into organization and purging mode. Let's get started.*

I got up early on day four, with six days left to go, and headed straight to Denice's apartment to dig in. Despite all the efforts over the past six years to help her maintain a one-bedroom apartment, her hoarding traits had gotten the best of her. While it wasn't a four-bedroom home, the amount of stuff she had accumulated was overwhelming.

I began sorting everything into piles—Goodwill, Good Riddance, or just plain Trash—keeping only the essentials and a few meaningful items. I spent twelve hours going through her belongings, calling her youngest son to ask what, if anything, he would like to keep for himself and his children, and if there was anything his older brother might want.

Mom came over to help, and at the same time, I was managing calls from Denice, from the consultant, and reaching out to anyone who could help with the tasks that needed to be done. I took a break and stepped outside to take a call from the consultant, just to escape the chaos of the apartment for a moment. There was so much to sort through—clothes, shoes, purses, jewelry—so much dust, hairballs, lint, food on the ground and in the carpet, things shoved under the bed and couch. Pills that had been dropped over time. The mess felt endless.

I was consumed with anger, wondering, *How the hell did she afford all of this on such a tight budget?* I knew she could buy a few new shirts here and there, and I'd given her a couple of pairs of shoes, but come on—there have only been six birthdays and six Christmases. You can't tell me she had that many people giving her gifts or gift cards to buy all this stuff. I was shocked, but not entirely surprised.

The anger kept building. I was trying to understand how she had acquired so much over the years. In the midst of my "angry cleaning," I lost it on Mom, trying to make sense of it all. That's when Mom told me she was aware that Debbie and April had been doing a lot for Denice because they felt sorry for her—because she didn't have much money to enjoy the good things in life.

That hit me like a Mack truck.

It all became clear. There had been so much manipulation happening behind my back, working against me for I don't know how long—all under the guise of "poor Denice" or, more accurately, "poor DeNaughty." I had been fighting a battle I couldn't win, being tricked and kept in the dark, all because Denice knew that if I found out, I would fix it—and then she wouldn't get her way. It wasn't a battle I was fighting for my pride; it was one I had been fighting in complete ignorance, believing I was doing what was best.

Let me just say, there were a hell of a lot more things I would have loved to spend my time and energy on over the past six years than re-raising Denice. Maybe like spending more time with my own adult children and my grandchildren. It was eye-opening to finally see the other side of this reality, once I woke up and my perspective shifted. Again, I felt used, mistreated, and misunderstood. I felt angry, disgusted, appalled, and resentful. I felt alone, defeated, and exhausted. And I just wanted to run away.

I took a break outside in the cold air, trying to gather myself after I had just imploded. I needed to pull myself together so I could go back inside and finish what I had started. This time, I told myself, would be the last.

Mom came to me and said, "Debbie and April are on their way over to help. I just told them if they don't come and help—if they don't help you, right now—we are going to lose you." She continued, "I told them that despite all their efforts to help Denice, we are where we are right now, in part, because they chose to help Denice work against you. They need to come get on the same page with you right now and do what you tell them needs to be done."

When they arrived, I was too tired to fight. So, instead of continuing to clash, we all resumed working together—

finally, working toward the same goal, instead of against each other.

Debbie and April went into full gear, starting with the piles I had made. April arranged for the Junk Man to come take the items we could repurpose. I saved back a few items that Denice's youngest son had asked for—old heirloom dolls from their Great-Grandmother on Jim's side—and a few keepsakes that belonged to Jim, in case his sons ever decided they wanted them. Later, I gave Jim's Bible college class ring to his youngest son, as he thought his older brother might like to have it.

By day seven, we had most of the apartment cleaned out. But we quickly realized that the furniture I had gotten for Denice's apartment wouldn't fit into the one-bedroom studio at the assisted living facility we had chosen for her.

Shifting gears, I began shopping for a new mattress, box spring, headboard, dresser, nightstand, and recliner for Denice's new place. I found a beautiful set that matched the new flooring and décor, and I arranged for delivery the day before move-in.

While at the apartment, a neighbor and her son came by to say hello and inquire about Denice. They had become friendly over the year or so while living next to her. The neighbor was saddened to hear about Denice, and told us to give her a hug from her. She said they would miss her.

As I continued the conversation, I mentioned that we weren't able to take most of Denice's furniture with us, and that I needed to find someone to pick it up. The neighbor shyly, but confidently, asked, "I would buy it from you, if that would be okay." She explained, "My son and I moved in here with nothing, and while we've picked up a few things here and there, I still don't have a bed or anywhere to put our clothes."

And just like that, God dropped another miracle into my lap.

I told her to please come in and take whatever she needed. The only payment I asked for was for her to move it from the apartment. I knew in Denice's pure heart, she would be happy to help someone in need, even after everything she had been through. The neighbor's eyes welled up with gratitude, and she arranged to pick up the furniture the very next day.

On day eight, I confirmed with Denice's youngest son that I would be seeing him on move-in day. He was flying in from out of state to pick her up from the mental hospital and move her directly to her new home. He wanted to see the place for himself so he could feel at ease and communicate to his older brother from his own perspective why this move was the best decision for their mother.

Day nine arrived, and the furniture was delivered. Debbie and April were there to help set up Denice's new place, while I returned to the apartment where Mom was still tidying up the last bits to prepare it for return and retrieve Denice's deposit. There was just one piece of furniture left: the couch. It had yet to be removed, and no new home had been found for it. I spoke with the property manager to let her know it was the final item I needed to handle. She mentioned that the maintenance man was in need of a couch and asked if I'd be willing to donate it. Without hesitation, I agreed. "Absolutely yes," I said.

And just like that, after nine whirlwind days of collaboration, we had unraveled the past six years of Denice's living situation and prepared her for a fresh start at assisted living.

Throughout the ten days, I communicated with Denice as much as I could, keeping her informed about everything happening in a way that she could process. The skills she learned at the residential treatment facility helped her manage the transition. Radical acceptance became her anchor during this time. She leaned into it as she adjusted to the fact that she was being moved, not moving herself. She was no longer living independently. No longer driving herself to appointments or shopping. She would have meals cooked for her, and she would choose from daily options instead of deciding on her meals herself.

Her apartment would no longer be her sanctuary to clean at her own pace. Housekeeping would come in regularly to tidy up, and she would have to keep her space organized according to the facility's standards. I decided to have the refrigerator removed from her studio apartment, and the facility enforced a rule of no food in the rooms—this was partly for health reasons, especially given Denice's dietary issues. She would only be allowed to eat in the dining room, which meant walking to and from each meal. It was a strategy designed to promote movement and exercise, especially for residents with weight concerns.

She no longer had me overseeing her, keeping her accountable. Instead, she had the entire staff at the facility to help manage her daily life. I would still be there to assist with the major decisions and manage her finances, but she would now be navigating the details of her life with the support of the facility and a new routine.

Move-in day was a major transition in Denice's life, and it brought forth many emotions for all of us. I confirmed that Denice's youngest son had traveled safely and met me at the mental health facility, still unbeknownst to Denice that he was coming. Much like the move from home to the residential facility six years prior, it had become a tradition for me and her son to handle the physical transition together, ensuring she understood it wasn't just me making decisions for her. Having the support of her youngest son helped Denice's system recognize that both he and his brother were on board with the plan. Her youngest son repeatedly said, "My brother doesn't want to be involved, so I'm representing both of us. I'll communicate with him so he knows what's happening with Mom—it's his choice."

We waited together in the lobby, and when Denice walked in and saw him, she cracked a small smile. Her body language said it all—hesitant, unsure, confused, yet cooperative. We waited for her attending psychiatrist to join us so the final discharge papers could be signed, and then we were off. Denice climbed into her son's truck, asking to ride with him to her new home. I pulled out in front of him, and together we made the short fifteen-minute drive to her new place.

Entering the building, Denice was excited but hesitant, as if she were absorbing every detail through a blank stare. We took her down the hallway to her new apartment, newly furnished with fresh, brand-new furniture. When she saw it, she gave a pleasantly surprised sigh and asked, "Wow, this is all mine?"

"Yes," I responded, as Debbie and April stepped in to show her all the new things they had set up, including how to use her new television. I took her to the closet where I'd put the clothes we kept, along with four pairs of shoes. I explained that this was all the space she had now, and that housekeeping would come in once a week to clean. All she needed to do was keep the space tidy and prepare her laundry for them.

Having just come from a DEFCON 5-level episode and leaving behind a life she knew to enter a totally new one, I knew how strange and overwhelming it would feel. I couldn't predict how she would react. There were parts of me hoping for excitement, while others were preparing for a negative response. What I witnessed from Denice was more neutral—interested but flat.

After about an hour of helping her settle in, I left her with Debbie and April to finish getting everything ready. Denice's youngest son and I then left the premises. I decided it was best not to overwhelm her any further and let her experience her new life on her own for a bit. It felt like a parent leaving their young adult at their first college dorm—letting them navigate this new chapter, make new friends, and explore the campus. I promised Denice I would check in a few days after she settled in, and we would go over the facility rules together, along with the care plan that had been set up for her.

Denice adjusted surprisingly well to her new environment. She made friends and began navigating her new life, but it wasn't without a few bumps. One of her strategies was testing the boundaries of the rules. She began negotiating with her friends during outings—offering to pick up items for them at the store if they couldn't go, in exchange for them letting her buy things for herself later. At first, it seemed harmless, but over time, it became a regular habit, and I noticed she started buying things that worked against her needs, cluttering her small space.

One day, she admitted to having "a small bag of candy" in her room. I decided to gently confront her during a meeting with the care manager. I asked, "Okay, when I go into your room and check your cupboards, what exactly am I going to find?" Denice hesitated before responding, "Okay, maybe a few bags of candy." She knew, just as I did, that she had been caught in a familiar pattern.

She confessed to having a bag of Hershey's Kisses in her room, and we discussed the situation with the facility manager. Together, we came up with a plan for Denice to keep her sweet treat in a more controlled way. Denice suggested that the exercise leader hold onto the bag for her, and after completing a week of the exercise program, she could "earn" a kiss or two. Everyone agreed with her plan. It seemed like a reasonable approach—Denice had created a motivational system for herself and a level of accountability.

But there was a part of me that felt uneasy. As Denice explained her plan, she added, with a sly flirtatious smile and a wink, "I can get a kiss or two from the exercise instructor." It was subtle, but her behavior triggered an immediate sense of caution in me. I knew this wasn't just about candy anymore; I could sense that DeNaughty was in play again. My trust level dropped, and my awareness was heightened.

After the meeting, I decided to follow up by checking her room. I found the bag of Hershey's Kisses, as well as what Denice had described as a "small" bag of mini PayDay candy bars. The "small" bag, however, turned out to be one of those large Halloween-sized bags with about fifty pieces in it. When I confronted her, she initially downplayed it, acting as if she had "forgotten" about the second bag. As we walked toward her room, she shrugged nonchalantly, knowing she'd been caught, and dismissed it as if to say, "You won, that's fine, because I already have a better plan for the kisses than this bag of candy."

A few weeks later, Denice suddenly stopped talking about participating in the exercise program. At first, her reasons were vague, but over time, her explanations became more inconsistent, especially in conversations with other team members. When I pieced the details together with information from mom, it became clear that Denice had been discussing how cute she thought the exercise leader was. She mentioned that he had been giving her more attention recently, which seemed to have caused her to become more interested in his presence. Eventually, she told mom that the exercise instructor had been moved to another facility or wasn't around as much.

I could smell DeNaughty's influence in all of this, and my suspicions grew. It was time to call a meeting with the facility manager to dig deeper into what had been happening.

As it turned out, the exercise leader had expressed concern about Denice's behavior toward him. He had become uncomfortable with the attention she was giving him, and despite attempts to manage her actions during the classes, his discomfort persisted. Eventually, he chose to move to another facility, and a female exercise instructor was brought in to replace him. For the facility, this resolved the issue professionally. However, for Denice and DeNaughty, the issue was far from resolved in my mind as her guardian.

I had a conversation with the facility staff about Denice's DEFCON 4 behaviors, helping them understand how her internal system works and how her different parts can hijack her decisions to get what they want. In this case, Denice's need for attention and affection—especially from someone of the opposite sex—was at the heart of her actions. She had defined this need in her mind as "love," and her pursuit of it began the moment she set out to get "a kiss or two" from the exercise leader each week for doing what she thought he wanted her to do.

For the next nine months, Denice adjusted fairly well to her life in assisted living. The medication management assistance provided helped control her Bipolar disorder symptoms, allowing her to stay on track with her medication and manage her mental health more effectively. While personality disorders can't be treated with medication alone, the consistency of her medication regimen helped mitigate the behaviors associated with her disorder.

Denice settled into a routine, which seemed to allow her to live within her means while working on managing the behavioral skills she was responsible for—with guidance. Over time, the facility staff got to know her better and understood the nuances of her condition. They learned to recognize when her behaviors raised concerns, prompting them to reach out for clarification or further guidance. There were moments, like the one I described earlier, when Denice tested the waters with her behavior, but this was to be expected for someone trying to manage internal systems on their own.

Denice showed great progress, particularly in situations where DeNaughty could have hijacked her system. One example was when she tripped over an outdoor rug and fell. Denice handled the incident remarkably well, asking for help and receiving it, while also appropriately advocating for herself and her needs. Despite the challenges, she was living her life to the best of her ability, supported by the staff and the structure of the facility.

Chapter 24

The Living Hell of Applying for Disability Assistance

The process of trying to apply for Denice's disability assistance nearly drove me to check in for a 72-hour mental hold. I honestly have no idea how anyone with an established mental disability can navigate the system without succumbing to an emotional death of frustration and rejection.

Over the years, Denice and I attempted three different times to get her qualified for disability assistance. The first attempt failed because she had too much money. She needed to spend down the death benefits she had received from Jim. This was going to take time, and rather than simply moving the money to someone else—which is illegal—we agreed she had no choice but to use what she had left to live, despite the tax penalties she would incur for withdrawing money from an IRA before the age of sixty-five.

Each attempt to qualify for financial assistance was met with failure. Denice had to go through the process multiple times, undergoing medical and mental tests conducted by Medicaid-approved physicians. The diagnosis provided by her own licensed physician and psychiatrist wasn't enough for the government to make a decision. Instead, they required further tests, which left Denice feeling worse about herself—ashamed, hopeless, and rejected, being told she wasn't "disabled enough" to qualify for financial assistance.

The final decision we received stated that her disability was in remission and that she was able to manage it well enough on her own. This decision ignored the reality that she had been determined by the court to be mentally disabled enough to need a Guardian and Conservator to manage her life—but somehow, she wasn't "disabled enough" to receive assistance. As my husband would say, "Makes no sense."

Despite the repeated setbacks, we worked hard to help Denice pick herself up emotionally. We focused on helping her find some pride in being able to live independently and support herself with Jim's money and her part-time work income.

As time passed and Denice was getting close to running out of her benefits, we were encouraged to try applying for assistance once more. This time, a gentleman reached out to us who actually took the time to review her case before making her go through the battery of tests again, sparing her further emotional grief and trauma. We took the meeting at a coffee shop in a small town where one of Mom's cousins had his 80th birthday party, a place we used to frequent for family reunions. The environment, with most of the family team present, was incredibly helpful for Denice, even though she was once again rejected for assistance.

However, this gentleman left Denice with hope. He encouraged her to continue for the next two years, spend down her finances, and when she turned sixty, she would be more likely to qualify for disability based on her age and financial status, rather than just her disability. If that didn't work out, she would also qualify for widow's benefits at sixty, regardless of her disability status. So, either way, if she could manage for a few more years, she would receive financial help.

Despite her best efforts, the episode Denice couldn't manage in 2022 forced her into assisted living, which drained her finances in less than half the time we had expected. This shifted the trajectory from the path the gentleman had outlined for us.

Once we got her settled into assisted living and had to redirect her finances to spend down faster than initially anticipated, we faced the need to try once more to get her qualified for disability financial assistance before she turned sixty. That's when God opened another door for us. We were referred to a private for-profit agency located about fifty miles south of our hometown. This agency specializes in helping people with barriers to successfully qualify for government financial assistance, individuals who would otherwise clearly be eligible for benefits.

Though I had reservations about the for-profit status, I figured it wouldn't hurt to contact them and find out more rather than just assuming it wouldn't work. Debbie and I made an appointment and drove down to learn about their business model. The presentation was very well done, and they also offered a 100% money-back guarantee if they couldn't get Denice qualified. I made sure, multiple times, that I understood everything correctly. On our drive back home, we arranged a family meeting to discuss what we had just learned.

Still in disbelief about the guarantee, Debbie kept reiterating it to me during the drive, until my mind could finally process it. "There's no way this couldn't work out. They'll deal with the government nonsense, and if they don't succeed,

Denice will get refunded. How could she lose?" I kept saying to myself and to Debbie.

With Denice and the rest of the team present, Debbie and I explained the process, the cost, and the conditions of the guaranteed refund to everyone. After much discussion and everyone sharing their thoughts and concerns, the decision was unanimous: Denice would spend the $10,000.00 on the service, which would either result in her obtaining the financial assistance she needed through disability payments to support herself until she was eligible for disability and widow's benefits at sixty, or she would get her money back, and we would have to figure out how to pay out of pocket for her $101,000.00 assisted living expenses until she turned sixty.

Debbie volunteered to take the lead with the organization, working diligently with them to gather the necessary documents to build Denice's case. Despite Denice's case taking four times longer than the average time to get someone qualified, the organization remained firm in their guarantee and worked tirelessly on her behalf. At the eleventh hour, we received the good news: Denice had been determined eligible for disability benefits and would begin receiving funds to manage her care on the 15th of the month—the exact month in which her benefits from Jim had completely depleted. "How can it be argued that God doesn't provide for those who are faithful?" Mom said, upon hearing the news.

At that point, I took back the reins. I began figuring out how to direct Denice's funds into my Conservator account, officially became her payee, and started managing her finances to pay her assisted living bill each month. I also helped her manage the allowance budget that was included in her monthly benefit payment. Overnight, I shifted from trying to make her finances stretch to avoid a zero balance, to managing them to stay under the low threshold set by the government. If she earned too much, she would lose her eligibility for benefits, which meant she couldn't save any money. All of this had to be reported to the Court annually, detailing exactly how her money was managed. I remained fiducially responsible, not only for Denice's money, but also for the government's funds. As I had in the past, I took this responsibility very seriously.

Part of the services this miracle organization helped us acquire included getting Denice determined eligible for healthcare coverage, psychiatric services, and nursing needs. They also offer mental health services, including regular therapy with a counselor and a social worker to help her navigate her service needs. Additionally, they provide physical and occupational therapy to work on her balance and coordination. The best part is that all of these services are available in one location, giving Denice a place to hang out and socialize with others, play games, do crafts, and participate in activities. They even provide breakfast and lunch if she wants to eat while there.

Wait, there's more! They also offer transportation to and from the facility from her assisted living home, ensuring she gets to her appointments on time and gets back home afterward. She can even go to the facility when she doesn't have an appointment, just to hang out with her friends. Genius! It's a one-stop shop for seniors to meet their medical and social needs.

This service was a huge benefit for Denice—everything she needed in one place. It allowed her to make friends, stay social, and remain active. However, the location we had moved her to, which was close to family, was not certified to accept

Medicaid. Fortunately, the company had multiple properties in different counties, and one of them had an open room for Denice. This would allow her to participate in the organization's services.

After gathering the family team, including Denice, to discuss the options—knowing that it would require her to move again—we all agreed that it would be best for her to relocate. The new facility was smaller, with only eight housemates, but it was a one-and-a-half to two-hour drive away from any of us. The distance would provide Denice with more independence, allowing her to live more autonomously and build her own relationships with others.

We moved her in December. After settling her into the new home and getting her acquainted with the new organization's processes, Denice began working toward gaining more control over her daily decisions, with support from both the facility staff and the service provider. This is where she was living when she started branching out, finding a new church, and transitioning into the episode I discussed in the chapter on establishing DEFCON 3 – Hyper-religiosity.

Chapter 25

Time to Quit – Coming To Terms with Terminating Responsibility

Coming full circle now, through the process that shaped Denice, it's time to share what brought me to my breaking point. I had done all I felt I could for Denice. The time and energy she spent trying to, what I felt was, constantly chip away at the united front, and her efforts to prove she could handle everything on her own, became a battle I could no longer fight. Debbie and I, with the support of Mom and Dad, had worked hard to assemble a professional team of caretakers for Denice, creating an environment where she could feel comfortable, cared for, and maintain some sense of independence from me—only to be involved when she entered a DEFCON phase.

Unfortunately, the last DEFCON episode, I believe, had a lot to do with her living in a smaller facility with fewer people. Denice was able to let DeNaugthy loose and manipulate others into following her unhealthy cognitive patterns. In a smaller setting, DeNaughty was more covert—able to carefully and strategically maneuver until the facility staff, who lacked mental health training, found themselves trapped in DeNaughty's web. The staff thought they were responding to Denice's needs, but these requests were often driven by DeNaughty's desire for control.

When things spiraled out of control, it led to the DEFCON 5 episode I mentioned earlier, where Denice trapped her caretaker in the community bathroom, insisting the caretaker follow her orders, even though another housemate's needs were a higher priority.

After being taken to the local ER near her assisted living home, the Friday after Thanksgiving, Denice was immediately placed on a mental health hold. They called to inform me that she would be moved to a bed at a different facility—one we hadn't worked with before. This part of Denice's journey was difficult, as she was still in a DEFCON 5 state, feeling trapped. She described how "Mrs. Hulk came out and ripped right through the restraining straps they had on me during the ambulance transport."

The new facility was about fifteen minutes away from my home, but due to her state and the intensity of the DEFCON episode, it took a few weeks before I could even consider visiting. This episode lasted about forty days, which spanned the Christmas holiday. Mom was upset and heartbroken that Denice had to be hospitalized over the holiday. Despite her desire to visit, she hesitated to go without me, her fears resurfacing from past trauma, as she had been the one most involved during Denice's DEFCON 5 experiences.

I went to pick Mom up from her home and took her to visit Denice, fulfilling her "momma bear" need to see for herself how Denice was doing and to spend time with her during such an emotionally charged holiday. This visit marked the moment

I began to approach Denice with the reality that she would likely have to move again. Due to the threat she posed at her current home, she wouldn't be eligible to return and would need a new place to live.

The hospital social worker was working to get Denice accepted into an assisted living facility that catered not only to elderly people needing daily living assistance, but also to individuals with mental health issues who required medication management and psychiatric care. I couldn't help but wonder—where was this place when we had first begun looking for a facility for Denice two years prior?

With the help of the hospital social worker and in collaboration with the service provider organization Denice had been working with, we moved her to yet another facility. This one was not far from where she had been living, but it was far better suited to help her with both her daily living support needs and mental health needs.

I was finally at the end of my capacity to help Denice. She now had all the support she needed from these two facilities. More than ever, I felt that this was the right time for me to terminate the legal guardianship and conservatorship responsibilities that Denice and I had been working toward—and sometimes against—for years.

The time and energy spent jumping through hoops to get her qualified for various assistance programs, alongside the intricate and often difficult decisions that needed to be made with her, and at times for her, felt at times harder than if we had been climbing Mt. Everest. We had accomplished the monumental task of building a support network for Denice, allowing her to live her life while also giving us the space to live ours, free from the constant worry about her well-being and the looming fear of her sliding into DEFCON behaviors, which would inevitably lead to chaos for all of us.

I had begun mentally preparing for the termination process during the 2022 episode, so deciding to move forward now was not a decision made out of spite or on impulse. It had been a process—first making the decision, then partially reversing it by terminating the conservatorship but keeping the guardianship. After researching the possibility of keeping the guardianship while dissolving the conservatorship, I discovered that, since Denice had no assets, the conservatorship would be terminated by default. Keeping the guardianship, however, would still require me to manage her financial matters. With that realization, I was back to the decision of remaining as her guardian.

When the 2023-2024 episode occurred, that was it for me. I needed to reinstate my decision to fully terminate my legal duties for Denice and completely relinquish her care to the system of caretakers we had worked so hard to set up for her over the past few years. Following through with this decision, I filed the necessary papers with the court to terminate my guardianship and conservatorship. As I had been told when I was granted these roles, I could terminate at any time, for any reason—or no reason at all.

The painful process of feeling like I had failed her, failed my family, and the humbling of my warrior spirit was an emotional journey, though it ended up being relatively short-lived. Within a few days, I received court papers and a phone call from the court clerk advising me that the judge required a hearing for me to explain why I wanted to terminate my position.

"Really, you have to be shitting me?" was what most—if not all—of my internal voices screamed. "I have to explain why I have to quit?" I yelled to my husband, who immediately stepped in to comfort me, saying, "It will be okay. You know you got this."

Unleashing the part of me in charge of logic, here's what was happening inside my mind, like a carnival of confusion. The court had provided Denice with an attorney and a guardian ad litem to represent her as the defendant in my petition to terminate. Now, I don't know about you, but for me, this situation was one of the strangest I'd ever found myself in. I became her guardian and conservator because she was determined to be incapable of making her own decisions. I spent nearly a decade helping her reach a point where she had sufficient support, allowing me to step back at any time—just as I was told I could do at the start of this journey. But now, I was being opposed for wanting to end my legal role after working to get her what she needed—and, by the way, what she wanted—by being intimidated and coerced by her attorney, who had been absent since the guardianship was granted. All this to keep working for, and being manipulated by, Denice. Last I checked, it was a violation of my Thirteenth Amendment rights to be subjected to involuntary servitude.

I followed the process I was required to, without legal representation, by the way. I prepared additional paperwork and sent it to the interested parties, informing them of the court hearing date, time, and location. I also prepared to explain to the court why I wanted to terminate my position and recommend that a new guardian be appointed to oversee Denice's care—once again, with no other family member stepping up to take my place, including either of Denice's adult sons. Everyone on the interested party list signed a waiver agreeing to the termination without a hearing—everyone except Denice's oldest son. When I contacted him to confirm that he had received the document, he told me he had reservations about my request to terminate and that he would see me in court.

I originally filed to terminate my positions in November 2023 and the hearing was set for mid-April 2024. All the interested parties, along with their spouses, attended. Denice's youngest son flew in for the short trip to be there in person with his brother and wife, Mom, Dad, Debbie, April, our sister-in-law, my husband, and my son. Denice's daughter-in-law, who had helped care for her after Jim's death, attended virtually, as did Denice and her social worker.

The judge began by asking Denice's attorney to present their concerns and the evidence supporting why I should not terminate my services. They remained firm in their belief that Denice needed a guardian due to her grave disability and her history of episodic behaviors. They argued that there were no public organizations that could offer guardian support without compensation. Hunh. They were actually arguing for me to remain in the position, providing unpaid support for Denice.

The judge then turned to me and asked me to state my position and explain why I wanted to terminate my role. I summed up my story and justification in a well-organized, concise, ten-minute statement. The judge then remarked, "I see that everyone has agreed to grant your termination without the need for a hearing, except for one interested party who appears to be contesting your request. Is that correct?"

"Yes, your honor, that is correct," I responded.

"Is that interested party present in the courtroom today?" the judge asked.

"Yes, your honor, that would be Denice's oldest son, and he is here," I said.

The judge called out his name and asked Denice's oldest son to rise and approach the podium. The judge had already reprimanded Denice's youngest son for not removing his ball cap when the judge entered the room and had everyone seated. Later, Denice's youngest son admitted his mistake, acknowledging he had been in the wrong and expressing appreciation for the judge's correction.

Denice's oldest son, confidently rising from his seat in the gallery, stood tall—his nearly seven-foot, easily three-hundred-pound frame clearing his throat as he buttoned his sharp-looking suit coat. He approached the podium as the judge asked him to state his name and his relation to Denice and me. He clearly and firmly stated that he was Denice's oldest son and my nephew.

The judge then asked him to explain why he felt the need to have a hearing set and to voice his concerns about my termination from taking care of his mother. Let me remind you, this wasn't the first time my nephew had appeared before a judge. In my opinion, by now at forty years old, he should have been well-primed to understand how to address a judge in a court of law.

Both surprised and yet not, the fight ensued, led by my nephew's gross misperceptions and clearly misguided opinions of my performance as a caretaker for his mother over the past eight years. He launched into a full-on attack of my character as Denice's sister and his aunt, questioning my integrity and my motivations for initially taking on the duties and responsibilities that many in the family believed he should have absorbed by now—responsibilities for his own mother. He questioned why I was now wanting to terminate my position.

He addressed the court, stating, "My aunt took on this responsibility despite my position from the beginning that my mom didn't need anyone to help her live her life, and now that my mom doesn't have any money left, my aunt shouldn't be allowed to just stop her duties because it's too hard for her."

He grew more agitated as he spoke, his voice rising. "I am extremely suspicious about how my aunt spent my mom's fucking money, and I'm requesting a forensic accounting audit because I think she fucked up and is hiding misappropriated spending. She's just trying to get out of it before she gets caught."

That was all the judge was willing to hear. The judge interrupted my nephew's tirade, asking sharply if he was willing to take on the responsibility of caring for his own mother. He responded, "HELL NO!"

The judge, in no uncertain terms, reprimanded him for his disrespectful behavior and outburst toward the court. He told my nephew that he was finished presenting his position and sternly ordered, "You will take your seat now."

He passed by me without looking at me, and I didn't look at him either, as he went to sit down next to his wife. Moments later, I heard rustling and erratic movement. Without turning around, I knew he had stood up and stormed out of the courtroom before the hearing had concluded.

Then I heard more commotion, but I chose not to let it distract me or turn around to see what was happening. It wasn't until I heard my mom begin to weep that I realized the emotional toll it had taken on her. Soon after, I heard her leave the hearing in an effort to regain control of her devastated, embarrassed, and ashamed emotions over how her oldest grandson had just behaved in a court of law, especially considering his own legal issues from twenty years ago.

Our sister-in-law hurried out after my mom, concerned that she had fallen, having heard the metallic clatter of my mom's cane as it accidentally dropped on the floor in her haste.

Maintaining my composure, I focused on the court hearing, knowing that despite not having witnessed what had just taken place behind me, the judge was well aware of everything that had occurred. I wondered whether the scene would influence his decision on the matter. However, the hearing was not yet over. He still needed to hear from Denice.

Turning his attention to her on the monitor, the judge asked Denice to state her position. She began calmly, addressing what we had all just witnessed. "While I am very disturbed by my adult son's behavior that we just all saw," she said, "I cannot allow myself to become distracted from why we are here today."

She went on to express that, although she still felt the need for a guardian, she had wanted to be free of one for a long time. She understood and agreed with my position—that I needed to be released from her affairs—and believed that I would continue helping her in the same way, even without the court's authority as her guardian and conservator.

That part… that stunned me. "Did we really just hear her say what we think we heard?" All my internal parts immediately broke into a low rumble. "Oh God," I thought to myself, "how do I respond to that on record if the judge goes straight from hearing Denice to making a decision?"

Before I could worry any longer, the judge turned to me and asked if I had anything else to add. "Of course we have more to add," my internal parts were screaming. I composed myself and responded, "Yes, your honor, I believe I just heard Denice state that I would continue helping her as I have, despite being terminated if that is the decision today."

I continued, "That will not be the case. I will not continue in this capacity, nor in any capacity once a termination is granted, except for completing what is necessary to resolve any outstanding tasks to remove myself from management of her affairs—such as closing the bank account so she can begin receiving her assistance funds on her own."

That statement threw a monkey wrench into the mix. I don't know how or why the judge wasn't aware that I had an open account for Denice in my name, which would need to be closed before I could fully be removed from her finances.

The judge then ordered me to be immediately terminated from performing as Denice's guardian. As for the conservatorship, he ordered me to remain in place until Denice could open a bank account for herself and I could legally close mine. He also ordered me to provide a final accounting report of the remaining funds and how they were distributed, once the account was closed. He gave us sixty days to complete the process and report back to the court in writing. Once that was done, he would grant the termination of the conservatorship through filing rather than requiring another court appearance.

He closed the hearing, and I took a deep breath. I paused to tell my internal parts, "We're halfway out. There's a little more work to do, but we're calling today a win."

Turning to those remaining in the gallery, I was filled in on the ruckus that had occurred. I learned that between

Denice's oldest son storming out and mom leaving the courtroom, the other noises I had heard were from Denice's daughter-in-law and youngest son—both had left the courtroom before the hearing had concluded, following Denice's oldest son's lead.

As you've probably gathered by now, Denice's oldest son hasn't played much of a role in this story, and that's no accident. His involvement in his mother's care has been minimal at best. I can count on two fingers the times he participated. The first time was at the beginning, when he vehemently opposed me being named her guardian and conservator. The second time was when he came to retrieve her from the hospital during an active DEFCON 5 mental state, putting her in my son's truck and leaving with a simple remark that he "had better things to do."

From the very start, he chose not to be involved. He avoided conversations, planning, or decisions about his mother's well-being. His brother, who was consistently active in Denice's care, informed me at one point that, between the two of them, he would be the designated representative. Denice's youngest son would handle everything, keeping her oldest son updated as he saw fit.

As required by the court, I continued to provide copies of all the annual guardian and conservator reports to the interested parties designated by the court. There was one year when I called him to get his physical address to send a report by mail, as the court didn't accept the electronic method I had used previously. He responded with indifference, saying, "I don't really care if I get it or not." Despite his lack of interest, I got his address from mom and sent it anyway.

The reports had a designated time frame during which any interested party could raise concerns. But not once, not one time, had Denice's oldest son ever contacted the court or me with concerns about anything written or submitted. His silence over the years spoke volumes.

As time went on, I informed Denice that she needed to open a bank account so I could stop the direct deposit of her disability and widow's benefits from being deposited into my account. She hadn't completed this task before the May payment came in, so I reminded her again that she needed to have it done by the end of May. I would be closing the account to finalize my reporting, as ordered by the judge with a sixty-day deadline.

Denice promised, "Ok, I'll talk with my social worker and have her help me get one opened this week." I sent another reminder the week before I planned to close the account to ensure she remembered. I went to the credit union, closed the account, and had them issue a check made out to Denice. This way, she could deposit the funds into her new account, and there would be a paper trail showing how the money was distributed and the exact amount.

I prepared all the documents and the final report I was ordered to complete, including an attestation for Denice to sign when I gave her the final check from my closed account. With everything in place, I scheduled a time for Debbie and me to make the two-hour drive to visit Denice at the new facility she had moved into.

Upon arriving, we sat and chatted for a few minutes before getting down to business. I requested the facility manager to join us, so she would be aware of what Denice was receiving and could assist her in case any questions arose after the meeting ended and Debbie and I had left.

The four of us gathered around the dining table, and I went over the final report with Denice, presenting her with the check for the remaining funds. It was written out for a little over three thousand dollars. I explained who she needed to distribute the money to and for how much, only transitioning one month's assisted living rent bill for her to pay after receiving her next month's benefit.

Denice would need to visit the Social Security office to provide them with the court orders removing me as her payee and to give them her new bank account number for the direct deposit transfer. I also planned to send the final orders to Social Security to close out my responsibility to inform them.

I had Denice sign the attestation confirming she had received her remaining funds, and both Debbie and the facility manager signed as witnesses to the exchange, affirming that I had outlined what Denice needed to do to take responsibility for herself.

"ERRRCH!" Denice suddenly interrupted. "I have a question," she said. "I don't understand how or where I'm supposed to cash this check."

Stunned, I replied, "Uh, you need to go to the bank where you opened your account and deposit it there so you can set up auto-payment for your assisted living facility to pay your monthly rent, just as we've been going over for the last forty-five minutes."

She looked at me squarely and said, "What bank account? I don't have a bank account."

My jaw dropped, and my chin jerked downward before halting. My eyes and eyebrows raised in confusion, and my head shook left to right as I tried to process what I had just heard. "What?" I asked firmly but calmly, my voice breathy. "The bank account that you and Debbie both told me you opened with your social worker's help—*that* account?"

Denice looked me squarely in the eye and responded, "I did not open an account, we started the process but didn't finish."

I sighed deeply and allowed my head to slowly tilt back, gazing upward as if the answer I was seeking might be written on the ceiling. Taking another deep breath, I found myself having an emergency "one-woman business meeting" with all the parts of me.

My firefighter instinct wanted to run to the rescue, take Denice out right away, and help her open a bank account. But no, I wasn't going to do that. My inner critic yelled at me, "I told you she wouldn't be able to handle all this." My Defender piped up, "Nope, she fought hard against me for years to regain responsibility for herself, and now that she has it, she needs to handle her own issues." My internal little sister part got pissed feeling lied to for having left the requirement unfinished by the deadline and feeling misled to believe it had been completed.

Another mom-like manager arrived, "Nope, not the time for a sister fight here." My business manager side wanted to outline a task list and calendar for the next day, laying out the steps Denice needed to take to fix her problem. But the Defender part screamed, "Nope, she needs to figure this out herself. It's time to learn how to problem-solve her own issues, starting now."

"Well, Denice," I said to her, "you have bills that need to be paid, and you have the money left over from my account in your hand. I suggest you think through it tonight and figure out your plan to deal with the problem you have."

I continued, "You, me, Debbie, and your social worker were all present at the hearing in February when the judge ordered that I close the account, submit a final report to the court within sixty days, and you would take over responsibility for yourself. It is unfortunate that you have not done your part yet."

We finished the meeting, and Debbie and I left, leaving Denice with her copy of the final papers and report that I needed to file with the courts the next day. I received the final orders of termination within forty-eight hours of filing—seven months after originally filing for termination—I was done and relieved of duty.

It has now been a year since the drama unfolded in the courtroom, and I've taken my time to withdraw and heal mentally from the last fifty years of trying to help Denice navigate her life with mental health diagnoses. I have requested to be left out of any drama or issues Denice may create or orchestrate over the past year as she continues to learn how to manage herself.

At one point, Dad confronted me and told me I needed to step in and help Denice sort out her Social Security payments because she still hadn't been able to establish herself as her own payee, even with Debbie's help, until just last month. Denice had gone ten months without receiving her benefits, despite assistance from the assisted living facility's accounting staff, who were trying to help her deal with the government Social Security offices.

I gently yet firmly told Dad that I had already sent copies of the court orders to Social Security twice, after receiving correspondence from them, and simply stated, "No." Mom would occasionally update me about Denice's progress, telling me how Debbie and April had once again loaned Denice money to catch up on her rent to prevent her from being evicted from the assisted living facility.

Debbie confirmed and justified loaning her the money, saying, "We worked too damn hard to get her qualified for receiving her services and benefits. I won't let her lose everything we got put in place for her."

I was in no position to argue with Debbie, nor did I have the energy to form an opinion on the matter.

Denice had to move again—this time from the assisted living facility I had last moved her into—because they were terminating their contract with the service provider who was handling her medical and mental health care services. Fortunately, she was able to be reconsidered and move back to the same company she had lived with when she first moved into assisted living. This move was not without its difficulties, though. The director of services had reservations about accepting her back due to the behavior issues Denice had shown, particularly the incident when she trapped a caretaker in the bathroom, leaving a trauma trail for the staff and caretakers.

It hasn't been easy for Denice since my termination was granted. Still, as I continue to work on healing myself internally, I sit here looking at the vase of pink and purple roses and carnations that arrived at my house yesterday on my birthday. When I got home from work, my husband was excited for me to open the card and find out who had sent them. Realizing they weren't from him, I opened the card with the Eiffel Tower stamped in silver shine and read the card aloud:

"Every day should have a little ooh-la-la in it."

Inside, it read, "Especially birthdays! Hope it's magnifique!"

The personal message inside read:

"Happy Birthday, Sis, and thank you again for taking care of me the way you did."

I still get periodic updates from Mom, who had talked to Denice and relayed, "Denice is really finding out every day how much work it was for you to take care of her. She appreciates it more and more as she runs into the stress of things you always did for her."

I still have trouble receiving these messages. They don't seem to have anywhere to park within my system yet. Maybe one day they will, but not just yet.

Chapter 26

Why Would You Tell Everyone

Why Did I Write This Book?

It began with a simple yet powerful opportunity: to offer encouragement to forgive those who came before us and to hope for those who come after. My wish is that each reader takes what resonates with them and uses it to open a pathway to broader perspectives. Embrace what fits, and adapt it as needed to consider more possibilities beyond your own. For the parts that don't align, use them to expand your understanding, knowing that what you may not have experienced personally may still have happened to someone else.

By broadening our knowledge of how goodness can triumph over evil, we increase our capacity for empathy and grace—toward ourselves and others.

When I first spoke to my mom about writing this book, she was hesitant, filled with fear. I can only guess it was fear of embarrassment. "Why would you write about all the things that happened?" she asked, her voice tinged with trepidation. "What is everyone going to say?" She repeated these concerns a few more times, adding, "I assume you'll let Denice read it first. But what if she reads something she doesn't know, or something she doesn't remember? What's that going to do to her?"

There was a moment, one that still lingers in my memory, when we were reviewing the timeline of events to ensure we had the facts right. During our conversation, I could hear the break in her voice as tears and trembling words escaped her. "It was so painful to watch these things happening to her, and there was nothing I could do except wait until I could finally call for help."

As we continued to talk through the events, my mom would often ruminate, asking herself, "What did I do wrong?" and "What should I have done differently?" There are no truer words to capture the love of a mother, enduring the unbearable pain of watching her child suffer, helpless to take away their pain. There are no words truer than the guilt of feeling like you could have been a better, more skilled parent.

When we find ourselves in the midst of these moments, we are forced to make a decision: to help the person who is suffering or to withdraw from them. Not everyone is equipped to help someone in such a state, and that's okay. For those of us who choose to help, we must never pass judgment on those who cannot. Judging others for choosing to remain distant from someone with a mental illness only brings condemnation upon ourselves through "pride, comparison, and belittling another" (Palmer, June 14, 2023). Similarly, those who decide they cannot help a mentally ill person should not pass judgment on those who do.

Now, you have before you my story—why, in the moment and over time, I chose to help Denice rather than withdraw. You will also encounter the stories of others I met along the way, some of whom chose to help and others who chose to step back. Judgment cast upon one another is the first act of harm. It places one person's opinion above another's and distracts from the real issue at hand: the mentally ill person's need for attention and support *(Holy Bible, NIV Romans 14:13).*

In Denice's case, the space for judgment becomes a playground for DeNaughty, who gains a sense of control over others. She takes on the role of director and producer of her own dramatic production, casting us into roles to play out the conflicts in her story. There are only two true judges in my story: God and Your Honor. These are the only ones who have the right to cast judgment on Denice, on me, and on everyone who helped or didn't help along the way.

When multiple people decide to help and act in what they believe to be the right way, they often feel a sense of satisfaction from doing a good deed. That is, until their efforts clash with the actions of others, and their good deeds become incompatible with the desired outcome. In Denice's case, this is when DeNaughty works to divide her "minions," ensuring they only receive the information necessary for her to extract what she needs from them. It becomes a disjointed orchestra, deliberately kept out of harmony to prevent the helpers from comparing notes. When transparency and unity eventually bring those notes together, some helpers become casualties. They realize they've been manipulated, lied to, and taken advantage of. They're left surprised, angry, violated, and emotionally wounded.

Denice must then cope with the devastating aftermath of this reality, once she regains her balance after each episode. This leads to shame, as DeNaughty checks out, leaving Denice to deal with the wreckage and destruction that DeNaughty has left behind.

The presentation of my story, our story, has always been intended to help us—and others—understand the purpose of mental illness, both within ourselves and in each other. I believe this story may help more of us grasp the therapeutic value of building perspective, developing distress tolerance skills, regulating emotions, and enhancing interpersonal effectiveness. It speaks to the need for us to continually seek understanding, not just of our varying levels of consciousness, but also of awareness and insight (Martin, 2023). Furthermore, it calls attention to the organization and management of the power and energy sources within our internal family system.

Gaining the wisdom to understand our internal relationships is vital to our personal maturation before we attempt to fix or control the external systems of our families or communities. Many of us are running on empty, constantly hoping to make it to the next fuel stop, where we scrounge the floorboards of our life's vehicle, searching for loose change to buy a mere drop of emotional fuel. This neglectful act is physically, mentally, emotionally, and spiritually draining. It leads individuals into major depression, uncontrollable anxiety, and unbearable trauma experiences, sometimes even dissociation—all in the name of trying to make sense of the differences between selfishness and selflessness.

We are taught that being selfish is sinful. Black-and-white thinking, also known as concrete thought, often leads us to swing into the opposite extreme of selflessness. This can result in us becoming someone's doormat, or falling into patterns of love addiction or love attachment (Real, 2022, p. 170). In search of human connection, we become boundaryless, exposing ourselves to others who are internally disorganized. This opens the door for them to inflict emotional pain, mental anguish, and, too often, physical harm. Concrete thinking then causes us to protect ourselves from others by walling off, withdrawing, and resigning into depression because fighting the perpetrator feels too difficult.

Once we regain strength and rise from the victimhood, concrete thinking still influences us. It leads us to seek what we need from others, sometimes behaving passively-aggressively or becoming indifferent toward others—appearing unharmed and resilient but actually under heavy protection from further emotional wounding.

When we feel sad and need to connect with others while in a victim state, to feel better and climb out of our low points, we may adopt manipulative behaviors, orchestrating others into giving us what we want and need. When we don't get what we want or feel we deserve, we might become controlling and angry. This can lead to us becoming the perpetrators, hurting our loved ones in the process, causing them to do anything they can to make us love them. Thus, the cycle of shame, control, grandiosity, and pain begins again—carrying on to the next relationship, the next family, the next generation of mental illness and sin (Real, 2022, p. 226).

None of us is immune to the emotional cycles we experience as humans. Rather than continuing the cycle of hiding behind shame and burying our heads in the sand, I—*we*—have taken this opportunity to expose our experiences with vulnerability, courage, and a willingness to be open and honest. Our message is simple: "You are not alone; there is help out there." Help exists for all of us—the hero children, the scapegoats, the wallflowers; the victims, the perpetrators; the loved, the unloved. Whoever you are, and wherever you fit into the grand scheme of relationships with yourself and others, we are all the same. You deserve to be loved, safely connected, and protected.

I hope you have found something in our story that has helped you in some way—to realize that you are loved for who you are, just as you are. You may find life a little easier to navigate once you look within and learn to love yourself. Since we are all subject to the Fall of Man, given the knowledge of good and evil, perhaps "knowing thyself is the beginning of all wisdom" ~Aristotle.

Chapter 27

Finding Professional Resources and Learning Skills

Calling 911:

I have yet to understand why calling 911 in an emergency creates such internal conflict for some people. Perhaps it's the instant realization that involving a third party—someone with authority over the situation—has something to do with it. To honor all readers who have experienced adverse or traumatic outcomes from calling 911, I will speak only to my own experience when having to involve first responders.

I firmly believe that it was only by the grace of God that Denice did not end up in jail, hurt anyone, or lose her life in any of these episodes. I stand behind that belief—God's grace made all the difference. Had it not been for the compassion and concern of those she encountered during her DEFCON 5 state, things could have turned out very differently. When first responders were called, Denice was fortunate to be met by officers who were not only aware but also skilled enough to recognize they were dealing with a very mentally ill woman. They never reached the point where deadly force was needed to contain her. Thank you, God!

Through these experiences, I learned that the best approach when calling 911 for help with Denice was to present the facts clearly. Here's how one of those 911 calls went, made on a three-way call while never losing contact with my mom:

"911 where is your emergency?".

"Hello, my name is DeAnna, I am currently in Phoenix, but the emergency is in [address, city, state]."

"Ok ma'm let me connect you directly to that location."

Seconds later "911 where is your emergency?"

"My mother's address is….she needs help, she is with my sister who is currently in a severely distressed bipolar episode, with mania and dissociated thoughts. My sister is 59 years old, my mother is 80. My dad is home but is sleeping in bed, he is 85."

"Ok we have first responders on the way, can you tell me what happened?"

"First, I need you to know that this has happened before and my sister has acted like she was complying but when she found a way to get out of it, she flees."

"Ok, thank you, we will make sure to let them know this."

"My sister is 5'1", about 280 lbs., and becomes superhumanly strong and fast in this mental state."

"Ok. Our responders are getting close, can you tell me what happened?"

Proceeding to briefly tell them why Denice was at moms I added "I have mom on the other phone so I can hear that she is doing a good job keeping my sister calm while they are waiting for help."

"My sister started going into her mania a few days ago and it became severely exacerbated when she started abusing her Albuterol inhaler, saying it was her 'emergency puffer the doctor gave me when I can't breathe'. Her condition made it impossible for her to decipher

between a panic attack and an asthma condition that she does not have. She is extremely high on this medication along with this mania."

"Ok, I have passed that information on to the responders, they are approaching the residence now."

"Thank you, I will wait with you until I know they have entered the home."

On the other phone, I had the call engaged with Mom. I heard her sternly telling Denice, "You sit down right there and behave. I'll answer the door when your 'boyfriend' gets here," using the same tone she had when we were little and in trouble. Denice complied. I could hear Mom directing the officers into the family room, where Denice was waiting for her "boyfriend" to arrive. Mom described Denice's reaction as one of total shock and surprise—uniformed officers were the last people she expected to see.

Once the initial shock wore off, Mom described how DeNaughty let out a chuckle, her facial expression shifting as she said, "Oh, I get what's happening here, okay," almost as if she were projecting her thoughts onto a screen, preparing her plan to comply and then escape.

Mom handed the phone to one of the officers, who went into another room to interview me. Mom had told them I was Denice's legal guardian, so they needed to speak with me about what had happened. I explained the details to the officer, and he returned the phone to Mom, who continued to update me on what was happening with Denice. It was like she became a play-by-play commentator, helping me follow what was unfolding.

"DeAnna, I kid you not, there are ten uniformed officers standing here in my family room all around Denice. They have gotten

her to agree to go with them and walk herself out of the house, God I hope it doesn't go again like it did last time."

"Denice is telling them she needs her shoes and wants to go get them from the laundry room, the lady officer told her she would get them for her, oh no, Denice doesn't like that, oh good, she just slapped her hands on her thighs and said 'fine', oh jeez here we go, now she is really showing them her DeNaughty side, thank God they are here to see this for themselves" mom said with internal conflict beginning to ease her inner critic who was beginning to tell her she didn't do enough for Denice before calling for help.

"It's ok mom, they are here to help you, help her, help us right now, just let them take over and deal with her. You just keep telling me what you are seeing, ok" I said working to console mom and let her know I was with her and we did the right thing by calling for help.

"Oh goodness" she said with a shaky tearful chuckle, *"you should see this DeAnna, all ten of the big, huge uniformed officers just formed a circle around her to take her out of here, there ain't no way she is going to break free this time, oh goodness, they got her on the gurney and are strapping her down, oh no, there she goes, screaming for me to help her"* mom began sobbing *"I can't do this, I can't listen to her beg me to help her get out of this."*

"Mom, it is out of your hands now, just shut the door and go sit down."

I believe it's crucial to emphasize that when you're on the call with 911, you should provide as many current details about your loved one as possible. This helps first responders know who and what they are coming to face. I believe this is one of the most important things you can do to keep your loved one safe. Understanding your loved one's erratic and triggering behaviors, and sharing past history of what they've done in similar situations, can be incredibly helpful. It ensures the responders are informed about the potential risks, allowing them to prepare to respond appropriately, rather than simply react.

Help with Decision Making:

Due to HIPAA privacy laws, it is nearly impossible for anyone to access someone's medical information without their consent. Each of us has a right to privacy regarding our health information. However, the other side of this law can create an impenetrable barrier when it comes to getting help for a loved one in their time of need. Despite technological advancements, such as portals that allow access to medical records, the inconsistency between healthcare providers and the fact that they are often not part of the same group makes it nearly impossible to manage your loved one's care consistently.

As Denice's legal guardian, I was able to access her medical records, which was invaluable in tracking her treatment over time—understanding what worked and what didn't. For those caring for loved ones who need help managing their medical care, there are a few options to consider before, or instead of, becoming a legal guardian.

One option is to have your loved one complete important documents while they are in a baseline, coherent state. A Medical Power of Attorney (POA) or Healthcare Proxy can be established. These documents, along with similar forms like an Advance Directive (medical or psychological), indicate that your loved one has given permission for someone else to make medical decisions on their behalf if they are no longer able to do so themselves. As Denice's guardian, it was also helpful for me to attend her doctor's appointments, helping manage her care and making medical decisions with or for her when necessary.

Medication Matching:

One of the critical steps I found important was for Denice to undergo genetic testing for medications. Some people argue that this process doesn't work, and that's understandable. My perspective, however, is that since each of us has a unique physiological and biological makeup, what harm is there in using science to explore and support the medications that might work better for an individual? This approach could save time and money compared to experimenting with medications in a critical situation.

In Denice's case, her ability to manage and balance her comorbid diagnoses always seemed precarious. If her treatment was left to trial and error, with new medications being tested without proper insight, it would inevitably lead to setbacks—time lost and chaos that spilled over into our lives as we tried to help her manage daily activities.

She was fortunate to have genetic testing as part of her residential treatment, which she paid a significant amount for. It seemed almost fatalistic to blindly follow any doctor's suggestion to try a new medication without considering the science behind it. Denice had already tried so many different medications, and she could clearly articulate how each one affected her. Interestingly, the results of her genetic testing confirmed that the medications she had been taking were, in fact, the best match for her all along.

Finding Treatment:

Finding the appropriate level of care for your loved one can be incredibly challenging, depending on the mental health resources available in your state. For our family, at the time, there was only one facility in our state that could provide extended care. Since then, the state has expanded the number of facilities that might have been helpful for Denice and her needs.

When looking for long-term residential care, I would advise you to be open-minded in your research, carefully considering a list of needs your loved one has and prioritizing them based on their level of urgency. For Denice, the top priority was for her to learn behavioral skills to manage her personality disorder, as it was the underlying issue causing the most difficulty in understanding and adhering to her medications for Bipolar disorder.

Once she had learned these skills, the next priority was to implement them. This process would take time—more time than the few weeks the facility in our state could offer for the same amount of money as the out-of-state facility. This decision was made after Denice had already participated in other shorter-term therapeutic programs, which had not been sufficient to meet her ongoing needs.

Short-term Treatment:

One of the other programs Denice participated in was the Intensive Outpatient Program (IOP). These programs typically span six to twelve weeks, with participants attending sessions during the weekdays and returning home in the evenings and on weekends. The curriculum covers a variety of topics, such as depression, anxiety, grief and loss, executive functioning, and others. The goal of the program is to teach participants coping skills for everyday issues, particularly for those who have struggled to develop these skills due to various mental health challenges.

Many community health organizations offer these services, and many of the programs are also covered by health insurance, helping to ease the financial burden.

Therapy Methods:

Throughout my story, I've discussed many therapeutic methods, with Internal Family Systems (IFS) being the foundational approach I subscribe to, believe in, and rely on when working with my own clients. Many therapists have invested time and resources to learn and integrate this method into their practices.

In addition to IFS, I highly recommend exploring other therapeutic approaches, such as Dialectical Behavior Therapy (DBT) and Cognitive Behavioral Therapy (CBT). Both focus on building skills for improved distress tolerance, interpersonal effectiveness, and emotional regulation. Another valuable tool is understanding genealogy and using genogram mapping to explore external and internal family systems, uncovering family history, generational patterns, and the burdens we inherit. These methods can help individuals sort through the historical reasons behind behaviors that may no longer be effective or healthy in their own lives.

Neuroscientific approaches are also incredibly useful, as they can help us understand how our bodies absorb and process trauma, and how we adapt to cope with traumatic events. Over time, these adaptive responses can shape the way we continue to handle life's challenges.

There are many other helpful therapies, and I encourage each reader to remain open when seeking help, honestly evaluating themselves throughout the process, and staying true to their own journey toward healing and peace. It's important to remember that it took a lifetime to reach the point of needing help, so even with dedicated effort during therapy, it can take time to truly feel better. Therapy is not a magic pill, but a journey of self-discovery and growth.

Self-Help Materials:

There are many self-help books available for readers seeking guidance on personal growth. I've included a few of my favorite resources in the reference list at the end of the book. It takes both courage and curiosity to read these materials, absorb their messages, and consider how they apply to one's own life.

One book in particular that I have found incredibly helpful, both for my clients and myself, is *The Body Keeps the Score* by Bessel van der Kolk. This book is among many that aim to help us understand how trauma impacts us and becomes stored in our bodies, often leading to physical ailments. I believe this book is essential for anyone working through trauma recovery, as it emphasizes the importance of reconnecting the body and mind to heal the whole self through a holistic approach.

Finding Laughter and Joy:

Use of laughter in times of sorrow can be very healing. No I am not encouraging use of laughter incongruently and during inappropriate times. However, proper use of laughter can be very helpful when working to normalize the level of trauma and reset the environment when it is time to move forward and regain control of normalcy. Laughter helps us change our moods rather than to stay in the state of trauma, depression and anxiety. It is also helpful in times where our system is in a state of confusion, being manipulated by another person who is in the midst of a mental illness state. Realization of unreal activities we find ourselves in when helping someone in a serious mentally ill state, sometimes simply laughing is helpful to see the humor in some behaviors in order to regain balance and control of our approach. I have often found myself laughing at myself, without judgement, seeing the silliness of my thoughts leading me to realize the silliness of my actions.

Faith and the Strength of Prayer:

Last, but certainly not least, the continued use of prayer—for strength, guidance, forgiveness, and support—has been the most important tool I can offer from all of this experience. Prayer has carried me through every moment of working with a loved one and with myself while navigating the realities of mental illness.

We are not alone. Ever. Our Creator—for me, that is God—is always with us. And when we truly listen, we can hear His voice. He shows up in the ways we need Him most, often in the smallest moments, or through the presence of others. When we are open to receiving His guidance and the support He sends, the path forward—though still difficult—feels more navigable.

This doesn't mean we won't experience pain, fear, anger, disgust, surprise, or sadness. But through prayer, we can also learn to experience happiness and kindness more fully, as well as recognize those moments of light when they come. Living by our core values helps lead us toward a virtuous life, grounded in faith, hope, and love—the greatest of these being love *(Holy Bible, NIV 1 Corinthians 13:13).*

Thank you, God, for bestowing upon me the grace and honor of these people—to walk beside me, guide me, and love me through this journey. I pray for all of them, and for all who now see my shame, our shame. May they take from this what they need, leave what they don't, and discern what is right for them.

Amen.

REFERENCES

American Psychological Association. (2025). Retrieved February 25, 2025 from www.apa.org/topica/trauma.

Bagwasi, B. (2011). Psychoanalysis of Ezekiel (Ezekiel 1-6). Reproduced by Sabinet Gateway. Johanesburg.

DSM-TR5. (2022). Diagnostic and Statistical Manual of Mental Disorders: 5th Edition text revision (DSM-TR5). Washington DC: American Psychiatric Association.

Gibran, K. (1923). The Prophet. Alfred A. Knopf.

Holy Bible, New International Version. (1994). Zondervan. (Original work published 1973).

Kadanoff, M. (2019). Everything you always wanted to know about Metformin but were afraid to ask. Retrieved February 10, 2025 from https://diatribe.org/diabetes-medications/everything-you-always-wanted-know-about-metformin-were-afraid-ask.

Linehan, M. (2014). DBT (R) skills training handouts and worksheets, second edition (2nd ed.). Guilford Publications.

Martin, S. (2023). Why using "consciousness" in psychotherapy: insight, metacognition and self-consciousness. Elsevier. Retrieved from: www.elsevier.com/locate/newideapsych.

MedlinePlus [Internet]. Bethesda (MD): National Library of Medicine (US); [updated 2023 October 15]. Albuterol. Available from: https://medlineplus.gov/druginfo/meds/a607004.html

Merriam-Webster. (n.d.). Word defined. In Merriam-Webster.com dictionary. Retrieved January 4, 2025 from www.merriam-webster.com/dictionary.

Newport Institute. (2022). Big T vs. Little t Trauma in Young Adults: Is There a Difference?. Retrieved February 25, 2025 from https://www.newportinstitute.com/resources/mental-health/big-t-little-t-trauma/

Palmer, P. (June 14, 2023). Is Judging others a sin. Bible Study Tools. Retrieved March 23, 2025 from https://www.biblestudytools.com/bible-study/topical-studies/is-judging-others-a-sin.html

Parker, G., Coroneo, M., Spoelma, M. (2023). BiPolar Eyes: windows to the pole? Australian and New Zealand Journal of Psychiatry, 57(11) 1405-106. DOI: 10.1177/00049674231195259.

Real, T. (2008). The New Rules of Marriage: What you need to know to make love work. Random House.

Real, T. (2024). Us: Getting past you & me to build a more loving relationship [Foreword by Bruce Springsteen]. Penguin Random House.

Real, T. Fierce Intimacy: Standing up to one another with love. September 4, 2018. (T. Real, Narr.) [Audiobook] Sounds True Publishing; unabridged edition.

Real, T. Working with Difficult Men: Where's the leverage for change. March 15, 2023. https://terryreal.com/articles/working-with-difficult-men/

Riemerrsma, J., Schwartz, R., et al., (2023). All Together Us: Integrating the IFS model with key modalities, communities and trends. Pivotal Press.

Riemersma, J. (2020). Altogether You: Experiencing personal and spiritual transformation with Internal Family Systems therapy. Pivotal Press.

Schwartz, R. (2019, March 5). Dr. Richard Schwartz explains Internal Family Systems (IFS) [Video]. YouTube. https://youtu.be/DdZZ7sTX840?si=X9DmjZrvruNT3lJQ

Sznycer, D., Tooby, J., Cosmides, L., Porat, R., Shalvi, S., & Halperin, E. (2016). Shame closely tracks the threat of devaluation by others, even across cultures. Proceedings of the National Academy of Sciences of the United States of America, 113(10), 2625–2630. https://doi.org/10.1073/pnas.1514699113s

Thomas, G. (2010). Zondervan. Sacred Pathways: Discover Your Soul's Path To God (Rev. ed.). Grand Rapids: Zondervan.

www.ingramcontent.com/pod-product-compliance
Lightning Source LLC
LaVergne TN
LVHW022153200926
848481LV00006B/1735